MW00717539

Interpreting Medical Reports

Claims Continuing Education Course

2nd Edition

At press time, this edition contains the most complete and accurate information currently available. Owing to the nature of license examinations, however, information may have been added recently to the actual test that does not appear in this edition. Please contact the publisher to verify that you have the most current edition.

We value your input and suggestions. If you found imperfections or incorrect information in this product, please let us know by sending an email to **errata@kaplan.com**.

We are always looking for ways to make our products better to help you achieve your career goals.

INTERPRETING MEDICAL REPORTS, 2ND EDITION
©2006 DF Institute, Inc. All rights reserved.

Published by DF Institute, Inc.

Printed in the United States of America.

ISBN: 1-4195-3752-0

PPN: 5392-5101

08   09   10   9   8   7   6   5   4   3   2
J   F   M   A   M   J   J   A   S   O   N   D

Contents

How to Use This Book

Interpreting Medical Reports is designed for insurance personnel whose responsibilities require a basic understanding of the structure and functions of the human body to analyze the medical reports that accompany trauma-related bodily injury claims.

This course does *not* purport to be all-inclusive, either in transmitting basic medical knowledge or in referring to all areas of medicine which come within the daily experience of insurance personnel. It *does* provide a solid foundation of basic medical-related knowledge which will enable you to make continuing progress in your career as a bodily injury claim examiner.

There are no specific prerequisites for this course. The material in this course is based on the assumption that you have no knowledge of medical terminology or human anatomy and begins at this level of understanding.

After completing this course, you should:

■ Have a broad, basic knowledge of the medical terminology, specialties, and abbreviations frequently used in medical reports.

■ Have a basic understanding of the anatomy, structures, and systems of the human body, including their location within the body and their functions.

■ Know about the most common types of injuries and other medical conditions found in bodily injury claim work, including their symptoms, treatment methods, possible healing complications, and other long- and short-term effects on the individual.

■ Be familiar with certain medical tests and signs used to diagnose injuries and medical conditions, including how they are performed and the type of information they provide.

At the end of the course, you will find several tear-out Job Aids for you to use in your work, including:

■ A list of common medical abbreviations seen in medical reports and claims

■ A summary of the medical terminology building blocks and their meanings discussed in Unit One

■ A phonetic pronunciation guide for many of the medical terms used in the course

■ A chart for estimating the amount of temporary disability time that may be required for certain medical conditions

This course is presented in programmed instruction format, which means you will first read increments of related information. We will then ask you to demonstrate your understanding of what you have read by answering a question, selecting the correct answer from a number of options, or in some other way responding to the material. As soon as you have written your response, you will be able to verify it. You can see how this works as you read the remainder of this section. Each numbered step in your study is called a "frame," and a series of frames makes up a study unit. Read the frames that follow and respond as requested.

PROGRAMMED INSTRUCTION BASICS

1. Three of the basic principles of programmed instruction are:

    1. The material is presented in sequence, one step at a time.

    2. The student is asked to respond frequently to the material, rather than just to read the text.

    3. The student receives immediate confirmation of each response.

    Each of the following statements corresponds to one of the three principles listed above. Mark a **1, 2,** or **3** in front of each statement to match it to the principle it represents.

    ____ A. You will know each step of the way whether you have understood the material up to that point.

    ____ B. The text takes you through the material step-by-step, in logical groupings.

    ____ C. Throughout the course, you will apply what you learned by answering questions.

    CHECKYOURANSWERHERECHECKYOURANSWERHERECHECKYOURANSWERHERE
    CHECKYOURANSWERHERECHECKYOURANSWERHERECHECKYOURANSWERHERE
    CHECKYOURANSWERHERECHECKYOURANSWERHERECHECKYOURANSWERHERE
    CHECKYOURANSWERHERECHECKYOURANSWERHERECHECKYOURANSWERHERE

2. Remove the red plastic response verifier from the inside front cover of this text. Check the answer to frame 1 above by placing the verifier over the red pattern in that frame. You should do this after completing each frame in the text, and if your answer matches the printed answer visible under the red overlay, go on to the next frame.

    If it does not match, read the material in the frame again, then respond differently. Check this response. You may need to follow this procedure more than once in a single frame. If the correct response still escapes you, try a fresh start. This is more likely to occur if you're returning to your study after a prolonged interruption.

    Some frame questions may have more than one correct answer. However, the questions in the course examination will only have one correct answer.

If the response you have made does not match the response under the red overlay, you should first (CHECK THE ONE ITEM THAT CORRECTLY COMPLETES THIS SENTENCE)

A. go on to the next frame.

B. go back several frames and start over.

C. reread the material in the frame and make a different response.

CHECKYOURANSWERHERECHECKYOURANSWERHERECHECKYOURANSWERHERE
CHECKYOURANSWERHERECHECKYOURANSWERHERECHECKYOURANSWERHERE
CHECKYOURANSWERHERECHECKYOURANSWERHERECHECKYOURANSWERHERE
CHECKYOURANSWERHERECHECKYOURANSWERHERECHECKYOURANSWERHERE

3. Once you understand the material in a frame, go on to the next frame and repeat the study-respond-verify cycle.

   Now arrange the following steps into the correct sequence by writing a number in the blank beside each statement to indicate how to proceed through a programmed instruction text. Write **1** for the first step, **2** for the second step, and so on.

   _____ A. Use the red plastic response verifier to check your response.

   _____ B. Read the material in the frame.

   _____ C. Go to the next frame.

   _____ D. Complete the response called for in the frame.

   _____ E. Repeat previous steps until you understand, reading the prior material again if necessary.

CHECKYOURANSWERHERECHECKYOURANSWERHERECHECKYOURANSWERHERE
CHECKYOURANSWERHERECHECKYOURANSWERHERECHECKYOURANSWERHERE
CHECKYOURANSWERHERECHECKYOURANSWERHERECHECKYOURANSWERHERE
CHECKYOURANSWERHERECHECKYOURANSWERHERECHECKYOURANSWERHERE

ILLUSTRATIONS

4. **Interpreting Medical Reports** blends programmed instruction with graphics to make your study more effective. Illustrations are used to:

   ■ Present concepts that are easier to understand when you can visualize them

   ■ Highlight key points

   ■ Summarize information for easy review

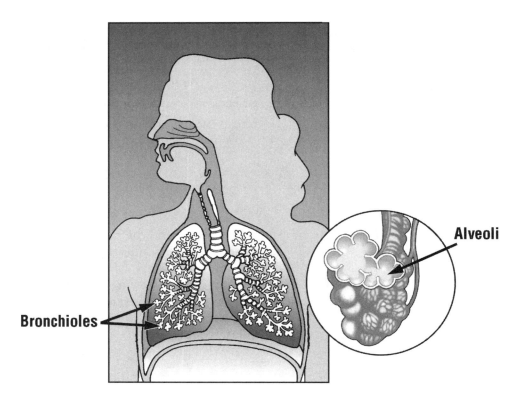

This approach serves to enhance learning, promote retention, and maintain your interest.

Which of the following statements are correct?

A. Illustrations might be used to explain certain concepts more effectively.

B. The use of graphics improves learning and retention while providing an interesting learning environment.

When you are ready to begin your study of **Interpreting Medical Reports,** go on to Unit One.

1

Introduction to Medical Terminology

HOW MEDICAL TERMS ARE DERIVED

1. In this first unit of *Interpreting Medical Reports*, we will introduce you to technical language you'll encounter and need to understand as you analyze medical reports and insurance claims.

   Of course, this unit does not contain all of the medical terminology you'll encounter during your career as a claim professional. Instead, this unit will demonstrate how Greek and Latin root words, prefixes, and suffixes are the *building blocks* of medical terminology. You will see how medical terms are derived from combining these building blocks in various ways, just as the English language does. For example, when most people encounter an English word such as *aerodynamics*, they recognize it as a combination of *aero*, meaning *air*, and *dynamics*, which deals with *motion or force*. By knowing the meaning of the building blocks used to create the word, they are able to interpret the meaning of the word.

   You'll see that medical terms are developed in the same way, and you will discover how easy it is to recognize the individual building blocks, learn their meanings, and combine them into new words. In addition to teaching you about medical terminology, the goal of this unit is to eliminate any concerns you might have about working with medical terms as you become confident of your ability to analyze and interpret these words. Finally, this unit will make it easier for you to use medical dictionaries and other tools on the job.

   After the discussion of basic medical terminology, you'll be introduced to some common types of medical specialists. Finally, you'll study some of the written medical abbreviations you are likely to encounter in medical reports and claims.

   Which of the following statements correctly expresses what you will learn about medical terminology as you study this unit? (CHECK ALL CORRECT STATEMENTS)

   A. You will learn the meaning of every medical term you will ever encounter on the job.

   B. You will be able to understand the meanings of medical terms because you can assign individual meanings to root words, prefixes, and suffixes.

   C. The terms you will study in this unit will provide a basis for learning other terms a claim professional must know.

   D. You will develop confidence about using tools such as medical dictionaries since you will know how medical terms are constructed.

COMMON ROOT WORDS, PREFIXES, AND SUFFIXES

2. In this section, we'll define some of the more common root words, prefixes, and suffixes used in medical terminology. After you memorize the meanings of these individual building blocks, you'll learn how to combine them to create medical terms.

    We'll start by defining **root words**. A root word is the *fundamental* building block of a medical term. It's what remains after you remove any prefixes (words that go *before* the root) and suffixes (words that go *after* the root) from the term.

3. We'll begin our discussion of root words with a group of terms that describe specific body parts:

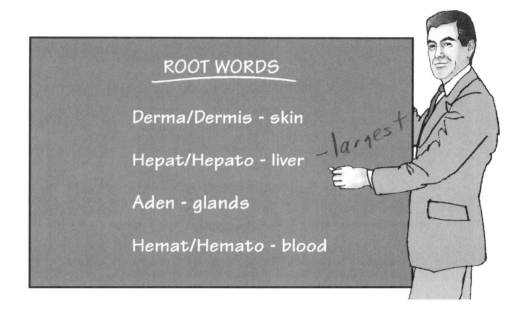

True or false?

A. The root word for any of the body's glands is **hemat**.
    ( ) True   (✗) False

B. The root word **hepat** means liver.   (✗) True   ( ) False

C. When you see a medical term containing the root word **derma**, you know that the term is describing the skin.   (✗) True   ( ) False

D. The definition of the root word **aden** is gland.   (✗) True   ( ) False

4. The next group of terms also describe specific body parts:

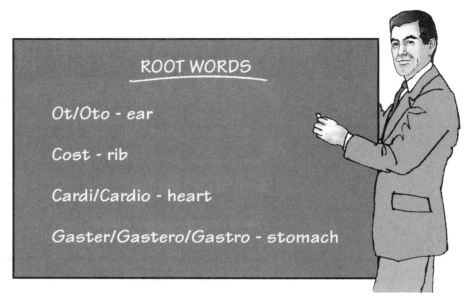

ROOT WORDS

Ot/Oto - ear

Cost - rib

Cardi/Cardio - heart

Gaster/Gastero/Gastro - stomach

Match the root word listed in the left-hand column with its correct definition in the right-hand column. **Some definitions may have more than one root word that applies**.

1. Cardi   _____ A. Rib
2. Gaster   _____ B. Stomach
3. Ot   _____ C. Ear
4. Cost   _____ D. Heart
5. Cardio
6. Gastero
7. Gastro
8. Oto

CHECKYOURANSWERHERECHECKYOURANSWERHERECHECKYOURANSWERHERE
CHECKYOURANSWERHERECHECKYOURANSWERHERECHECKYOURANSWERHERE
CHECKYOURANSWERHERECHECKYOURANSWERHERECHECKYOURANSWERHERE
CHECKYOURANSWERHERECHECKYOURANSWERHERECHECKYOURANSWERHERE

5. Write in the correct definition of the following terms.
    A. Cardi/Cardio _____
    B. Derma/Dermis _____
    C. Ot/Oto _____
    D. Aden _____
    E. Hepat/Hepato _____
    F. Gaster/Gastero/Gastro _____
    G. Hemat/Hemato _____
    H. Cost _____

CHECKYOURANSWERHERECHECKYOURANSWERHERECHECKYOURANSWERHERE
CHECKYOURANSWERHERECHECKYOURANSWERHERECHECKYOURANSWERHERE
CHECKYOURANSWERHERECHECKYOURANSWERHERECHECKYOURANSWERHERE
CHECKYOURANSWERHERECHECKYOURANSWERHERECHECKYOURANSWERHERE

6. Let's define some more common root words:

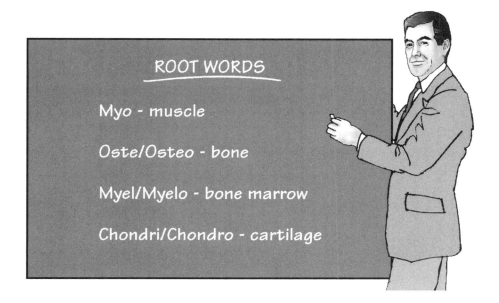

A. When you see a medical term containing the root word **oste** or **osteo**, you know that the term is describing something to do with
    1. bone marrow.
    2. cartilage.
    3. bones.
    4. muscles.

B. What does the root word **myo** mean?
    1. Bones
    2. Muscles
    3. Bone marrow
    4. Cartilage

C. What root word is used to describe cartilage?
    1. Oste/Osteo
    2. Myo
    3. Chondri/Chondro
    4. Myel/myelo

D. What do the root words **myel** and **myelo** mean?
    1. Bones
    2. Cartilage
    3. Muscles
    4. Bone marrow

CHECKYOURANSWERHERECHECKYOURANSWERHERECHECKYOURANSWERHERE
CHECKYOURANSWERHERECHECKYOURANSWERHERECHECKYOURANSWERHERE
CHECKYOURANSWERHERECHECKYOURANSWERHERECHECKYOURANSWER
CHECKYOURANSWERHERECHECKYOURANSWERHERECHECKYOURANSWERHERE

7. Here are the root words for the head, brain, and skull:

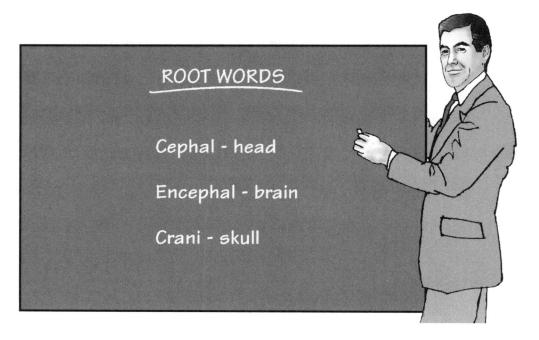

ROOT WORDS

Cephal - head

Encephal - brain

Crani - skull

Although **cephal** and **encephal** are separate and distinct words, each with their own meaning, the two are often used interchangeably in medical reports and claims.

Match the medical term in the left-hand column with its correct definition in the right-hand column.

1. Crani   _____ A. Brain
2. Encephal   _____ B. Head
3. Cephal   _____ C. Skull

CHECKYOURANSWERHERECHECKYOURANSWERHERECHECKYOURANSWERHERE
CHECKYOURANSWERHERECHECKYOURANSWERHERECHECKYOURANSWERHERE
CHECKYOURANSWERHERECHECKYOURANSWERHERECHECKYOURANSWERHERE
CHECKYOURANSWERHERECHECKYOURANSWERHERECHECKYOURANSWERHERE

8. Take a minute to review the terms you have learned in the last few frames. Match the term in the left-hand column with its correct definition in the right-hand column.

1. Crani   _____ A. Cartilage
2. Myel/myelo   _____ B. Bone
3. Ot/Oto   _____ C. Ear
4. Cephal   _____ D. Head
5. Myo   _____ E. Brain
6. Chondri/Chondro   _____ F. Muscle
7. Encephal   _____ G. Bone marrow
8. Oste/Osteo   _____ H. Skull

9. You've learned enough medical terminology now to start combining root words to create new words.

   In an earlier frame, you learned that the root word *crani* means *skull*. The **cranium** is the part of the skull that encloses the brain. The skull is composed of both **bones** and **cartilage**. You already know the root words for bones *(oste/osteo)* and cartilage *(chondro/chondri)*.

   A. Based on these terms, the part of the skull that is composed of bones is the

      1. osteocranium.

      2. chondrocranium.

   B. Based on these terms, what is the correct term for the part of the skull that is composed of cartilage?

      1. Osteocranium

      2. Chondrocranium

10. Two more common root words are:

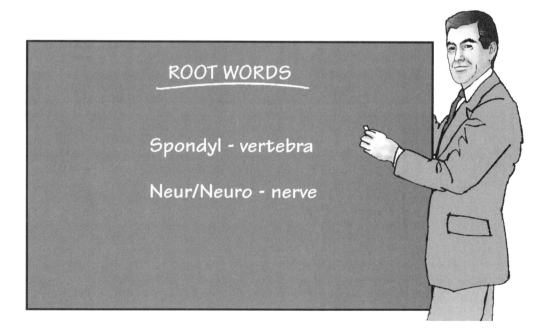

ROOT WORDS

Spondyl - vertebra

Neur/Neuro - nerve

Vertebrae (singular is **vertebra**) are the bony parts that make up your spinal column. You will encounter many medical terms in claims and medical reports that incorporate the common word *vertebra*, as well as the root word for vertebra, **spondyl**.

A. Medical terms that incorporate the root word *spondyl* are describing diseases or conditions involving the (nerves/vertebrae) _____.

B. When you see a medical term that contains the root word *neur* or *neuro*, you know that the term is describing something to do with the (nerves/vertebrae) _____.

CHECKYOURANSWERHERECHECKYOURANSWERHERECHECKYOURANSWERHERE
CHECKYOURANSWERHERECHECKYOURANSWERHERECHECKYOURANSWERHERE
CHECKYOURANSWERHERECHECKYOURANSWERHERECHECKYOURANSWERHERE
CHECKYOURANSWERHERECHECKYOURANSWERHERECHECKYOURANSWERHERE

Root Words

11. Three more common root words are:

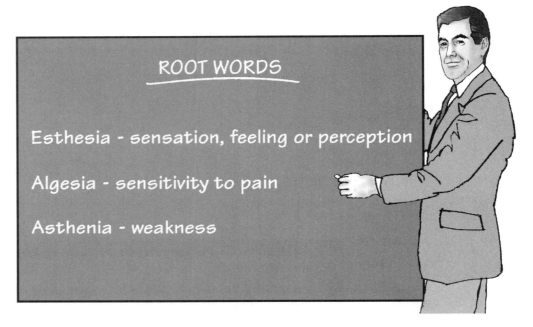

ROOT WORDS

Esthesia - sensation, feeling or perception

Algesia - sensitivity to pain

Asthenia - weakness

Which of the following statements are correct?

A. The root word for sensation, feeling, or perception is **esthesia**.

B. **Algesia** means weakness.

C. **Asthenia** means sensitivity to pain.

CHECKYOURANSWERHERECHECKYOURANSWERHERECHECKYOURANSWERHERE
CHECKYOURANSWERHERECHECKYOURANSWERHERECHECKYOURANSWERHERE
CHECKYOURANSWERHERECHECKYOURANSWERHERECHECKYOURANSWERHERE
CHECKYOURANSWERHERECHECKYOURANSWERHERECHECKYOURANSWERHERE

12. Here are some additional terms for you to learn:

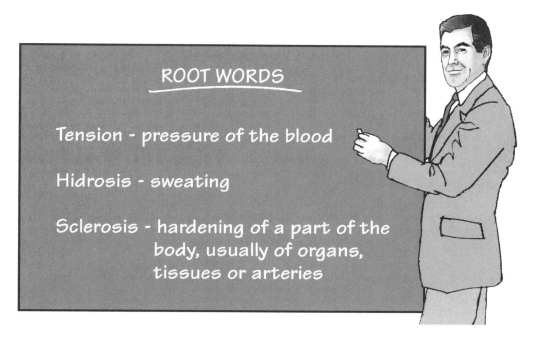

ROOT WORDS

Tension - pressure of the blood

Hidrosis - sweating

Sclerosis - hardening of a part of the
            body, usually of organs,
            tissues or arteries

True or false?

A. **Tension** means sweating.   ( ) True   (X) False
B. The term **sclerosis** means hardening, usually of organs, tissues, or arteries in a part of the body.   (X) True   ( ) False
C. **Hidrosis** refers to the pressure of the blood.   ( ) True   (X) False

CHECKYOURANSWERHERECHECKYOURANSWERHERECHECKYOURANSWERHERE
CHECKYOURANSWERHERECHECKYOURANSWERHERECHECKYOURANSWERHERE
CHECKYOURANSWERHERECHECKYOURANSWERHERECHECKYOURANSWERHERE
CHECKYOURANSWERHERECHECKYOURANSWERHERECHECKYOURANSWERHERE

13. This completes our discussion of some common root words. Take a minute to review some of the terms you've learned in this section by completing the following review exercise.

Which of these statements are true?

A. The term *spondyl* means brain.
B. Although the terms *cephal* and *encephal* are separate and distinct words with their own meanings, they are sometimes used interchangeably in medical reports and claims.
C. A medical term containing the root word *crani* is describing a disease or condition involving the skull.
D. The root words for nerve are *neur* and *neuro*.
E. The term *hidrosis* means sweating.
F. The term *tension* refers to hardening of organs, tissues, or arteries.

CHECKYOURANSWERHERECHECKYOURANSWERHERECHECKYOURANSWERHERE
CHECKYOURANSWERHERECHECKYOURANSWERHERECHECKYOURANSWERHERE
CHECKYOURANSWERHERECHECKYOURANSWERHERECHECKYOURANSWERHERE
CHECKYOURANSWERHERECHECKYOURANSWERHERECHECKYOURANSWERHERE

Prefixes

14. Now that you're familiar with root words, you're ready to learn some common **prefixes** that are added to the beginning of root words to build medical terms. In this section, we'll define common prefixes in medical terminology, combine them with the root words presented in the last section, and ask you to define the resulting word.

    We'll begin with these common prefixes:

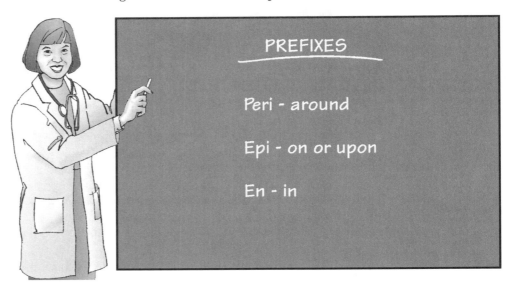

PREFIXES

Peri - around

Epi - on or upon

En - in

Earlier, you learned that the root word for brain is *encephal*. As you can now see, the *literal* translation of encephal is **in the head**.

Note that **peri** usually refers to a **covering around a part of the body**. Sometimes, it refers to the *area* around a part, and less frequently, to the *surface* of a part.

Define the following words.

A. Epicostal _____

B. Periosteum _____

C. Epidermis _____

D. Epicranium _____

E. Pericardium _____

F. Encranial _____

CHECKYOURANSWERHERECHECKYOURANSWERHERECHECKYOURANSWERHERE
CHECKYOURANSWERHERECHECKYOURANSWERHERECHECKYOURANSWERHERE
CHECKYOURANSWERHERECHECKYOURANSWERHERECHECKYOURANSWERHERE
CHECKYOURANSWERHERECHECKYOURANSWERHERECHECKYOURANSWERHERE

15. The next two prefixes are:

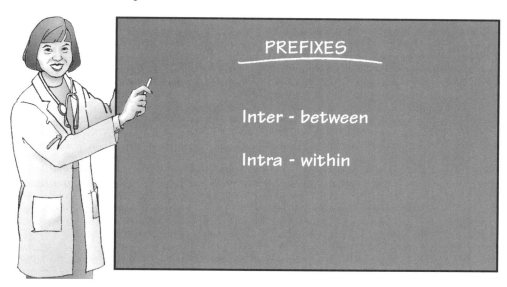

PREFIXES

Inter - between

Intra - within

A. The prefix **inter** means ___between___, and the prefix **intra** means
    ___within___.

B. Write in the correct medical term for each of the following descriptions.
    1. Between the ribs ___intercostal___
    2. Within the stomach ___intra gastro___
    3. Between two vertebrae _____
    4. Within the liver _____

CHECKYOURANSWERHERECHECKYOURANSWERHERECHECKYOURANSWERHERE
CHECKYOURANSWERHERECHECKYOURANSWERHERECHECKYOURANSWERHERE
CHECKYOURANSWERHERECHECKYOURANSWERHERECHECKYOURANSWERHERE
CHECKYOURANSWERHERECHECKYOURANSWERHERECHECKYOURANSWERHERE

16. The next three prefixes are:

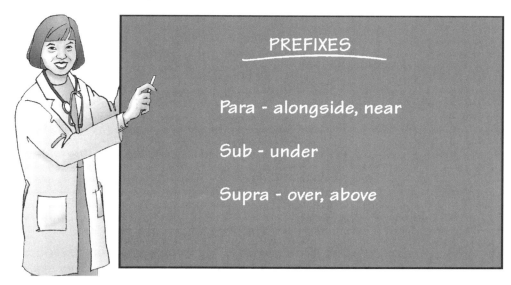

PREFIXES

Para - alongside, near

Sub - under

Supra - over, above

What are the definitions of these terms?

A. Paravertebral _____

B. Subvertebral _____

C. Supravertebral _____

CHECKYOURANSWERHERECHECKYOURANSWERHERECHECKYOURANSWERHERE
CHECKYOURANSWERHERECHECKYOURANSWERHERECHECKYOURANSWERHERE
CHECKYOURANSWERHERECHECKYOURANSWERHERECHECKYOURANSWERHERE
CHECKYOURANSWERHERECHECKYOURANSWERHERECHECKYOURANSWERHERE

17. Review the prefixes you've learned by matching the prefix in the left-hand column with its definition in the right-hand column.

1. En	____ A.	Around
2. Para	____ B.	Alongside, near
3. Peri	____ C.	On or upon
4. Epi	____ D.	Between
5. Inter	____ E.	In
6. Intra	____ F.	Within
7. Sub	____ G.	Over, above
8. Supra	____ H.	Under

CHECKYOURANSWERHERECHECKYOURANSWERHERECHECKYOURANSWERHERE
CHECKYOURANSWERHERECHECKYOURANSWERHERECHECKYOURANSWERHERE
CHECKYOURANSWERHERECHECKYOURANSWERHERECHECKYOURANSWERHERE
CHECKYOURANSWERHERECHECKYOURANSWERHERECHECKYOURANSWERHERE

18. Two more prefixes for you to learn are:

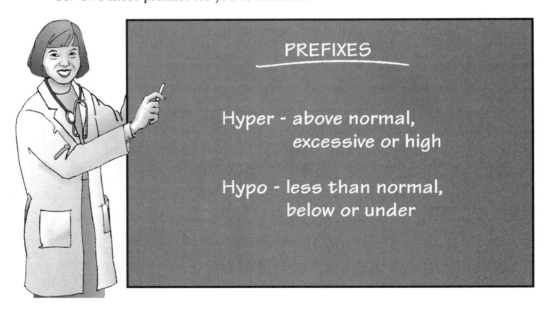

PREFIXES

Hyper - above normal, excessive or high

Hypo - less than normal, below or under

When **hypo** is combined with a root word or suffix that begins with a vowel, the "o" is sometimes dropped. For example, earlier you learned that the root word *algesia* means *sensitivity to pain.* When used in combination with *hypo,* the word becomes **hypalgesia,** without the letter "o."

In other cases, the "o" is retained, such as with the root word *esthesia*. In this case, the resulting word is **hypoesthesia**. Don't be alarmed by minor inconsistencies such as these. You'll soon learn to interpret them without conscious effort, just as you've learned to cope with the inconsistencies of the English language.

Match the medical term in the left-hand column with its correct definition in the right-hand column.

1. Hypertension   _____   A. Excessive sweating
2. Hypodermic   _____   B. Below the skin
3. Hyperhidrosis   _____   C. High blood pressure
4. Hypalgesia   _____   D. Less than normal sensitivity to pain

CHECKYOURANSWERHERECHECKYOURANSWERHERECHECKYOURANSWERHERE
CHECKYOURANSWERHERECHECKYOURANSWERHERECHECKYOURANSWERHERE
CHECKYOURANSWERHERECHECKYOURANSWERHERECHECKYOURANSWERHERE
CHECKYOURANSWERHERECHECKYOURANSWERHERECHECKYOURANSWERHERE

19. The last two prefixes for you to learn are:

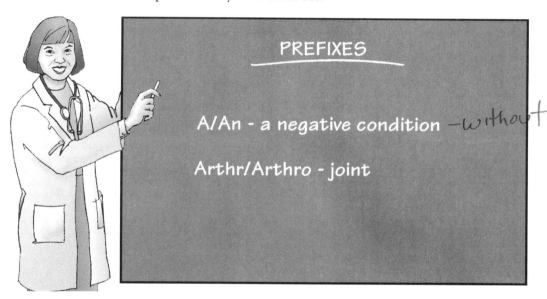

PREFIXES

A/An - a negative condition —without

Arthr/Arthro - joint

A term you learned earlier in this chapter was *esthesia*, which refers to *sensation*, *feeling*, *or perception*. Adding the prefix **an** to this word gives us the word **anesthesia**, which means **a lack of or absence of sensation, feeling, or perception.**

Define the following terms.

A. Anadenia _____

B. Anhidrosis _____

C. Arthrosclerosis _____

CHECKYOURANSWERHERECHECKYOURANSWERHERECHECKYOURANSWERHERE
CHECKYOURANSWERHERECHECKYOURANSWERHERECHECKYOURANSWERHERE
CHECKYOURANSWERHERECHECKYOURANSWERHERECHECKYOURANSWERHERE
CHECKYOURANSWERHERECHECKYOURANSWERHERECHECKYOURANSWERHERE

20. Define the following prefixes.

    A. A/An _____

    B. Hyper _____

    C. Hypo _____

    D. Arthr/Arthro _____

Suffixes

21. Now you're ready to build your medical vocabulary even more by learning about the **suffixes** that are added to the end of root words to build medical terms. In this section, we'll define common suffixes used in medical terminology and have you combine them with the root words and prefixes discussed earlier in this unit to build new words.

    We'll start with three suffixes that are used to describe surgical techniques:

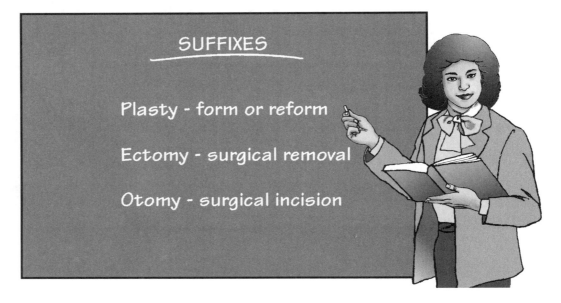

SUFFIXES

Plasty - form or reform

Ectomy - surgical removal

Otomy - surgical incision

    Note that the suffix **ectomy** may be used to describe the *partial* surgical removal of a structure. For example, it is highly unlikely that a person having a **craniectomy** would have his or her entire skull removed.

    A. Which term describes the procedure used to form or reform a person's joint?

    1. Arthroplasty

    2. Arthrotomy

    3. Arthrectomy

B. Which term means the partial surgical removal of the skull?
   1. Craniotomy
   2. Craniectomy
   3. Craniplasty

C. Which term refers to a surgical incision into the brain?
   1. Encephalotomy
   2. Encephoplasty
   3. Encephalectomy

CHECKYOURANSWERHERECHECKYOURANSWERHERECHECKYOURANSWERHERE
CHECKYOURANSWERHERECHECKYOURANSWERHERECHECKYOURANSWERHERE
CHECKYOURANSWERHERECHECKYOURANSWERHERECHECKYOURANSWERHERE
CHECKYOURANSWERHERECHECKYOURANSWERHERECHECKYOURANSWERHERE

22. Both of the suffixes listed below mean **pain**:

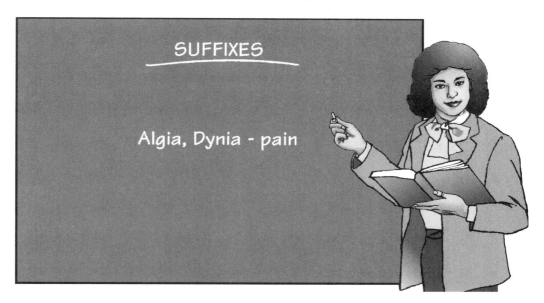

Of the terms listed below, select all that mean **pain in the ear**.
A. Otalgia
B. Otoplasty
C. Otodynia
D. Otectomy

CHECKYOURANSWERHERECHECKYOURANSWERHERECHECKYOURANSWERHERE
CHECKYOURANSWERHERECHECKYOURANSWERHERECHECKYOURANSWERHERE
CHECKYOURANSWERHERECHECKYOURANSWERHERECHECKYOURANSWERHERE
CHECKYOURANSWERHERECHECKYOURANSWERHERECHECKYOURANSWERHERE

23. The following suffixes are used in medical terms to describe a condition or disease of a specific body part:

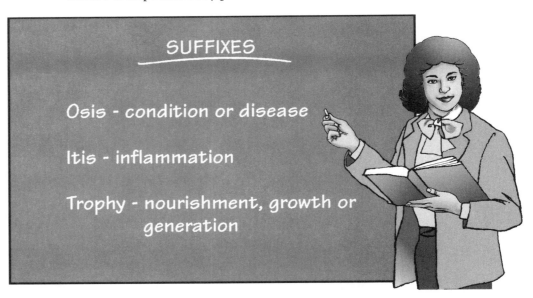

SUFFIXES

Osis - condition or disease

Itis - inflammation

Trophy - nourishment, growth or generation

Combining the suffix **osis** with the root word for nerve, **neuro**, gives us the term **neurosis**, which means a **condition of the nerves**.

Earlier, you learned that the prefix *arthr* means *pertaining to a joint*. Joints are places where bones join together, or *articulate*. Adding the suffix **itis** to this prefix gives you the word **arthritis**, which means **inflammation of a joint**.

You may see *arthritis* combined with the root word for bone, *osteo*. **Osteoarthritis** sounds like an inflammation of a bone and a joint. However, since there would be no joints without bones to form them, the terms *osteo* and *arthr* together mean the *joint end of a bone*; that is, the end of a bone that forms a joint with another bone. So, the most accurate definition of osteoarthritis is the **inflammation of the joint, or articular, end of a bone**.

You're probably familiar with the word **atrophy**, which is a combination of the prefix *a*, which means a *negative condition*, and the suffix *trophy*. The term **atrophy** literally means without nourishment. Without nourishment, living things will waste away, and this is the usual concept of the term atrophy—wasting away from lack of nourishment.

True or false?

A.   The suffix *trophy* means inflammation.   ( ) True   ( ) False

B.   The suffix *itis* means inflammation.   ( ) True   ( ) False

C.   *Osis* means a condition or disease.   ( ) True   ( ) False

D.   *Trophy* refers to the nourishment, growth, or generation of organs or other structures.   ( ) True   ( ) False

CHECKYOURANSWERHERECHECKYOURANSWERHERECHECKYOURANSWERHERE
CHECKYOURANSWERHERECHECKYOURANSWERHERECHECKYOURANSWERHERE
CHECKYOURANSWERHERECHECKYOURANSWERHERECHECKYOURANSWERHERE
CHECKYOURANSWERHERECHECKYOURANSWERHERECHECKYOURANSWERHERE

24. Define the following medical terms.

    A. Hepatitis _____

    B. Spondylosis _____

    C. Neuritis _____

    D. Neuroplasty _____

    E. Craniotomy _____

    F. Ostectomy _____

    G. Cephalalgia _____

    H. Myodynia _____

    I. Osteoarthritis _____

    J. Atrophy _____

CHECKYOURANSWERHERECHECKYOURANSWERHERECHECKYOURANSWERHERE
CHECKYOURANSWERHERECHECKYOURANSWERHERECHECKYOURANSWERHERE
CHECKYOURANSWERHERECHECKYOURANSWERHERECHECKYOURANSWERHERE
CHECKYOURANSWERHERECHECKYOURANSWERHERECHECKYOURANSWERHERE
CHECKYOURANSWERHERECHECKYOURANSWERHERECHECKYOURANSWERHERE
CHECKYOURANSWERHERECHECKYOURANSWERHERECHECKYOURANSWERHERE
CHECKYOURANSWERHERECHECKYOURANSWERHERECHECKYOURANSWERHERE

25. Two other common suffixes are:

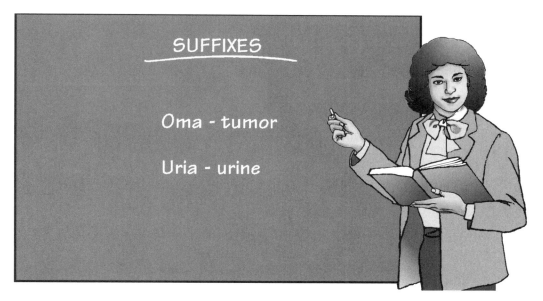

SUFFIXES

Oma - tumor

Uria - urine

These suffixes are frequently combined with the root word for blood, *hemat*, to create the terms **hematoma** and **hematuria**.

Define these terms.

    A. Hematoma _____

    B. Hematuria _blood in urine_____

CHECKYOURANSWERHERECHECKYOURANSWERHERECHECKYOURANSWERHERE
CHECKYOURANSWERHERECHECKYOURANSWERHERECHECKYOURANSWERHERE
CHECKYOURANSWERHERECHECKYOURANSWERHERECHECKYOURANSWERHERE
CHECKYOURANSWERHERECHECKYOURANSWERHERECHECKYOURANSWERHERE

26. You know that the root word for blood is *hemat* or *hemato*. Both of these suffixes also refer to blood:

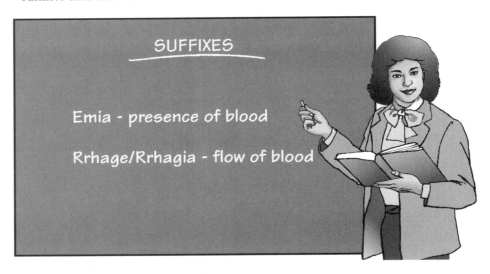

SUFFIXES

Emia - presence of blood

Rrhage/Rrhagia - flow of blood

Since you now know three terms related to blood, let's reiterate the use of these terms. *Hemat* or *hemato* means *the blood itself*. *Emia* means the *presence* of blood. Finally, *rrhage* or *rrhagia* refers to a *flow* of blood.

Let's combine each of these with some terms you already know and define them.

A. The presence of blood in a bone is
    1. ostemia.
    2. hematemia.
    3. osteorrhagia.

B. Osteorrhagia is
    1. the presence of blood in a bone.
    2. the flow of blood from a bone.
    3. a blood tumor in a bone.

C. A blood tumor is a
    1. hematoma.
    2. omarrhagia.
    3. hematemia.

CHECKYOURANSWERHERECHECKYOURANSWERHERECHECKYOURANSWERHERE
CHECKYOURANSWERHERECHECKYOURANSWERHERECHECKYOURANSWERHERE
CHECKYOURANSWERHERECHECKYOURANSWERHERECHECKYOURANSWERHERE
CHECKYOURANSWERHERECHECKYOURANSWERHERECHECKYOURANSWERHERE

27. The last set of suffixes for you to learn includes these terms:

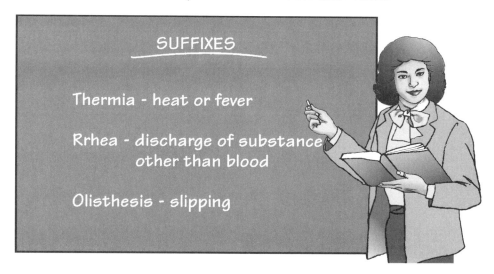

SUFFIXES

Thermia - heat or fever

Rrhea - discharge of substance other than blood

Olisthesis - slipping

When you combine the suffix **thermia** with the prefix **hyper**, you get the word for **high fever**, which is **hyperthermia**.

Rrhea, as you will note, refers to a **discharge of a substance other than blood**. For example, a patient who has an earache might suffer from **otorrhea**, which is a **discharge from the ear**.

You may see the suffix **olisthesis** combined with the root word **spondyl**. The literal translation of the resulting term, **spondylolisthesis**, is a slipped vertebra. However, the precise definition is a condition in which a vertebra has slipped *forward* over the vertebra below it.

Write in the medical suffix used to describe each of the following conditions.

A. Slipping _____

B. Heat or fever _____

C. Discharge of a substance other than blood _____

28. Write in the correct medical term for each of the following conditions.

A. Low fever _____

B. Blood in a bone _____

C. Blood in the urine _____

D. Flow of blood from the ear _____

E. Flow of blood from a bone _____

F. Vertebra has slipped over the one below it _____

29. This concludes our discussion of basic root words, prefixes, and suffixes. Before you continue with the next topic—medical specialties—complete the following review exercises.

The left-hand column below contains a list of medical terms with a root word, suffix, prefix, or definition missing. The right-hand column lists the missing part of each term. Write in the correct letter of the missing part in the space provided.

1. Oto + _____ = discharge of something besides blood from the ear.

2. _____ + tension = low blood pressure.

3. Hyper + hidrosis = _____.

4. Hyper + _____ = excessive blood.

5. Hypo + thermia = _____.

6. _____ + algia = nerve pain.

7. Arthr + itis = _____.

8. Encephal + _____ = swelling in the brain.

9. Crani + _____ = surgical removal of part of the skull.

10. Osteo + myel + itis = _____.

11. Osteo + _____ + itis = inflammation of bone and cartilage.

12. Osteo + arthr + otomy = _____.

13. _____ + esthesia = lack of sensation, perception, or feeling.

14. _____ + osteum = covering around a bone.

15. Myo + sclerosis = _____.

16. _____ + otic = on the ear.

17. Epi + _____ = on the skin.

18. _____ + vertebral = alongside a vertebra.

19. Intra + cranial = _____.

20. Myo + _____ + itis = inflammation of the heart muscle.

21. Gastr + itis = _____.

22. _____ + costal = between a rib.

23. My + asthenia = _____.

A. Ectomy

B. Hardening of muscle

C. Rrhea

D. Inflammation of a joint

E. Itis

F. Inflammation of stomach

G. Epi

H. Weakness in muscle

I. Hypo

J. Chondr

K. Peri

L. Emia

M. Excessive sweating

N. Within the skull

O. Inter

P. Inflammation of bone and bone marrow

Q. Neur

R. Low fever

S. An

T. Dermis

U. Card

V. Para

W. Surgical incision into bone end of joint

TERMS RELATED TO MEDICAL SPECIALTIES

30. After a patient has received the initial treatment for a medical problem, he or she is often referred to a specialist in some area for ongoing medical treatment. In this section, you'll learn some more medical terms which apply to medical specialists in various fields.

Cardiologist, Dermatologist, Neurologist, Otologist

31. We'll begin with some easy ones—those you can easily identify based on the medical terms you just learned. Define each of the following types of specialists.

   A. Cardiologist _____

   B. Dermatologist _____

   C. Neurologist _____

   D. Otologist _____

Ophthalmologist

32. You probably noticed that all of the specialist names in the preceding frame ended in the suffix **ologist**, which comes from this Greek term:

SUFFIXES

Ology - study or science of

So, to use an example from the preceding frame, **cardiology** is the **study or science of** the heart.

Changing the **gy** to **gist** changes the meaning to **one who studies or one who specializes.** So, a *cardiologist* is someone who *studies or specializes in the heart*.

Here is another root word for you to learn:

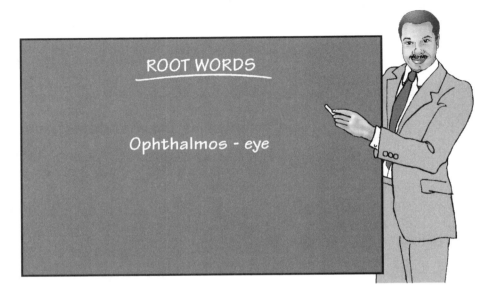

Based on the illustrations in this frame, which one of the terms in the following list means an eye specialist?

A. Ophthalmologist

B. Otologist

C. Cardiologist

CHECKYOURANSWERHERECHECKYOURANSWERHERECHECKYOURANSWERHERE
CHECKYOURANSWERHERECHECKYOURANSWERHERECHECKYOURANSWERHERE
CHECKYOURANSWERHERECHECKYOURANSWERHERECHECKYOURANSWERHERE
CHECKYOURANSWERHERECHECKYOURANSWERHERECHECKYOURANSWERHERE

Laryngologist, Otolaryngologist

33. Here are two new types of specialists for you to learn, both of which are based on the Greek word for **voice box**, or **larynx**, which is **larynges:**

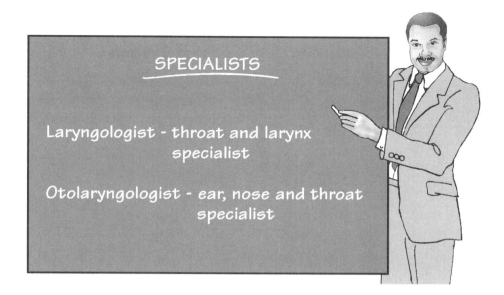

Note that while the *literal* translation of **otolaryngologist** is an ear, throat and larynx specialist, the term actually means an ear, nose and throat specialist.

A. A specialist in diseases of the throat and larynx is a/an _____ gologist.

B. A specialist in diseases of the ear, nose and throat is a/an _____ gologist.

CHECKYOURANSWERHERECHECKYOURANSWERHERECHECKYOURANSWERHERE
CHECKYOURANSWERHERECHECKYOURANSWERHERECHECKYOURANSWERHERE
CHECKYOURANSWERHERECHECKYOURANSWERHERECHECKYOURANSWERHERE
CHECKYOURANSWERHERECHECKYOURANSWERHERECHECKYOURANSWERHERE

Radiologist

34. A **radiologist** is a physician who specializes in interpreting x-rays. The name is derived from this Latin word:

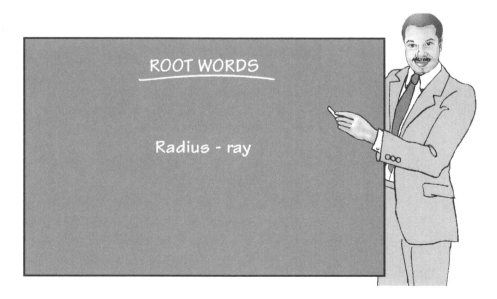

Because x-rays are sometimes used to treat diseases (to kill cancer cells, for example), the term *radiologist* may also be used to refer to a physician who uses x-rays in a therapeutic manner.

A radiologist

A. is strictly an interpreter of the x-rays someone else has taken.

B. not only interprets x-rays, but may also administer them to treat certain diseases.

C. may administer x-rays to treat diseases, but is never involved in interpreting x-rays.

CHECKYOURANSWERHERECHECKYOURANSWERHERECHECKYOURANSWERHERE
CHECKYOURANSWERHERECHECKYOURANSWERHERECHECKYOURANSWERHERE
CHECKYOURANSWERHERECHECKYOURANSWERHERECHECKYOURANSWERHERE
CHECKYOURANSWERHERECHECKYOURANSWERHERECHECKYOURANSWERHERE

Oncologist

35. The word **oncologist** is derived from this Greek prefix:

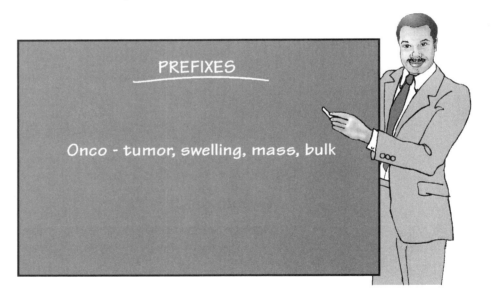

Although the prefix **onco** technically refers to any type of tumor, swelling, or mass, it is commonly used to specifically describe **cancerous** tumors.

Based on what you just read, a physician who specializes in the treatment of cancer is a/an _____logist.

CHECKYOURANSWERHERECHECKYOURANSWERHERECHECKYOURANSWERHERE
CHECKYOURANSWERHERECHECKYOURANSWERHERECHECKYOURANSWERHERE
CHECKYOURANSWERHERECHECKYOURANSWERHERECHECKYOURANSWERHERE
CHECKYOURANSWERHERECHECKYOURANSWERHERECHECKYOURANSWERHERE

Pathologist

36. You may see references in medical reports and claims to the **pathology** of a disease. This word is derived from the following Greek term:

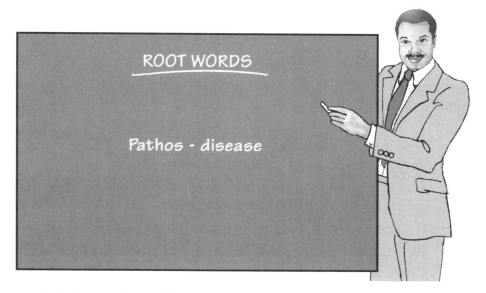

ROOT WORDS

Pathos - disease

Pathology is the **study of** the nature and cause of a disease, so a **pathologist** is someone who **specializes** in the _____
_____.

CHECKYOURANSWERHERECHECKYOURANSWERHERECHECKYOURANSWERHERE
CHECKYOURANSWERHERECHECKYOURANSWERHERECHECKYOURANSWERHERE
CHECKYOURANSWERHERECHECKYOURANSWERHERECHECKYOURANSWERHERE
CHECKYOURANSWERHERECHECKYOURANSWERHERECHECKYOURANSWERHERE

Internist

37. Another medical specialty you'll see frequently in claim work is **internist**.

ROOT WORDS

Intern - inside

An internist is a physician who specializes in internal medicine, treating diseases of the internal organs by *nonsurgical means*.

How do internists treat medical problems?

A. Through surgical treatment

B. Through nonsurgical treatment

C. Through a combination of surgical and nonsurgical treatment

CHECKYOURANSWERHERECHECKYOURANSWERHERECHECKYOURANSWERHERE
CHECKYOURANSWERHERECHECKYOURANSWERHERECHECKYOURANSWERHERE
CHECKYOURANSWERHERECHECKYOURANSWERHERECHECKYOURANSWERHERE
CHECKYOURANSWERHERECHECKYOURANSWERHERECHECKYOURANSWERHERE

Orthopedist

38. The last medical specialist we'll discuss is an **orthopedist**. The term is a combination of these Greek words:

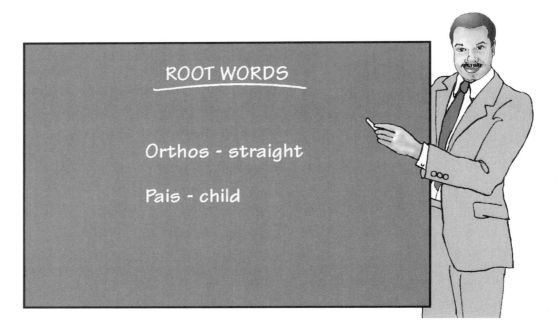

ROOT WORDS

Orthos - straight

Pais - child

From the illustration, you'd think that an orthopedist specializes in straightening out children, and this is actually where the term comes from. At one time, bone deformities were so common in children that the entire branch of orthopedics was devoted to correcting bone-deformed children. The term has since been broadened to include all ages and all disorders of the skeleton and joints.

Today's orthopedist treats disorders of the skeleton and joints in

A. children only.

B. adults only.

C. both children and adults.

CHECKYOURANSWERHERECHECKYOURANSWERHERECHECKYOURANSWERHERE
CHECKYOURANSWERHERECHECKYOURANSWERHERECHECKYOURANSWERHERE
CHECKYOURANSWERHERECHECKYOURANSWERHERECHECKYOURANSWERHERE
CHECKYOURANSWERHERECHECKYOURANSWERHERECHECKYOURANSWERHERE

Physical and Occupational Therapists

39. Two other "specialists" you'll probably encounter in claim work are not physicians, but medically trained persons who assist in the rehabilitation process. They are **physical therapists** and **occupational therapists**.

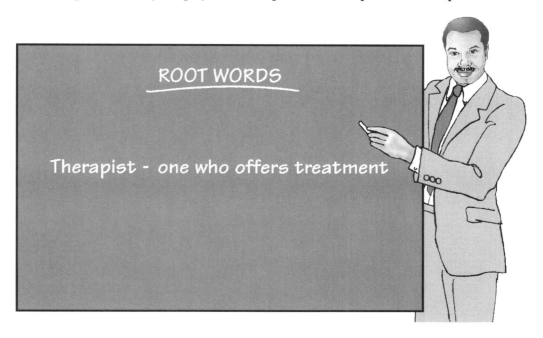

ROOT WORDS

Therapist - one who offers treatment

A **physical** therapist treats disease through the use of **physical agents** such as massage, heat, radiation, water, electricity, and exercise.

An **occupational** therapist takes into consideration elements of the patient's life—not just the disease elements—in **evaluating and helping plan work, play, and self-care activities** to treat the physically or emotionally ill person and to prevent or minimize disability.

A. A therapist who uses physical agents to restore health is a/an (physical/occupational) _____ therapist.

B. A therapist who takes into consideration the elements of a person's life as part of the treatment plan is a/an (physical/occupational) _____ therapist.

CHECKYOURANSWERHERECHECKYOURANSWERHERECHECKYOURANSWERHERE
CHECKYOURANSWERHERECHECKYOURANSWERHERECHECKYOURANSWERHERE
CHECKYOURANSWERHERECHECKYOURANSWERHERECHECKYOURANSWERHERE
CHECKYOURANSWERHERECHECKYOURANSWERHERECHECKYOURANSWERHERE

Chiropractor

40. Another type of health care professional is a **chiropractor**. The name is derived from these Greek terms:

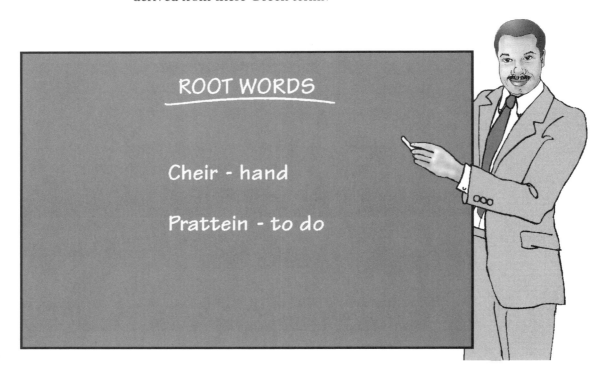

Based on the illustration, it appears that a chiropractor specializes in treating diseases of the hand. Actually, the term is more descriptive of **how a chiropractor treats patients**, which is usually through the **use of the hands**. Chiropractors focus on the relationship between the structure of the human body, particularly the spinal column, and how the body functions, primarily the nervous system, in order to preserve health. Chiropractors treat most medical conditions by manipulating and adjusting the body, particularly the spinal column.

How does a chiropractor treat diseases? _____

_____

_____

CHECKYOURANSWERHERECHECKYOURANSWERHERECHECKYOURANSWERHERE
CHECKYOURANSWERHERECHECKYOURANSWERHERECHECKYOURANSWERHERE
CHECKYOURANSWERHERECHECKYOURANSWERHERECHECKYOURANSWERHERE
CHECKYOURANSWERHERECHECKYOURANSWERHERECHECKYOURANSWERHERE

41. Match the name of the specialist in the left-hand column with its correct definition in the right-hand column.

1.	Physical therapist	____ A.	Specialist in nature and cause of diseases
2.	Dermatologist	____ B.	Heart specialist
3.	Otologist	____ C.	Uses physical agents to treat diseases
4.	Occupational therapist	____ D.	Ear specialist
5.	Chiropractor	____ E.	Cancer specialist
6.	Oncologist	____ F.	Treats disease by manipulating and adjusting the body
7.	Cardiologist	____ G.	Treats diseases of the internal organs through nonsurgical means
8.	Orthopedist	____ H.	Larynx and throat specialist
9.	Radiologist	____ I.	Eye specialist
10.	Neurologist	____ J.	Takes patient's life activities into consideration when treating diseases
11.	Laryngologist	____ K.	Ear, nose and throat specialist
12.	Otolaryngologist	____ L.	Specialist in bones and joints of the skeleton
13.	Ophthalmologist	____ M.	Specialist who interprets x-rays and may use x-rays in treatment
14.	Pathologist	____ N.	Specialist in diseases of the nerves
15.	Internist	____ O.	Skin specialist

CHECKYOURANSWERHERECHECKYOURANSWERHERECHECKYOURANSWERHERE
CHECKYOURANSWERHERECHECKYOURANSWERHERECHECKYOURANSWERHERE
CHECKYOURANSWERHERECHECKYOURANSWERHERECHECKYOURANSWERHERE
CHECKYOURANSWERHERECHECKYOURANSWERHERECHECKYOURANSWERHERE

COMMON MEDICAL ABBREVIATIONS

42. The medical reports you will be required to analyze on the job will contain a variety of written abbreviations. In this section, we will introduce some of the medical abbreviations you are likely to encounter on the job.

    While most medical abbreviations have their basis in Latin, you don't need to be a Latin scholar to understand them. That's because many words in the English language are derived from Latin, so it's easy to make logical connections between the Latin abbreviations and their meanings. A few abbreviations commonly used today come directly from the English language.

True or false?

A. All medical abbreviations have their basis in Latin.
( ) True   ( ) False

B. In order to understand medical abbreviations, you must first study Latin.   ( ) True   ( ) False

C. Some abbreviations come directly from English.   ( ) True   ( ) False

CHECKYOURANSWERHERECHECKYOURANSWERHERECHECKYOURANSWERHERE
CHECKYOURANSWERHERECHECKYOURANSWERHERECHECKYOURANSWERHERE
CHECKYOURANSWERHERECHECKYOURANSWERHERECHECKYOURANSWERHERE
CHECKYOURANSWERHERECHECKYOURANSWERHERECHECKYOURANSWERHERE

43. Let's begin our study of medical abbreviations with the letter $\bar{s}$:

This abbreviation is based on the Latin word *sine*, which also means *without*.

You're reviewing a medical report that notes, "the patient left the hospital $\bar{s}$ prescribed medication." This patient left the hospital

A. before medication was prescribed.

B. with the medication that was prescribed.

C. without the medication that was prescribed.

CHECKYOURANSWERHERECHECKYOURANSWERHERECHECKYOURANSWERHERE
CHECKYOURANSWERHERECHECKYOURANSWERHERECHECKYOURANSWERHERE
CHECKYOURANSWERHERECHECKYOURANSWERHERECHECKYOURANSWERHERE
CHECKYOURANSWERHERECHECKYOURANSWERHERECHECKYOURANSWERHERE

44. Another common abbreviation is the letter c̄:

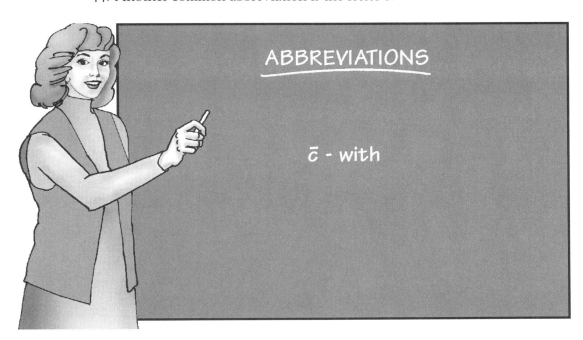

This abbreviation represents the Latin word *cum*, which means *with*. When someone graduates from college "with distinction," we use the phrase straight from Latin: *cum laude*. In English, the spelling has been changed to *com*, and it is used in a number of words that use the concept of *with*, such as *composure* or *compassion*.

An excerpt from a medical report says, "this medication must be taken c̄ water." This patient must take the medication

A. without drinking any water.

B. with water.

C. before drinking water.

CHECKYOURANSWERHERECHECKYOURANSWERHERECHECKYOURANSWERHERE
CHECKYOURANSWERHERECHECKYOURANSWERHERECHECKYOURANSWERHERE
CHECKYOURANSWERHERECHECKYOURANSWERHERECHECKYOURANSWERHERE
CHECKYOURANSWERHERECHECKYOURANSWERHERECHECKYOURANSWERHERE

45. Another medical abbreviation you should be familiar with is **ss**.

This abbreviation comes from the Latin word *semis*, which means *half*. Note the *s* at the beginning and end of semis, and you'll see the origin of this abbreviation. *Semis* is similar to *semi*, the English word that means half. Think of words such as semiannual and semicircle, each signifying a half of something.

A medical report states, "patient should receive ss of a dosage of prescribed medication." This patient should receive

A. a half dosage of the prescribed medication.

B. a full dosage of the prescribed medication.

C. none of the prescribed medication.

CHECKYOURANSWERHERECHECKYOURANSWERHERECHECKYOURANSWERHERE
CHECKYOURANSWERHERECHECKYOURANSWERHERECHECKYOURANSWERHERE
CHECKYOURANSWERHERECHECKYOURANSWERHERECHECKYOURANSWERHERE
CHECKYOURANSWERHERECHECKYOURANSWERHERECHECKYOURANSWERHERE

46. Abbreviations are sometimes used in conjunction with instructions for **how often something is to be done**. For example, a patient might be instructed to take a prescribed medication three times a day, or someone might be required to have a certain procedure performed every day during a hospital stay. Let's begin with this abbreviation:

This abbreviation is based on the Latin phrase *in die*. Note how similar *in die* is to the English derivative, *in a day*.

Another letter is then added at the beginning of the abbreviation *i.d.* to complete the instruction. The most commonly used are:

What does the abbreviation i.d. stand for? _____

47. The *b* in *b.i.d.* comes from the Latin word *bis*, from which the English language derives the prefix *bi*, as in biannual or bilateral.

    Based on this explanation, what do you think b.i.d. means? _____

CHECKYOURANSWERHERECHECKYOURANSWERHERECHECKYOURANSWERHERE
CHECKYOURANSWERHERECHECKYOURANSWERHERECHECKYOURANSWERHERE
CHECKYOURANSWERHERECHECKYOURANSWERHERECHECKYOURANSWERHERE
CHECKYOURANSWERHERECHECKYOURANSWERHERECHECKYOURANSWERHERE

48. Another abbreviation is *t.i.d.*. This stands for *ter in die*. One English word that uses the Latin word *ter* is tertiary, which means *third*. Other English words use its derivative *tri*, such as tricycle or triangle.

    Based on this information, what does t.i.d. mean? _____

CHECKYOURANSWERHERECHECKYOURANSWERHERECHECKYOURANSWERHERE
CHECKYOURANSWERHERECHECKYOURANSWERHERECHECKYOURANSWERHERE
CHECKYOURANSWERHERECHECKYOURANSWERHERECHECKYOURANSWERHERE
CHECKYOURANSWERHERECHECKYOURANSWERHERECHECKYOURANSWERHERE

49. The final abbreviation is *q.i.d.*, meaning *quater in die*. The term *quater* is very close to the English words *quarter* and *quadruple*.

    You can probably figure out the meaning of q.i.d. without any more information. What is it? _____

CHECKYOURANSWERHERECHECKYOURANSWERHERECHECKYOURANSWERHERE
CHECKYOURANSWERHERECHECKYOURANSWERHERECHECKYOURANSWERHERE
CHECKYOURANSWERHERECHECKYOURANSWERHERECHECKYOURANSWERHERE
CHECKYOURANSWERHERECHECKYOURANSWERHERECHECKYOURANSWERHERE

50. You know that q.i.d. means four times a day. There are two other abbreviations that are very close in construction, but different in meaning. They are:

With these abbreviations, the *q* stands for *quaque*, which means *every*. There isn't a similar-sounding English word to help you remember what the *q* means in this case, so you'll have to rely on memorization. When *q* is used alone, it *always* means *every*.

Use these hints to help you remember the difference between q.d. and q.o.d.:

■ The *d* in q.d. refers to the Latin word *die*, or *day*, so q.d. means *every day*.

■ For q.o.d., associate the letter *o* with the word *other*, then translate q.o.d. to *every other day*.

The letter *q* is sometimes used in other ways to designate *every*. For example, the letter **h** stands for **hour** or **hours**, so an order to give medication every two hours might be abbreviated as **q2h**.

Study the following medical report excerpt, then go on to the questions below.

Patient was given medication to control high blood pressure q.d. for two weeks beginning August 1. Patient's blood pressure was checked q.o.d.

A. How often did the patient receive medication to control high blood pressure? _____

B. How often was the patient's blood pressure checked? _____

CHECKYOURANSWERHERECHECKYOURANSWERHERECHECKYOURANSWERHERE
CHECKYOURANSWERHERECHECKYOURANSWERHERECHECKYOURANSWERHERE
CHECKYOURANSWERHERECHECKYOURANSWERHERECHECKYOURANSWERHERE
CHECKYOURANSWERHERECHECKYOURANSWERHERECHECKYOURANSWERHERE

51. Here is another abbreviation for you to learn:

ABBREVIATIONS

h.s. - at bedtime

This abbreviation is based on the Latin phrase *hora somni*, which translates literally as *hour of sleep*. You can connect *somni* with the English word *somnolent*.

If a medical report notes that a patient has been prescribed medication to be taken *h.s.*, this means that the medicine must be taken

A. with food.

B. with water.

C. every other day.

D. at bedtime.

CHECKYOURANSWERHERECHECKYOURANSWERHERECHECKYOURANSWERHERE
CHECKYOURANSWERHERECHECKYOURANSWERHERECHECKYOURANSWERHERE
CHECKYOURANSWERHERECHECKYOURANSWERHERECHECKYOURANSWERHERE
CHECKYOURANSWERHERECHECKYOURANSWERHERECHECKYOURANSWERHERE

52. Some medications are available in a variety of forms, such as suppositories, capsules, pills, or liquids. The abbreviation used to indicate that medicine should be taken **by mouth** is:

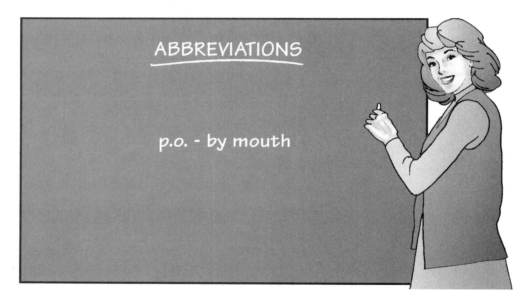

ABBREVIATIONS

p.o. - by mouth

This abbreviation stands for the Latin terms *per os* or *per ora*. In English, *oral* means *by mouth*, so this abbreviation should be easy for you to remember.

When a patient is instructed to take medication p.o., this means that the medicine should be taken

A. every day.

B. at bedtime.

C. every four hours.

D. by mouth.

CHECKYOURANSWERHERECHECKYOURANSWERHERECHECKYOURANSWERHERE
CHECKYOURANSWERHERECHECKYOURANSWERHERECHECKYOURANSWERHERE
CHECKYOURANSWERHERECHECKYOURANSWERHERECHECKYOURANSWERHERE
CHECKYOURANSWERHERECHECKYOURANSWERHERECHECKYOURANSWERHERE

53. Before surgery and certain types of tests, patients are not allowed to have anything to eat or drink; that is:

ABBREVIATIONS

n.p.o. - nothing by mouth

Mrs. Li is scheduled for surgery at 8:00 Monday morning. Her physician doesn't want her to have anything to eat or drink after midnight on Sunday. How will this order be listed on her doctor's report? _____

CHECKYOURANSWERHERECHECKYOURANSWERHERECHECKYOURANSWERHERE
CHECKYOURANSWERHERECHECKYOURANSWERHERECHECKYOURANSWERHERE
CHECKYOURANSWERHERECHECKYOURANSWERHERECHECKYOURANSWERHERE
CHECKYOURANSWERHERECHECKYOURANSWERHERECHECKYOURANSWERHERE

54. Orders for medication and treatment may be referred to in the following way:

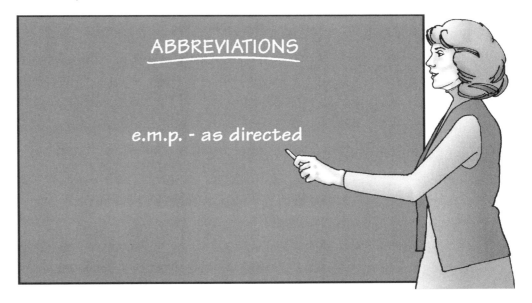

ABBREVIATIONS

e.m.p. - as directed

This abbreviation represents the first three initials of the Latin phrase *ex modo prescripto*, which means *in the mode prescribed*.

Translate the following instructions.

Patient is to have n.p.o. after midnight e.m.p. _____

_____

55. Medication is sometimes administered by drops. The medical abbreviation for drops is:

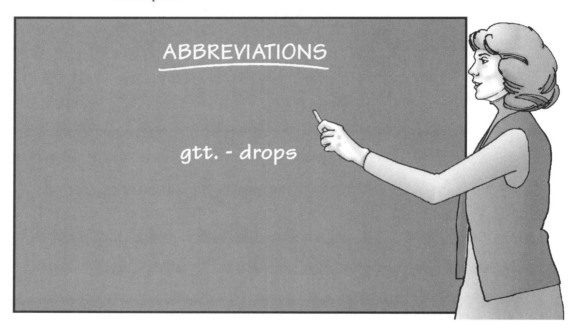

ABBREVIATIONS

gtt. - drops

The Latin term for drops is *guttae*. An English word derived from this Latin word is *gutters*, the troughs that drop down from the eaves of roofs to carry away rain water. While this may seem to be far removed from the concept of medicine, the spelling of the word gutter can help you remember *guttae* and the abbreviation *gtt*.

What do the following instructions mean?
Four gtt. in each ear e.m.p. _____

56. The next two groups of abbreviations are all based on English words. They are either shortened versions of the actual word or made up of one or two key letters.

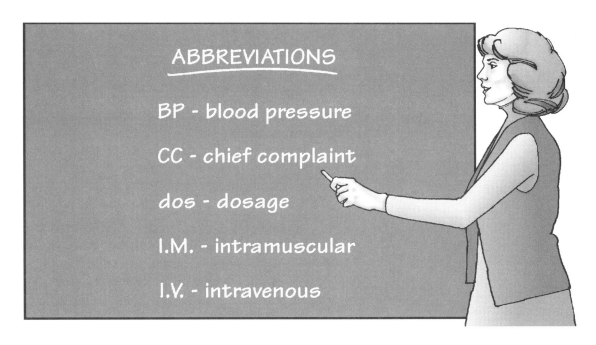

ABBREVIATIONS

BP - blood pressure

CC - chief complaint

dos - dosage

I.M. - intramuscular

I.V. - intravenous

Write in the correct abbreviation for each of the following words.

A. Blood pressure _____

B. Intramuscular _____

C. Chief complaint _____

D. Intravenous _____

E. Dose _____

CHECKYOURANSWERHERECHECKYOURANSWERHERECHECKYOURANSWERHERE
CHECKYOURANSWERHERECHECKYOURANSWERHERECHECKYOURANSWERHERE
CHECKYOURANSWERHERECHECKYOURANSWERHERECHECKYOURANSWERHERE
CHECKYOURANSWERHERECHECKYOURANSWERHERECHECKYOURANSWERHERE

57. Here are some more English-based medical abbreviations:

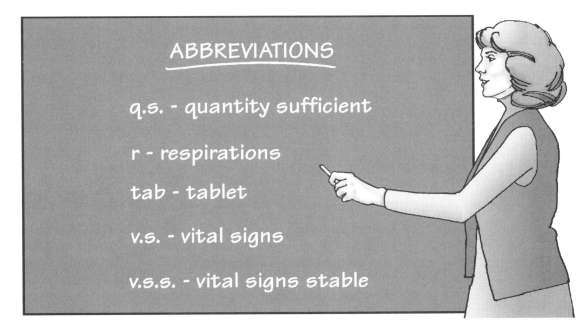

ABBREVIATIONS

q.s. - quantity sufficient

r - respirations

tab - tablet

v.s. - vital signs

v.s.s. - vital signs stable

Abbreviate these terms.

A. Tablet _____

B. Vital signs _____

C. Vital signs stable _____

D. Respirations _____

E. Quantity sufficient _____

CHECKYOURANSWERHERECHECKYOURANSWERHERECHECKYOURANSWERHERE
CHECKYOURANSWERHERECHECKYOURANSWERHERECHECKYOURANSWERHERE
CHECKYOURANSWERHERECHECKYOURANSWERHERECHECKYOURANSWERHERE
CHECKYOURANSWERHERECHECKYOURANSWERHERECHECKYOURANSWERHERE

58. Review your knowledge of medical abbreviations by translating the follow-
    ing medical report excerpts.

A. Medication should be taken h.s. s̄ food or milk. _____

    _____

    _____

B. Patient's back injury was treated c̄ medication and physical therapy.

    _____

    _____

    _____

C. Patient's v.s. must be checked q2h. _____

    _____

    _____

D. Patient should take ss dos of medicine q.i.d. e.m.p. _____

    _____

    _____

E. Patient should have n.p.o. two hours prior to examination. _____

    _____

    _____

CHECKYOURANSWERHERECHECKYOURANSWERHERECHECKYOURANSWERHERE
CHECKYOURANSWERHERECHECKYOURANSWERHERECHECKYOURANSWERHERE
CHECKYOURANSWERHERECHECKYOURANSWERHERECHECKYOURANSWERHERE
CHECKYOURANSWERHERECHECKYOURANSWERHERECHECKYOURANSWERHERE
CHECKYOURANSWERHERECHECKYOURANSWERHERECHECKYOURANSWERHERE
CHECKYOURANSWERHERECHECKYOURANSWERHERECHECKYOURANSWERHERE
CHECKYOURANSWERHERECHECKYOURANSWERHERECHECKYOURANSWERHERE
CHECKYOURANSWERHERECHECKYOURANSWERHERECHECKYOURANSWERHERE

REVIEW

59. This completes your study of the terminology, specialties, and abbreviations
    unique to the medical field. Complete the following review exercises before
    you go on to the next unit. You may also want to turn to the back of the
    book and review the tear-out Job Aids for medical abbreviations and medi-
    cal terminology.

Write in the correct medical term for the following descriptions of diseases and medical conditions.

A. Wasting away of the brain _____

B. Inflammation of bone marrow _____

C. Muscle weakness _____

D. Brain tumor _____

E. Inflammation of articular cartilage _____

F. Sweat contains blood _____

CHECKYOURANSWERHERECHECKYOURANSWERHERECHECKYOURANSWERHERE
CHECKYOURANSWERHERECHECKYOURANSWERHERECHECKYOURANSWERHERE
CHECKYOURANSWERHERECHECKYOURANSWERHERECHECKYOURANSWERHERE
CHECKYOURANSWERHERECHECKYOURANSWERHERECHECKYOURANSWERHERE

60. In the left-hand column are examples of claimants with specific diseases or conditions. Match each example with the type of specialist listed in the right-hand column that the claimant is likely to consult for his or her condition.

1. Rupert Young, heart disease	_____ A.	Otologist
2. Ashley Perkins, acne	_____ B.	Cardiologist
3. Geneveive DeShannon, lung cancer	_____ C.	Oncologist
4. Martin Wilson, arthritis	_____ D.	Ophthalmologist
5. Brittany Lester, ear infection	_____ E.	Neurologist
6. James Irwin, glaucoma (a disease which affects the eye)	_____ F.	Orthopedist
	_____ G.	Dermatologist
7. Monty Abbott, nerve damage caused by a back injury		

CHECKYOURANSWERHERECHECKYOURANSWERHERECHECKYOURANSWERHERE
CHECKYOURANSWERHERECHECKYOURANSWERHERECHECKYOURANSWERHERE
CHECKYOURANSWERHERECHECKYOURANSWERHERECHECKYOURANSWERHERE
CHECKYOURANSWERHERECHECKYOURANSWERHERECHECKYOURANSWERHERE

61. Define the following medical abbreviations.

A. s̄ _without_ _____

B. c̄ _with_ _____

C. ss _half_ _____

D. b.i.d. _____

E. t.i.d. _____

F. q.i.d. _____

G. q.d. _____

H. q.o.d. _____

I. q4h _____

J. h.s. _____

K. p.o. _____

L. n.p.o. _____

M. e.m.p. _____

N. gtt. _____

O. BP _____

P. CC _____

Q. dos _____

R. I.M. _____

S. I.V. _____

T. q.s. _____

U. r _____

V. tab _____

W. v.s. _____

X. v.s.s. _____

2

Medical Usage
of Common Terms

FLESH AND SOFT TISSUE INJURIES

Bruises, Contusions, Abrasions

1. In everyday life, people speak of bruises, wounds, sprains and other types of injuries with a common understanding about what the terms generally mean. In medical cases, however, such words have very specifically defined meanings that are important in analyzing the severity of injuries. In this unit you will learn how certain terms are defined when used by medical personnel.

   A **bruise** and a **contusion** are the same thing: An injury that does *not* break the skin but which discolors it and also spreads into the tissue below the skin. The rupture of superficial blood vessels directly below the skin causes the discoloration. A contusion may be painful and cause swelling as well. Bruising may be referred to as **ecchymosis**. Bruise, contusion or ecchymosis, this is typically a nonthreatening injury in healthy people without other medical problems.

   Unlike a bruise, an **abrasion** scrapes away some of the skin and could include bleeding. Think about rubbing your knuckles along a rough cement surface, and you'll be able to visualize an abrasion. Again, this is a minor injury in healthy people. A scab forms quickly, preventing or minimizing infection.

   For each description below, write in a **B** if it refers to a bruise or an **A** if it refers to an abrasion. Write in both letters if the description applies to both bruises and abrasions.

   _____ A. Another term for a contusion

   _____ B. Protected during healing by scab formation

   _____ C. Scrapes away the skin

   _____ D. May cause swelling and pain, but the skin is unbroken

   _____ E. Nonthreatening in healthy individuals

   _____ F. Sometimes described as ecchymosis

CHECKYOURANSWERHERECHECKYOURANSWERHERECHECKYOURANSWERHERE
CHECKYOURANSWERHERECHECKYOURANSWERHERECHECKYOURANSWERHERE
CHECKYOURANSWERHERECHECKYOURANSWERHERECHECKYOURANSWERHERE
CHECKYOURANSWERHERECHECKYOURANSWERHERECHECKYOURANSWERHERE

Wounds

Lacerated Wounds

2. **Wounds** cause a break in the continuity of the soft parts of the body as the result of traumatic injury to soft tissue. Various kinds of wounds are specified by descriptive adjectives.

   A **lacerated wound** or **laceration** is an irregular tear of the flesh as opposed to a clean cut. Which of these illustrations shows a lacerated wound?

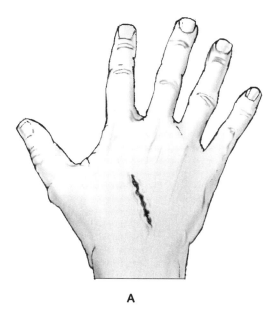

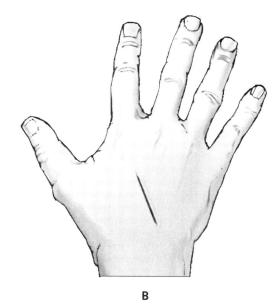

A **B**

CHECKYOURANSWERHERECHECKYOURANSWERHERECHECKYOURANSWERHERE
CHECKYOURANSWERHERECHECKYOURANSWERHERECHECKYOURANSWERHERE
CHECKYOURANSWERHERECHECKYOURANSWERHERECHECKYOURANSWERHERE
CHECKYOURANSWERHERECHECKYOURANSWERHERECHECKYOURANSWERHERE

Incised Wounds

3. An **incised wound** is a clean, straight cut caused by a sharp-edged instrument. Incised wounds do not have the irregular tearing that characterizes lacerations. An incised wound might result from a surgical incision but may also be caused by other means, such as stabbing.

   Complete the following sentences.
   A. The type of wound characterized by a clean, straight cut from a sharp-edged object is (lacerated/incised) _____.
   B. The type of wound characterized by irregular tearing is (lacerated/incised) _____.

CHECKYOURANSWERHERECHECKYOURANSWERHERECHECKYOURANSWERHERE
CHECKYOURANSWERHERECHECKYOURANSWERHERECHECKYOURANSWERHERE
CHECKYOURANSWERHERECHECKYOURANSWERHERECHECKYOURANSWERHERE
CHECKYOURANSWERHERECHECKYOURANSWERHERECHECKYOURANSWERHERE

Puncture Wounds

4. **Puncture wounds** are caused by a sharp, pointed instrument. Punctures leave a deep narrow hole penetrating the flesh, which makes proper cleansing difficult. Since germs and bacteria thrive in this environment, puncture wounds are prime sources for infection. A bullet wound is an example of a puncture wound.

   When an object breaks the skin and enters under the skin or deeper into the body, as a bullet might do, the wound is often referred to as a **penetrating** wound. Furthermore, in the case of a bullet or other object that not only penetrates but also exits at another point, such a wound is known as a **perforating** wound.

Each illustration below represents a kind of puncture wound. Label each as either a puncture wound **(PUNC)**, a penetrating wound **(PEN)**, or a perforating wound **(PERF)**.

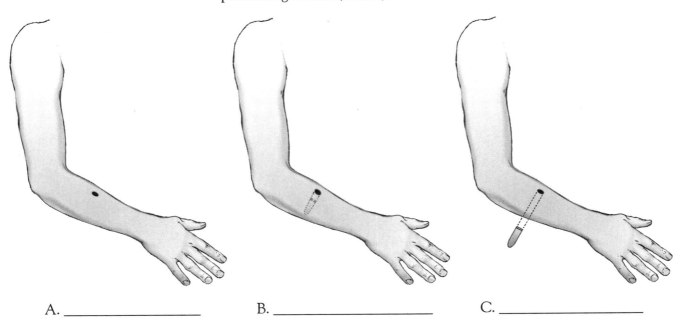

A. _____   B. _____   C. _____

Crushing Wounds

5. A **crushing wound** is caused by trauma of sufficient force to smash or compress the tissues but sometimes without lacerating the skin. If the skin *is* broken, bleeding may occur. Broken bones are common with crushing wounds because of the extreme force that caused the injury.

    Answer these questions concerning crushing wounds.

    A. What occurs to tissue when a crushing wound occurs?_____
    _____
    _____

    B. What other type of injury occurs frequently with crushing wounds?
    _____

    C. Is the skin broken with a crushing wound?_____

6. Match the type of wound in the left-hand column with the injury it corresponds to in the right-hand column. **Some answers may be used more than once**.

1. Skin is scraped	_____ A. Multiple contusions of right cheek
2. Deep, narrow hole caused by sharp pointed instrument	_____ B. Penetrating wound in upper left thigh
3. Irregular tear in the flesh	_____ C. Incised wound, right index finger
4. Skin is bruised but not broken	_____ D. Abrasion and contusion, tip of left ring finger
5. Clean, straight cut caused by sharp-edged instrument	_____ E. Severe lacerations, right eyebrow and right chin
6. Object causing the wound has passed completely through the body	_____ F Crushing wound with lacerations, upper right shoulder
7. Soft tissue is smashed	_____ G. Perforating wound in left forearm; ecchymosis and abrasions on left elbow
8. Wounding object is lodged beneath the skin	_____ H. Puncture wound, right thigh; multiple abrasions and contusions, left thigh and knee

CHECKYOURANSWERHERECHECKYOURANSWERHERECHECKYOURANSWERHERE
CHECKYOURANSWERHERECHECKYOURANSWERHERECHECKYOURANSWERHERE
CHECKYOURANSWERHERECHECKYOURANSWERHERECHECKYOURANSWERHERE
CHECKYOURANSWERHERECHECKYOURANSWERHERECHECKYOURANSWERHERE

Implications of Flesh and Soft Tissue Injury

Infection and Scarring

7. Whenever the skin is broken, as it is with a wound, there is danger of infection. Some types of wounds are more likely to become infected than others—puncture wounds for example. However, infection can usually be controlled with drugs or other medical care appropriate to the situation.

In addition to infection, scarring may have an adverse effect on the injured person even though the medical significance of a scar could be slight. For example, a fairly minor facial wound might cause no ongoing health problems but could pose a psychological problem concerning scarring on the face.

While superficial scars usually disappear over time, deep or jagged wounds can result in a lasting scar. It is difficult to determine the end result of such a wound until several months have passed since most wounds appear severe immediately after they occur.

The long-term evaluation of a scar, especially on the face, therefore, should be made

A. as soon as the injuries are reported to the insurance company since the severity is most apparent at that time.

B. on the basis of the psychological effect on the injured person.

C. sometime after healing has progressed sufficiently to determine the severity and extent of the scarring that will result.

CHECKYOURANSWERHERECHECKYOURANSWERHERECHECKYOURANSWERHERE
CHECKYOURANSWERHERECHECKYOURANSWERHERECHECKYOURANSWERHERE
CHECKYOURANSWERHERECHECKYOURANSWERHERECHECKYOURANSWERHERE
CHECKYOURANSWERHERECHECKYOURANSWERHERECHECKYOURANSWERHERE

8. In very severe injuries, plastic surgery might be needed for any part of the body. However, facial scars are those for which people are more likely to seek corrective plastic surgery since society places great emphasis on physical attractiveness.

Of the following injuries, which are *very* likely to result in plastic surgery?

A. Severe abrasions, contusions and lacerations of the left inner thigh

B. Multiple lacerations of the cheek and neck

C. Extensive lacerations on the jaw, cheek and forehead

D. Deep abrasions on the left shoulder

CHECKYOURANSWERHERECHECKYOURANSWERHERECHECKYOURANSWERHERE
CHECKYOURANSWERHERECHECKYOURANSWERHERECHECKYOURANSWERHERE
CHECKYOURANSWERHERECHECKYOURANSWERHERECHECKYOURANSWERHERE
CHECKYOURANSWERHERECHECKYOURANSWERHERECHECKYOURANSWERHERE

Keloid Scarring

9. One type of scarring that might not respond positively to plastic surgery or other treatment is called **keloid**. Keloid is scar tissue that occurs more massively than is necessary for normal healing, resulting in a thick, raised, irregularly-shaped red scar, which is often painful to the touch. In general, darker pigmented individuals are more likely to develop keloid. Certain steroids, drugs and laser therapy are treatments that have had some success in removing keloid scars, but keloid sometimes recurs after apparently successful treatment.

Which statements below are true concerning keloid scarring?

A. Some methods for removing keloid are drugs, steroids and laser treatment.

B. Keloid is an irregular mass of tissue that is disfiguring but never painful.

C. Although treatment is difficult, once keloid is removed, it never returns.

CHECKYOURANSWERHERECHECKYOURANSWERHERECHECKYOURANSWERHERE
CHECKYOURANSWERHERECHECKYOURANSWERHERECHECKYOURANSWERHERE
CHECKYOURANSWERHERECHECKYOURANSWERHERECHECKYOURANSWERHERE
CHECKYOURANSWERHERECHECKYOURANSWERHERECHECKYOURANSWERHERE

STRAINS AND SPRAINS

10. Strains and sprains are two different injuries that are sometimes confused if for no other reason than the similarity of the names. A **strain** is a minor injury with no lasting effects, although there may be significant pain when a strain first occurs. It involves stretching of muscles or tendons beyond their usual limits. Muscles can be strained simply by excessive use or by accidental or traumatic means. Taping is sometimes required to immobilize the strained part.

   A **sprain**, on the other hand, is a serious injury to a joint, such as the elbow or knee joint, wherein the ligaments are partly or totally torn from the bone. **Ligaments** are connective tissues that help joints work properly. A sprained joint will become hot, swell rapidly and become limited in movement. Discoloration usually occurs as well. Sprains are typically treated like bone fractures by immobilizing the injured part of the body. Common methods used to immobilize sprains include elastic bandages, casts, and splints. In less severe cases, the affected area may be taped.

   Each statement following refers to a sprain, a strain, or both. Write in **SP** if the statement refers to a sprain, **ST** if it refers to a strain, or **B** if it refers to both a sprain and a strain.

   _____ A. Muscles or tendons are stretched beyond their normal limits

   _____ B. Causes rapid swelling and limits movement

   _____ C. May require immobilization

   _____ D. Has no lasting adverse effects

   _____ E. Might be immobilized with a cast as if it were a fractured bone

   _____ F. Injures a joint by pulling the ligaments away from the bone

CHECKYOURANSWERHERECHECKYOURANSWERHERECHECKYOURANSWERHERE
CHECKYOURANSWERHERECHECKYOURANSWERHERECHECKYOURANSWERHERE
CHECKYOURANSWERHERECHECKYOURANSWERHERECHECKYOURANSWERHERE
CHECKYOURANSWERHERECHECKYOURANSWERHERECHECKYOURANSWERHERE

11. The swelling, discoloration and inflammation that characterize a sprain will disappear slowly or rapidly, depending upon the severity of the injury. However, returning the affected joint—the knee, for example—to normal movement and function may be difficult or impossible. The effects of any kind of joint injury can vary greatly. We'll be talking more about joint injuries throughout this course.

   Another problem that can occur with a sprain is the possible weakening of the joint, increasing the chance that a similar injury might occur to the same area.

   A sprain, then, is severe not only in its immediate consequences, but also because

   A. the affected joint will remain inflamed even when the swelling and discoloration have disappeared.

   B. swelling typically remains long after other symptoms have disappeared.

C. it may be difficult or even impossible to return the joint to normal effectiveness.

D. a joint becomes more susceptible to a future similar injury because the joint is weaker following the sprain.

CHECKYOURANSWERHERECHECKYOURANSWERHERECHECKYOURANSWERHERE
CHECKYOURANSWERHERECHECKYOURANSWERHERECHECKYOURANSWERHERE
CHECKYOURANSWERHERECHECKYOURANSWERHERECHECKYOURANSWERHERE
CHECKYOURANSWERHERECHECKYOURANSWERHERECHECKYOURANSWERHERE

REVIEW

12. Briefly review what you have learned about flesh and soft tissue injuries by completing the following exercises.

    Complete these sentences.

    A. Contusion and ecchymosis are terms that refer to (wounds/bruises) _____.

    B. Of a bruise or an abrasion, which one involves scraping away of the skin? (Bruise/Abrasion) _____

CHECKYOURANSWERHERECHECKYOURANSWERHERECHECKYOURANSWERHERE
CHECKYOURANSWERHERECHECKYOURANSWERHERECHECKYOURANSWERHERE
CHECKYOURANSWERHERECHECKYOURANSWERHERECHECKYOURANSWERHERE
CHECKYOURANSWERHERECHECKYOURANSWERHERECHECKYOURANSWERHERE

13. Match each term in the left-hand column with its correct description in the right-hand column.

1. Laceration	_2_ A.	Bruised, no break in the skin
2. Contusion	_1_ B.	Irregular tear in the skin
3. Incised wound	_4_ C.	Soft tissue compressed, with or without bone fracture
4. Crushing wound	_3_ D.	Clean, straight cut caused by a sharp-edged instrument

CHECKYOURANSWERHERECHECKYOURANSWERHERECHECKYOURANSWERHERE
CHECKYOURANSWERHERECHECKYOURANSWERHERECHECKYOURANSWERHERE
CHECKYOURANSWERHERECHECKYOURANSWERHERECHECKYOURANSWERHERE
CHECKYOURANSWERHERECHECKYOURANSWERHERECHECKYOURANSWERHERE

14. Complete these sentences regarding puncture wounds.

    A. This type of wound is susceptible to infection because it is (deep and narrow/long and irregular) _____, making cleansing difficult.

    B. If such a wound involves an object lodged in the tissue, it is called a (penetrating/perforating) _____ wound.

C. If such a wound involves an object entering at one point in the body and passing completely through, it is called a (penetrating/perforating) _____ wound.

15. Answer these questions concerning sprains and strains.

A. Of strains and sprains, the one that is most like a fractured bone in terms of damage to a joint is a (strain/sprain) _____.

B. An injury involving excessive stretching of muscles or tendons is called a (strain/sprain) _____.

C. If a sprain causes weakness in a joint, to what condition is the joint more susceptible?_____

_____

3

The Skull and the Brain

BONES OF THE SKULL

Large Cranial Bones

1. In the remaining units of this course, we'll discuss the various parts of the body. We'll begin with a discussion of the **skull**, which is composed of cranial bones, facial bones and teeth. Its primary function is to protect the brain. Later, you'll learn about the brain and how brain injuries can affect a claimant.

    We'll begin our discussion with the larger bones of the cranium—those which cover the brain.

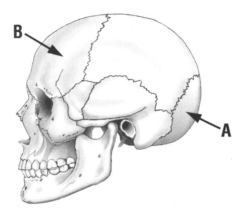

    The cranial bone that is the simplest to remember is the **frontal bone**, because the name describes the location of the bone. The frontal bone is located at the front of the head and is also referred to as **the forehead bone**.

    Here is a picture of a skull, with arrows indicating two different bones at Point A and Point B. Which arrow points to the frontal bone? (A or B)

    _____

CHECKYOURANSWERHERECHECKYOURANSWERHERECHECKYOURANSWERHERE
CHECKYOURANSWERHERECHECKYOURANSWERHERECHECKYOURANSWERHERE
CHECKYOURANSWERHERECHECKYOURANSWERHERECHECKYOURANSWERHERE
CHECKYOURANSWERHERECHECKYOURANSWERHERECHECKYOURANSWERHERE

Parietal Bones

2. There are two bones which join on the top of the head and extend part way down the sides, forming a "roof" and "walls" around the brain. These are the **parietal bones**, which form a protective covering around a large portion of the brain. The highlighted area in this illustration is the left parietal bone.

    Describe the parietal bones. _____
    _____
    _____

Left Parietal Bone

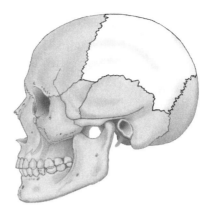

Temporal Bones

3. Two bones, one on either side of the head, extend from the occipital bone forward on the lower part of the skull. These bones, which are called the **temporal bones**, terminate near the front of the skull, roughly in the region of the temples. The highlighted area in the illustration at the left indicates the left temporal bone.

Left Temporal Bone

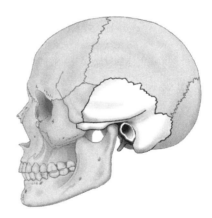

Which bones extend from the occipital bone on the lower part of the skull and terminate near the front of the skull near the temples?

A. Parietal bones

B. Temporal bones

C. Frontal bones

Occipital Bone

4. The **occipital bone** forms the lower back portion of the skull. It is located between the parietal and temporal bones.

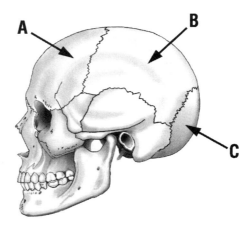

Which one of the bones in this illustration is the occipital bone? (A, B, or C) _____

CHECKYOURANSWERHERECHECKYOURANSWERHERECHECKYOURANSWERHERE
CHECKYOURANSWERHERECHECKYOURANSWERHERECHECKYOURANSWERHERE
CHECKYOURANSWERHERECHECKYOURANSWERHERECHECKYOURANSWERHERE
CHECKYOURANSWERHERECHECKYOURANSWERHERECHECKYOURANSWERHERE

Sphenoid Bone

5. The **sphenoid bone** is a large bone which extends through the skull, but is visible from both sides only as a small wedge in front of the temporal bones.

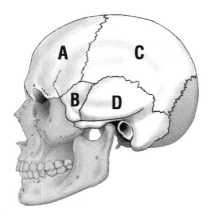

Which one of the bones in this illustration is the sphenoid bone? (A, B, C, or D) _____

CHECKYOURANSWERHERECHECKYOURANSWERHERECHECKYOURANSWERHERE
CHECKYOURANSWERHERECHECKYOURANSWERHERECHECKYOURANSWERHERE
CHECKYOURANSWERHERECHECKYOURANSWERHERECHECKYOURANSWERHERE
CHECKYOURANSWERHERECHECKYOURANSWERHERECHECKYOURANSWERHERE

6. Now, let's review the large bones of the skull. Identify the bones marked as A, B, C, D, and E in the illustration at the right.

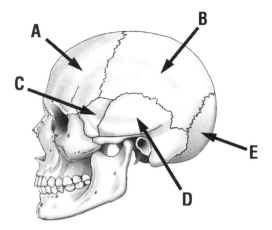

A. _____

B. _____

C. _____

D. _____

E. _____

CHECKYOURANSWERHERECHECKYOURANSWERHERECHECKYOURANSWERHERE
CHECKYOURANSWERHERECHECKYOURANSWERHERECHECKYOURANSWERHERE
CHECKYOURANSWERHERECHECKYOURANSWERHERECHECKYOURANSWERHERE
CHECKYOURANSWERHERECHECKYOURANSWERHERECHECKYOURANSWERHERE

Facial Bones

Malar/Zygomatic Bones

7. There are 14 facial bones in the skull, but we'll limit our discussion to a few of the larger, more commonly injured bones.

    The two **cheekbones** are located directly below the eyes on both sides of the face. The cheekbones are known as either **malar bones** or **zygomatic bones**. Both terms refer to the same bones. In this illustration, the left cheekbone is highlighted.

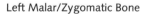

Left Malar/Zygomatic Bone

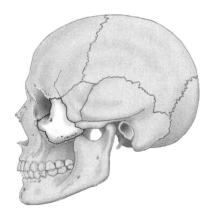

The two terms used to describe the cheekbones are

A. occipital bones and parietal bones.

B. malar bones and zygomatic bones.

C. sphenoid bones and temporal bones.

D. frontal bones and cranial bones.

CHECKYOURANSWERHERECHECKYOURANSWERHERECHECKYOURANSWERHERE
CHECKYOURANSWERHERECHECKYOURANSWERHERECHECKYOURANSWERHERE
CHECKYOURANSWERHERECHECKYOURANSWERHERECHECKYOURANSWERHERE
CHECKYOURANSWERHERECHECKYOURANSWERHERECHECKYOURANSWERHERE

Maxilla and Mandible

8. There are two **jawbones** in the skull. A jawbone is known as a **maxilla**, and since there are two of them, one above the other, they are distinguished by calling one **superior** and the other **inferior**. The upper jawbone, which is located below the nose and extends to each side of the skull, is called the **superior maxilla**; the lower jawbone is called the **inferior maxilla**.

Left Maxilla and Mandible

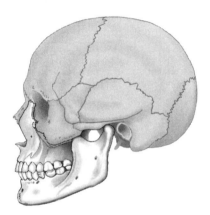

As a rule, the superior maxilla, or upper jawbone, is referred to simply as the **maxilla**. The inferior maxilla, the lower jawbone, is commonly called the **mandible**.

The superior maxilla is called the (maxilla/mandible) _____ and the inferior maxilla is called the _____ (maxilla/mandible).

CHECKYOURANSWERHERECHECKYOURANSWERHERECHECKYOURANSWERHERE
CHECKYOURANSWERHERECHECKYOURANSWERHERECHECKYOURANSWERHERE
CHECKYOURANSWERHERECHECKYOURANSWERHERECHECKYOURANSWERHERE
CHECKYOURANSWERHERECHECKYOURANSWERHERECHECKYOURANSWERHERE

9. The following describe the facial bones we've just discussed. For each description, write in a **C** if it refers to a cheekbone or a **J** if it refers to a jawbone.

_____ A. Located directly below the eyes on each side of the face

_____ B. Located below the nose, extends to each side of the skull

_____ C. Commonly referred to as malar bones and zygomatic bones

_____ D. Commonly referred to as maxilla and mandible

INJURIES TO THE SKULL

Temporomandibular Joint Disorders (TMJ)

10. The term **temporomandibular joint disorders (TMJ)** refers to a variety of disorders related to the **temporomandibular joints**.

    The temporomandibular joints are located on both sides of the head between the mandible (the lower jaw) and the temporal bones. They are sliding "ball and socket" joints that provide a gliding action between your upper and lower jaws, allowing you to open and close your mouth. In this illustration, the left temporomandibular joint is circled.

Left Temporomandibular Joint

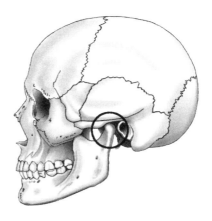

Describe the temporomandibular joints. _____
_____
_____

11. There are many causes of TMJ disorders, so any claim for this condition should be examined carefully to determine if it is compensable.

EXAMPLE

TMJ disorders can be caused by problems with the patient's jaw muscles and "bite" or by problems with the TMJ joint itself. **Emotional stress** and even **clenching of the teeth (bruxism)** can cause the muscles in the jaw to tighten, pulling the upper and lower jaws closer together and putting pressure on the TMJ. A **"bad bite" (malocclusion)** can also affect the proper functioning of the TMJ. For example, a malocclusion could displace the **condyle** (the round end of the mandible which moves in and out of the TMJ socket). Problems in the TMJ itself can be caused by **trauma**, such as a blow to the head, jaw, or neck, or by **disease**, such as arthritis.

Name five common causes of a TMJ disorder.

A. _____

B. _____

C. _____

D. _____

E. _____

CHECKYOURANSWERHERECHECKYOURANSWERHERECHECKYOURANSWERHERE
CHECKYOURANSWERHERECHECKYOURANSWERHERECHECKYOURANSWERHERE
CHECKYOURANSWERHERECHECKYOURANSWERHERECHECKYOURANSWERHERE
CHECKYOURANSWERHERECHECKYOURANSWERHERECHECKYOURANSWERHERE
CHECKYOURANSWERHERECHECKYOURANSWERHERECHECKYOURANSWERHERE
CHECKYOURANSWERHERECHECKYOURANSWERHERECHECKYOURANSWERHERE

12. A TMJ disorder can produce a variety of symptoms. Some of the more common ones are:

■ Severe pain in the area of the TMJ

■ Grating or clicking sounds when opening the mouth

■ Difficulty in opening the mouth

■ Increase in pain when clenching the teeth

■ Headaches or neck aches

■ Increase in pain during emotional stress

■ Sensitive, loose, broken, or worn teeth

■ Sore, stiff muscles around the jaw area upon awakening

Which of the following are common symptoms of a TMJ disorder?

A. Memory loss

B. Vomiting

C. Difficulty in opening the mouth

D. Grating or clicking sounds when opening the mouth

E. Increase in pain when clenching the teeth

F. Hemorrhaging

CHECKYOURANSWERHERECHECKYOURANSWERHERECHECKYOURANSWERHERE
CHECKYOURANSWERHERECHECKYOURANSWERHERECHECKYOURANSWERHERE
CHECKYOURANSWERHERECHECKYOURANSWERHERECHECKYOURANSWERHERE
CHECKYOURANSWERHERECHECKYOURANSWERHERECHECKYOURANSWERHERE

13. Treatment of a TMJ disorder depends on the cause of the disorder. The patient can relieve many of the symptoms of a TMJ disorder by resting the jaw, applying ice or heat, or taking medication. Other common treatments include:

- Stress management techniques

- Physical therapy

- A dental splint, which can be used to reduce bruxism or stabilize a malocclusion

- Various methods used to correct malocclusions, such as orthodontic braces, bridges and crowns

In severe cases, surgery may be required to repair the TMJ.

Which of the following methods may be used to treat TMJ disorders?
A. Stress management techniques
B. Dental splints
C. Orthodontic braces, bridges and crowns
D. Surgery
E. All of the above

CHECKYOURANSWERHERECHECKYOURANSWERHERECHECKYOURANSWERHERE
CHECKYOURANSWERHERECHECKYOURANSWERHERECHECKYOURANSWERHERE
CHECKYOURANSWERHERECHECKYOURANSWERHERECHECKYOURANSWERHERE
CHECKYOURANSWERHERECHECKYOURANSWERHERECHECKYOURANSWERHERE

Common Types of Skull Fractures

Linear Skull Fractures

14. A **fracture** is a break in a bone. Various descriptive terms are used to identify fractures by their appearance and location. You need to know some of these terms before you can learn about the effects fractures have on the skull, head and brain.

    Fractures fall into two broad categories:

- **Simple fractures**, in which the bone is broken, but there is no external wound

- **Compound fractures**, in which the bone is broken, and an external wound leads down to the fracture site, or a piece of the bone extends through the skin

Simple and compound fractures may be further defined by various terms which describe the appearance or condition of the fractured bones. Most of these terms will be discussed later in the course, but several are used to describe fractures which often occur to the skull. The first, a **linear skull fracture**, is the least serious type of skull fracture. A linear skull fracture is merely a crack in the bone, which does not break it into pieces. It is the easiest type of fracture to treat because a bone that has only been cracked does not require surgical treatment.

Linear Skull Fracture

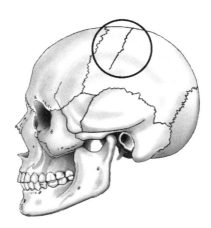

A simple, or closed, linear skull fracture is usually the least dangerous type of skull fracture. A crack in the skull with no head wound will usually heal on its own. However, on rare occasions, the crack may occur on the inner surface of the skull near the brain covering and cross a blood vessel. This causes bleeding between the skull and the brain and puts pressure on the brain.

Select the correct description of a linear skull fracture.

A. A skull bone is broken or splintered into more than two pieces.

B. A skull bone is broken or splintered into more than two pieces, and one or more of the bone pieces are driven inward and press on the brain.

C. A skull bone is cracked but not broken into pieces.

Comminuted Skull Fractures

15. When a skull bone is broken or splintered into more than two pieces, the fracture is said to be **comminuted**. Because it takes a tremendous blow to cause a comminuted fracture to the skull, it is nearly impossible for such a fracture to occur *without* a wound to the head. You may never hear of a *simple* comminuted skull fracture.

    A comminuted skull fracture is treated surgically by realigning the bone pieces and holding them together by some means until the bone pieces adhere. Any time a surgical incision into the head is required, there is some danger to the patient.

Which one of these illustrations shows a comminuted skull fracture?

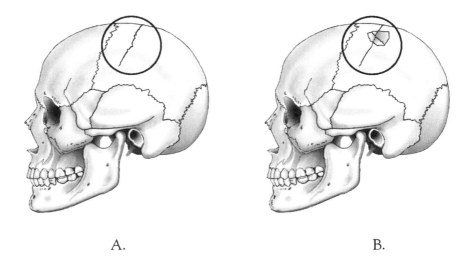

A.   B.

CHECKYOURANSWERHERECHECKYOURANSWERHERECHECKYOURANSWERHERE
CHECKYOURANSWERHERECHECKYOURANSWERHERECHECKYOURANSWERHERE
CHECKYOURANSWERHERECHECKYOURANSWERHERECHECKYOURANSWERHERE
CHECKYOURANSWERHERECHECKYOURANSWERHERECHECKYOURANSWERHERE

Depressed Skull Fractures

16. The third and **potentially most serious** type of skull fracture is a **depressed skull fracture**. A depressed skull fracture is actually a comminuted fracture in which one or more of the bone pieces are driven inward and press on the brain. The brain or its covering may or may not be torn, but the pressure on the brain remains until the bone is returned to its proper position.

    A depressed skull fracture must be treated surgically. With this type of fracture, the patient faces both the danger of injury to the brain from the depressed skull fracture itself and the additional possibility of damage to the brain when correcting the fracture.

    Which of the following statements concerning depressed skull fractures are correct?

    A. Depressed skull fractures do not require surgical treatment.

    B. Depressed skull fractures are the least serious type of skull fracture.

    C. The risk of brain damage is present when a depressed skull fracture is treated surgically.

    D. Depressed skull fractures put pressure on the brain.

CHECKYOURANSWERHERECHECKYOURANSWERHERECHECKYOURANSWERHERE
CHECKYOURANSWERHERECHECKYOURANSWERHERECHECKYOURANSWERHERE
CHECKYOURANSWERHERECHECKYOURANSWERHERECHECKYOURANSWERHERE
CHECKYOURANSWERHERECHECKYOURANSWERHERECHECKYOURANSWERHERE

Basal Skull Fractures

17. When the cranium, which encloses the brain, is fractured, the location of the fracture can be as important as the type of fracture. The most common

is the **basal skull fracture**, which refers to a fracture at the base of the skull on which the brain rests. This can be at any point extending from behind the eyes to the back of the head, and includes the occipital, sphenoid, and temporal bones.

Which of the following might be classified as a basal skull fracture?

A. Compound fracture of the right frontal bone

B. Depressed fracture of the occipital bone

C. Two-inch simple linear fracture of the left parietal, extending from the center top of the bone

D. Compound comminuted fracture of the sphenoid, right side

18. A basal skull fracture is potentially the most dangerous type of skull fracture. As you've learned, most skull fractures, other than linear fractures, require surgery to realign the bones. However, cranial nerves, major blood vessels to the brain and head, and nerve centers are all located in and around the basal skull area. The proximity of these vital parts to the basal skull area makes surgery impossible in most cases.

A basal skull fracture is usually accompanied by bleeding from one or both ears and sometimes from the mouth or nose. While these symptoms alone do not necessarily prove a basal skull fracture, they are indicative signs to be considered when such a fracture is suspected.

Which of the following statements regarding basal skull fractures are correct?

A. One of the symptoms of a basal skull fracture is bleeding from one or both ears.

B. Fractures in the basal area of the skull are extremely rare.

C. Bleeding from one or both ears or the mouth or nose always indicates a basal skull fracture.

D. The biggest potential danger of a basal skull fracture is that the fracture may not be able to be corrected surgically.

E. The basal skull area extends from behind the eyes to the back of the head.

19. Following are six descriptions of skull fractures. Mark each description with an **L** if it refers to a linear skull fracture, a **C** if it refers to a comminuted skull fracture, a **D** if it refers to a depressed skull fracture, or a **B** if it refers to a basal skull fracture.

_____ A. Usually heals on its own without surgical treatment

_____ B. Usually includes symptoms such as bleeding from the ears, nose or mouth

_____ C. Skull bone is broken or splintered into more than two pieces

_____ E. Skull bone is broken or splintered into more than two pieces, and one or more of the bone pieces are driven inward and press on the brain

_____ F. Difficult to treat surgically because cranial nerves, major blood vessels to the brain and head, and nerve centers are in close proximity to the area of the fracture

_____ G. Type of fracture where a bone in the skull is cracked, but not broken into pieces

CHECKYOURANSWERHERECHECKYOURANSWERHERECHECKYOURANSWERHERE
CHECKYOURANSWERHERECHECKYOURANSWERHERECHECKYOURANSWERHERE
CHECKYOURANSWERHERECHECKYOURANSWERHERECHECKYOURANSWERHERE
CHECKYOURANSWERHERECHECKYOURANSWERHERECHECKYOURANSWERHERE

20. We have suggested dangers to the brain resulting from skull fractures, without really explaining much about the brain and what can happen to it. We'll discuss this in the next section. At this point, it seems appropriate to emphasize that _any brain injury is the most important aspect of a skull fracture, which, without brain injury, is relatively minor._

    With that in mind, continue to the next section, where you'll learn more about common brain injuries.

INJURIES TO THE BRAIN

The Meninges

21. The brain is a large mass of nerve tissue located within the skull that controls all of the thought processes and physical actions of the human body. While the skull provides the brain with its main protection against outside forces, the brain is also surrounded by coverings which form a sort of padding between the brain and the skull. These are three soft layers of tissue, or membranes, and combined, the three are called the **meninges**. Beginning with the membrane nearest the brain and moving outward to the skull, the three are:

    1. **Pia mater**

    2. **Arachnoid**

    3. **Dura mater**

The Meninges

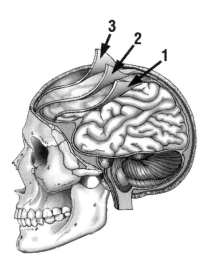

On the left is a sketch of a brain inside a skull. The arrows labeled 1, 2, and 3 point to each membrane. Look at the sketch, then go to the questions that follow.

A. The dura mater is indicated by Arrow (1/2/3) _____.

B. The pia mater is indicated by Arrow (1/2/3) _____.

C. The arachnoid is indicated by Arrow (1/2/3) _____.

CHECKYOURANSWERHERECHECKYOURANSWERHERECHECKYOURANSWERHERE
CHECKYOURANSWERHERECHECKYOURANSWERHERECHECKYOURANSWERHERE
CHECKYOURANSWERHERECHECKYOURANSWERHERECHECKYOURANSWERHERE
CHECKYOURANSWERHERECHECKYOURANSWERHERECHECKYOURANSWERHERE

Cerebral Hemorrhages

22. A traumatic injury to the skull often results in a **cerebral hemorrhage**, which is an abnormal flow of blood in the brain or meninges. One cause of a cerebral hemorrhage is a fractured bone breaking blood vessels. In addition, a blow to the skull can break blood vessels even if the bone itself is not broken. Injuries to the brain which cause hemorrhaging are commonly one of two types: a contusion or a laceration. We'll take a closer look at brain contusions and brain lacerations in the next frame.

Other factors besides trauma can cause a cerebral hemorrhage, such as the rupture of a diseased blood vessel. You'll learn more about nontraumatic causes of cerebral hemorrhages in a later unit.

Name the two most common trauma-related causes of cerebral hemorrhages.

A. _____

B. _____

CHECKYOURANSWERHERECHECKYOURANSWERHERECHECKYOURANSWERHERE
CHECKYOURANSWERHERECHECKYOURANSWERHERECHECKYOURANSWERHERE
CHECKYOURANSWERHERECHECKYOURANSWERHERECHECKYOURANSWERHERE
CHECKYOURANSWERHERECHECKYOURANSWERHERECHECKYOURANSWERHERE

Brain Contusions

23. A **brain contusion** is usually considered less serious than a brain laceration. A contusion bruises the brain and resembles a bruise anywhere else on the body. It does not tear or break the brain or its coverings.

    Contusions to the brain usually cause a period of unconsciousness which is usually longer in duration than, say, fainting or a "blackout." The length of the period of unconsciousness will depend on the severity of the bruise. In most cases, a slight bruise with little swelling and a relatively quick return to consciousness will result in a short (about three weeks) period of recuperation with no brain damage.

    On the other hand, severe bruises, a lengthy period of unconsciousness, and swelling causing pressure on the brain can impair the brain either temporarily or permanently. This condition is often characterized by malfunctioning vocal cords, vision, or body movements as a result of pressure from the swollen brain. Swelling is usually reduced in about eight weeks, after which the brain begins to function normally again. More severe degrees of contusion can cause death.

    Which of the following statements regarding brain contusions are correct?

    A. A brain contusion is considered more serious than a brain laceration.

    B. A contusion bruises the brain and resembles a bruise anywhere else on the body.

    C. A brain contusion usually causes a period of unconsciousness.

    D. A brain contusion always results in permanent brain damage.

CHECKYOURANSWERHERECHECKYOURANSWERHERECHECKYOURANSWERHERE
CHECKYOURANSWERHERECHECKYOURANSWERHERECHECKYOURANSWERHERE
CHECKYOURANSWERHERECHECKYOURANSWERHERECHECKYOURANSWERHERE
CHECKYOURANSWERHERECHECKYOURANSWERHERECHECKYOURANSWERHERE

Brain Lacerations

24. A **brain laceration** tears into the substance of the brain. It is an even more severe injury than a brain contusion. In order for the brain to be lacerated, there must be an extremely severe blow to the head. The probability of a brain laceration without a skull fracture is nearly nonexistent. In fact, a laceration usually results from a depressed skull fracture. Hemorrhaging is inevitable, and contusions to other parts of the brain near the laceration are very probable. A brain laceration is also accompanied by all of the symptoms of a brain contusion.

    While a patient who suffers a brain contusion may be able to recover from the injury without permanent brain damage, this is not likely for a patient with a brain laceration. If the laceration occurs in one of the few areas of the brain where no nerve impairment can result, the patient may recover from the injury completely. However, considering that a depressed skull fracture and additional hemorrhaging and contusions are probably present, this is a fairly remote possibility.

    Frequently, the swelling does not subside even after eight weeks, which means that a massive blood clot has formed and put gradually increasing pressure on the brain. This pressure on the brain causes permanent damage to the nerves. Depending on the location of the laceration, there may be impairments in sight, hearing, speech, movement, or any other area of brain function. Even surgery cannot guarantee a reversal of these conditions.

So, a brain laceration is considered more dangerous than a brain contusion because

A. it is usually accompanied by a depressed skull fracture.

B. contusions to nearby areas of the brain are likely.

C. nerve damage which cannot be corrected surgically is likely.

D. all of the above are correct.

CHECKYOURANSWERHERECHECKYOURANSWERHERECHECKYOURANSWERHERE
CHECKYOURANSWERHERECHECKYOURANSWERHERECHECKYOURANSWERHERE
CHECKYOURANSWERHERECHECKYOURANSWERHERECHECKYOURANSWERHERE
CHECKYOURANSWERHERECHECKYOURANSWERHERECHECKYOURANSWERHERE

Cerebral Hematomas

25. A cerebral hemorrhage can cause a **cerebral hematoma**, which is a blood tumor located somewhere within the brain or meninges. Cerebral hematomas are further defined by where they are located in the brain or meninges.

   Earlier in this unit, we discussed the possibility that a linear skull fracture could cause bleeding between the skull and brain covering. We also discussed how this bleeding will cause pressure on the brain. This happens because the bleeding causes a hematoma to form and, because the space in the skull is already filled, there is no room for the hematoma. Since the hematoma can't exert pressure on the hard skull bones, it presses on the soft brain and its coverings. This type of hematoma, which is located **on or above** the dura mater, is called an **epidural hematoma**. When the hematoma is located **under** the dura mater, it is called a **subdural hematoma**.

   Both epidural and subdural hematomas cause pressure on the brain, which can cause nerve damage. In addition, a hematoma can be fatal as pressure builds from the growing blood clot. This is especially true of epidural hematomas, because epidural bleeding comes from arteries which, when torn, spurt blood with great force. This force creates large clots, resulting in great pressure which can cause rapid death if not relieved by surgery.

   While a subdural hematoma can also be fatal, it does not present such a great urgency as an epidural hematoma. This is because subdural bleeding comes from veins rather than arteries, and veins ooze blood instead of spurting it. Consequently, it takes longer for a hematoma to form and press on the brain. Nevertheless, subdural hematomas must also be treated surgically.

A. A cerebral hematoma located on or above the dura mater is called a/an _____ hematoma.

B. A cerebral hematoma located below the dura mater is called a/an _____ hematoma.

CHECKYOURANSWERHERECHECKYOURANSWERHERECHECKYOURANSWERHERE
CHECKYOURANSWERHERECHECKYOURANSWERHERECHECKYOURANSWERHERE
CHECKYOURANSWERHERECHECKYOURANSWERHERECHECKYOURANSWERHERE
CHECKYOURANSWERHERECHECKYOURANSWERHERECHECKYOURANSWERHERE

Cerebral Concussion

26. The least complicated and least damaging injury to the brain is the **cerebral concussion**. This term means the brain has been violently shaken about, usually as a result of a blow to the head. No hemorrhaging occurs. There is usually a short period of unconsciousness, although in some cases the victim is momentarily dazed but does not lose consciousness.

   In addition to the brief period of unconsciousness or dazed condition, a concussion may also produce symptoms such as sudden vomiting, dizziness, and temporary loss of either sensation or movement in some area of the body. These symptoms usually diminish or disappear entirely within 24 hours. However, both the symptoms produced by a concussion and the time frame in which these symptoms disappear can vary greatly among individuals.

   Which of the following are common symptoms of a concussion?
   A. Hemorrhaging
   B. Brief period of unconsciousness
   C. Dazed condition
   D. Permanent impairment of sensation or movement
   E. Sudden vomiting
   F. Dizziness
   G. Extended unconsciousness

CHECKYOURANSWERHERECHECKYOURANSWERHERECHECKYOURANSWERHERE
CHECKYOURANSWERHERECHECKYOURANSWERHERECHECKYOURANSWERHERE
CHECKYOURANSWERHERECHECKYOURANSWERHERECHECKYOURANSWERHERE
CHECKYOURANSWERHERECHECKYOURANSWERHERECHECKYOURANSWERHERE

Residual Symptoms

27. After a patient has apparently recovered, and the concussion is all but forgotten, its effects sometimes reappear in some other mode. The various forms it may take are often called **residual symptoms**, which vary greatly among individuals.

   The most common residual symptom is a **headache**, which may be either a dull overall ache or a sharp, stabbing sensation which begins in the area where the blow to the head occurred. Concussion-related headaches may occur after physical activity or when the individual is very tired or under emotional stress. A period of quiet rest will usually relieve the headaches if they are related to the concussion.

   Another residual symptom is **nervousness**, a category which can include many problems such as fear, irritability, insomnia, absent-mindedness, lack of concentration, and physical weakness. Whatever the symptoms, they were generally not usual to the character of the individual before the concussion occurred.

   A third residual symptom of a concussion is what the patient usually describes as dizziness, meaning the **sensation of swaying, lightheadedness, or feeling faint**. This usually occurs after physical exertion or shifting position (such as standing up or turning abruptly).

Two final residual symptoms involve hearing and sight. A **ringing in the ears** is not uncommon, but an actual decrease in hearing ability should not occur unless there has been injury to the ear, in which case the ear injury and not the concussion is responsible for the symptoms. **Blurred vision** for short periods is another common complaint. Headaches or physical exertion may precede the blurred vision, but do not necessarily do so.

Which of the following conditions are common residual symptoms of a concussion?

A. Paralysis

B. Blurred vision

C. Sensation of lightheadedness or feeling faint

D. Headaches

E. Hemorrhaging

F. Brief periods of unconsciousness

G. Ringing in the ears

H. Insomnia

CHECKYOURANSWERHERECHECKYOURANSWERHERECHECKYOURANSWERHERE
CHECKYOURANSWERHERECHECKYOURANSWERHERECHECKYOURANSWERHERE
CHECKYOURANSWERHERECHECKYOURANSWERHERECHECKYOURANSWERHERE
CHECKYOURANSWERHERECHECKYOURANSWERHERECHECKYOURANSWERHERE

28. To review what you've just learned about brain injuries, match the term in the left-hand column with its correct description in the right-hand column.

1. Meninges
2. Cerebral hemorrhage
3. Brain contusion
4. Brain laceration
5. Cerebral hematoma
6. Epidural hematoma
7. Subdural hematoma
8. Cerebral concussion

____ A. Extremely serious injury where the substance of the brain is torn

____ B. Blood tumor located somewhere within the brain or meninges

____ C. Coverings surrounding the brain

____ D. Abnormal flow of blood in the brain or meninges

____ E. Injury where brain has been violently shaken about, usually as a result of a blow to the head

____ F. Blood tumor located on or above the dura mater

____ G. Bruise on the brain

____ H. Blood tumor located below the dura mater

CHECKYOURANSWERHERECHECKYOURANSWERHERECHECKYOURANSWERHERE
CHECKYOURANSWERHERECHECKYOURANSWERHERECHECKYOURANSWERHERE
CHECKYOURANSWERHERECHECKYOURANSWERHERECHECKYOURANSWERHERE
CHECKYOURANSWERHERECHECKYOURANSWERHERECHECKYOURANSWERHERE

DIAGNOSTIC TESTS

X-Rays

29. Medical personnel use many types of diagnostic tests to provide information about the physical condition of a patient. In this section, you'll learn about several tests used to diagnose skull and brain injuries. Many of these tests are also used to diagnose injuries in other parts of the body.

   One of the most common types of diagnostic tests is the **x-ray**. X-rays are high energy, high frequency electromagnetic waves that can penetrate a variety of structures. Here's how an x-ray is obtained:

X-Ray

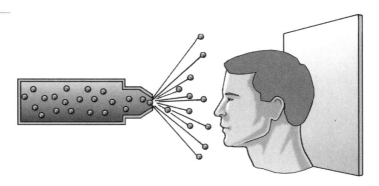 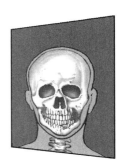

Electrons pass rapidly through a vacuum tube, impacting a metal target beneath the area of the body being examined and producing an image on photographic film.

To get an accurate image of the injured area, x-rays may be made from several angles. The four most common are:

- **A. P. or anteroposterior**—Rays pass through the body from the front (anterior) to the back (posterior).

- **P. A. or posteroanterior**—Rays pass from the back of the body to the front of the body.

- **Lateral**—Rays pass from one side of the body to the other.

- **Oblique**—Rays slant diagonally through the body.

Study the following illustrations. The arrows indicate the direction of the x-rays. Label each illustration as A.P., P.A., lateral, or oblique.

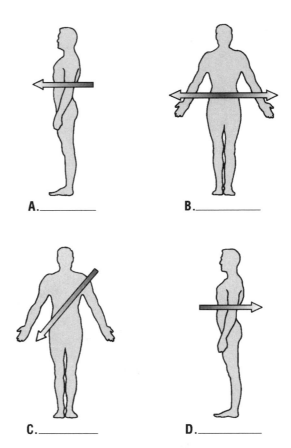

30. Although there are more definitive tests than x-rays for examining the skull and brain, x-rays are still used to detect such conditions as skull fractures, cerebral hemorrhaging, and increases in intracranial pressure (which can suggest other conditions). In fact, x-rays are routinely taken after most types of traumatic injuries to check for fractures, and they should be performed before more advanced testing techniques, such as CT scans and MRIs, are used.

What three conditions related to the brain and skull can be detected using x-rays?

A. _____

B. _____

C. _____

Computerized Tomography (CT)

31. More sophisticated x-ray techniques have resulted from combining existing procedures with computer technology. One of these is **computerized tomography**, commonly called a **CT scan**. Other names used to describe this same test are:

    ■ CAT scan (Computerized Axial Tomography)

    ■ CTT scan (Computerized Transverse Axial Tomography)

    Tomography is a technique that uses x-rays in a special way to capture the details in a selected structure by *blurring* other images or shadows that surround the part being examined.

    Here's how a CT scan works:

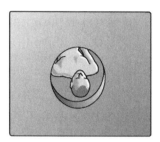

The part of the body (or the entire body) being examined is placed in a gantry, which is the housing for the CT scanners and detectors.

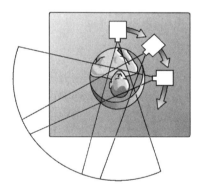

The x-ray tube revolves around the patient, making a series of x-rays, rather than a single, one-dimensional view. The CT scanner converts the series of x-rays into digital code which the computer interprets and reproduces on a separate video screen as a two-dimensional image. Color enhancements are usually used to differentiate various structures.

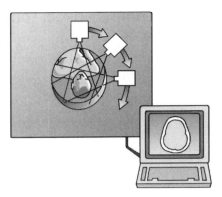

The two-dimensional image results from the computer's comparing and assembling the many x-rays into a single image of a selected "slice" of the part being examined. The computer can then reassemble and show sections from many different angles, allowing precise visualization of the part being examined and comparison from different angles.

A characteristic feature of CT is

A. no x-rays are used.

B. many different views of the body part are made, rather than just one or two different angles.

C. both of the above are true.

32. One of the greatest advantages of the CT scan is that it is usually *noninvasive*, which means it usually does not involve entering the body or puncturing the skin. Before the development of the CT scan, it was often necessary to use invasive techniques when conventional procedures, such as x-rays, could not diagnose the problem. This was especially dangerous when the only alternative was a surgical incision into the skull or brain in order to make a satisfactory diagnosis. Because the CT scan is usually noninvasive, there is no significant risk or discomfort to the patient, and it can be performed on an outpatient basis.

    Contrast agents are sometimes used with CT scans. A contrast agent is material, such as dye, that is injected into the body before the test is performed to enhance details of certain parts of the body.

    A major disadvantage of the CT scan is that it produces higher radiation doses than plain x-rays. Women who are pregnant should not undergo CT scans.

    Which of the following statements concerning the CT scan are true?

    A. The CT scan is a dangerous, invasive procedure which should not be used unless other diagnostic techniques have failed to diagnose the patient's condition.

    B. The CT scan can be performed on an outpatient basis.

    C. The CT scan poses no significant risk or discomfort to the patient.

    D. The CT scan is usually a noninvasive test.

33. The CT scan is effective at diagnosing many conditions in the skull and brain, including:

    ■ Subdural and epidural hematomas

    ■ Brain tumors

    ■ Cerebral infarcts (dead tissue resulting from lack of blood supply to the area)

    The CT scan is frequently used to diagnose problems in the skull and brain because of its relative safety and thus, the potential to be used frequently on the same patient. Invasive procedures into the brain, on the other hand, are dangerous and cannot be repeated frequently.

    In addition, the CT scan has a very high accurate diagnostic rate. Overall, the error rate for intracranial conditions diagnosed by CT scan is less than 5%. This accuracy can mean earlier diagnosis and treatment without using more dangerous procedures. But even if invasive procedures are subsequently required, the CT scan typically will have given the patient a start on treatment and recovery. Because it is noninvasive, the CT scan is often used to monitor treatment or monitor the progress of a condition after the diagnosis has been made.

    A. The intracranial CT scan is an effective diagnostic tool for (many/only a few) _____ problems.

    B. For diagnosis and followup on a single patient, the intracranial CT can be used (frequently/infrequently) _____.

    C. The diagnostic accuracy of the intracranial CT is (high/low) _____.

    D. Early diagnosis (is/is not) _____a benefit of CT.

Magnetic Resonance Imaging (MRI)

34. Before we discuss specifically how **magnetic resonance imaging,** or **MRI,** works, let's first consider the full term, **nuclear magnetic resonance imaging,** and the meaning of each descriptive word as a way to begin understanding the procedure.

    This test uses certain atomic principles in conjunction with an external magnetic field. The **nuclear** terminology refers, in this case, to the **nuclei of hydrogen atoms**. All of the body's atoms have magnetic properties, but hydrogen atoms predominate numerically, and hydrogen is also the most magnetically sensitive. These qualities prompted researchers to focus the MRI test on hydrogen atoms rather than other atoms. The word **magnetic** refers to the **magnetic properties of atomic nuclei**, and an **external magnetic field** created as an integral part of the MRI technology. **Resonance** means an intensified reaction of the nuclei to the magnetic field, a response that occurs when radio frequency (RF) energy is directed toward the body's atoms. The result of the resonance ultimately produces the **imaging,** or the computer-generated video image of the part of the body being tested.

With this terminology in mind, study the following information about how the MRI is actually administered.

MRI

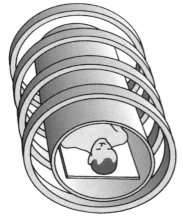 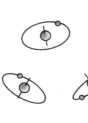 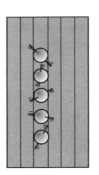 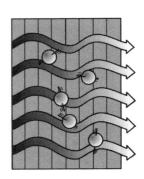

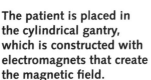

The patient is placed in the cylindrical gantry, which is constructed with electromagnets that create the magnetic field.

Before the scanner is activated, the nuclei of the body's hydrogen atoms (called protons) are in their normal spinning state, pointing in random directions.

When the scanner is activated, the magnetic field created by the electromagnets causes the protons to align uniformly in the direction of the magnetic field's poles. Though aligned, the protons gyrate or wobble at a certain frequency. The stronger the magnetic field, the greater the frequency.

Radio frequency (RF) energy, at the same frequency as the wobble, passes through RF coils in the cylinder, knocking the protons out of alignment.

 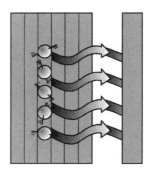

As soon as the RF pulse stops, the protons realign themselves, emitting their own RF energy as they do so.

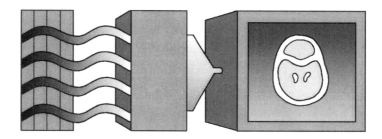

The computer detects and interprets the protons' energy emission and transfers it to the computer screen, forming the MRI image. The variations in hydrogen atoms in different parts of the body permit visual distinction between various soft tissue structures.

Like the CT scan, MRI images result from many different views combined into a single two-dimensional slice of the part being examined. Complete the following mix and match exercise to test your knowledge of the basic characteristics of the MRI.

1. The nuclei involved in the test are those of this atom

2. Intensified response of nuclei to the magnetic field when RF energy is applied

3. Computer-generated "picture" that results

____ A. Resonance

____ B. Imaging

____ C. Hydrogen

CHECKYOURANSWERHERECHECKYOURANSWERHERECHECKYOURANSWERHERE
CHECKYOURANSWERHERECHECKYOURANSWERHERECHECKYOURANSWERHERE
CHECKYOURANSWERHERECHECKYOURANSWERHERECHECKYOURANSWERHERE
CHECKYOURANSWERHERECHECKYOURANSWERHERECHECKYOURANSWERHERE

35. The MRI is especially valuable for diagnosing problems within the nervous system, which includes the brain. Neurology remains one of the primary uses for MRI. Because MRI focuses on hydrogen atoms, it is particularly effective for examining soft tissues with high fluid content or for detecting any condition that *increases* fluid content. The specific areas where MRI is especially useful include:

- Brainstem abnormalities that are less visible on a CT scan

- Brain contusions or bruises

- Brain edema or swelling

- Hemorrhages and hematomas

Contrast agents are sometimes used in an MRI test. The MRI poses no known danger to the patient. The major limitations of MRI are that it cannot be used with patients who are dependent on a respirator or on patients who have any type of metallic prosthesis or implant, including metal staples used in some types of surgery.

Select the correct statement.

A. MRI is a dangerous, invasive procedure which should not be used unless other diagnostic techniques have failed to diagnose the patient's condition.

B. MRI is rarely effective at diagnosing conditions affecting the brain.

C. MRI is especially effective for diagnosing neurological disorders, such as brain contusions and hemorrhages.

CHECKYOURANSWERHERECHECKYOURANSWERHERECHECKYOURANSWERHERE
CHECKYOURANSWERHERECHECKYOURANSWERHERECHECKYOURANSWERHERE
CHECKYOURANSWERHERECHECKYOURANSWERHERECHECKYOURANSWERHERE
CHECKYOURANSWERHERECHECKYOURANSWERHERECHECKYOURANSWERHERE

Electroencephalography (EEG)

36. **Electroencephalography**, or **EEG**, is a diagnostic test that records the electrical activity occurring in the brain. It is a noninvasive test that poses no risk to the patient. Here's how the EEG works:

Electroencephalography

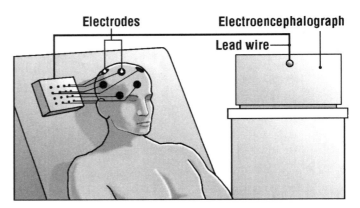

Electrodes on the scalp are attached to leads to the electroencephalograph equipment, which records the brain's electrical activity.

The EEG measures brain waves for abnormalities. Some abnormalities that appear in brain waves indicate specific problems, while others only indicate a problem that requires further investigation.

An EEG records _____.

CHECKYOURANSWERHERECHECKYOURANSWERHERECHECKYOURANSWERHERE
CHECKYOURANSWERHERECHECKYOURANSWERHERECHECKYOURANSWERHERE
CHECKYOURANSWERHERECHECKYOURANSWERHERECHECKYOURANSWERHERE
CHECKYOURANSWERHERECHECKYOURANSWERHERECHECKYOURANSWERHERE

37. The EEG is successful for identifying changes in the brain related to:

■ Head trauma

■ Seizure disorders such as epilepsy

■ Sleep disorders

■ Structural dysfunctions of the brain

■ Lesions and tumors in the cerebrum

While EEG has been successful for identifying some problems, a normal EEG does not necessarily indicate there is no intracranial disease or other abnormalities. The opposite is also true; an EEG sometimes records abnormal waves that have no basis in disease or injury.

Select the correct statement.

A. EEG is better than CT scan and MRI for diagnosing all types of problems associated with the brain.

B. EEG is often used to assess an individual following traumatic injury to the head.

C. A normal EEG automatically rules out diseases and other abnormalities.

D. EEG never records abnormal brain waves that have no basis in disease or injury.

CHECKYOURANSWERHERECHECKYOURANSWERHERECHECKYOURANSWERHERE
CHECKYOURANSWERHERECHECKYOURANSWERHERECHECKYOURANSWERHERE
CHECKYOURANSWERHERECHECKYOURANSWERHERECHECKYOURANSWERHERE
CHECKYOURANSWERHERECHECKYOURANSWERHERECHECKYOURANSWERHERE

Echoencephalography (Ultrasonography)

38. An early application of the ultrasonographic techniques that are now so common was **echoencephalography**. Before we discuss echoencephalography in detail, let's take a look at the basic principles of ultrasonography.

An ultrasonographic test uses sound waves to produce an image of a particular area of the body. These images are similar to those produced by CT scans or MRI, although a few ultrasonographic techniques produce a one-dimensional image. Ultrasonographic tests are sometimes referred to informally as **ultrasound**, which is descriptive, if not technically correct. The graphic image produced by ultrasonographic tests is called a **sonogram**. Another term used in connection with ultrasonography is **echo**, which refers to the sound waves reflecting back, or echoing, during the test.
The basic procedure for all ultrasonographic tests is this:

- A transducer moves across the area being examined, sending ultrasound waves into the tissue.

- The transducer receives sound waves echoed back from the tissue and converts them to electrical energy that forms images on an oscilloscope screen.

A **transducer** is a piece of equipment designed to send and receive energy and, if necessary, convert the energy to another form to make it usable. An **oscilloscope** is an instrument that records electrical oscillations, or waves, on the screen of a cathode ray tube.

Which of the following are correct?

A. In ultrasonography, the transmission of sound waves is a one-way process.

B. Tissue being examined by ultrasonography reflects sound waves back to a transducer as a result of the sound waves directed into the tissue.

C. When the transducer receives the echo from the tissue, it must first convert the wave to electrical energy before the result can appear on the oscilloscope.

D. The image resulting from ultrasonography always resembles a one-dimensional x-ray picture.

CHECKYOURANSWERHERECHECKYOURANSWERHERECHECKYOURANSWERHERE
CHECKYOURANSWERHERECHECKYOURANSWERHERECHECKYOURANSWERHERE
CHECKYOURANSWERHERECHECKYOURANSWERHERECHECKYOURANSWERHERE
CHECKYOURANSWERHERECHECKYOURANSWERHERECHECKYOURANSWERHERE

39. For echoencephalography, the basic principles of ultrasonography apply, with the following specific procedures for echoencephalography:

Echoencephalography

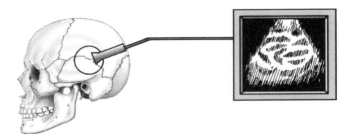

Transducer moves over the temporoparietal area. When midline cerebral structures echo the ultrasonic beam, the time required for reflection is converted to an electrical impulse that displays on the oscilloscope screen.

The **temporoparietal area** refers to the place where the temporal and parietal bones of the skull converge above the ear, as indicated by the circle on the illustration.

Midline cerebral structures are various cavities or **ventricles** in the brain. These structures are typically more or less centered within the skull, with no more than a two- or three-millimeter variation from center. However, when some abnormality is present, such as a hemorrhage, there may be a shift in the midline structures as the foreign presence crowds into the space they normally occupy. For example, with a hemorrhage, the accumulation of blood in the brain might cause midline structures to shift.

Although echoencephalography plays an important diagnostic role under certain circumstances, CT and MRI scans are more frequently used for cerebral testing. CT and MRI are considerably more effective, especially when an intracranial tumor is suspected. Echoencephalography excels, however, at evaluating midline structure shifts. Other situations for which echoencephalography may be preferred include:

■ Displaying the midline structures of the brain

■ Evaluating traumatic head injuries for suspected internal damage

■ Detecting hemorrhages, lesions, and cerebral edema (hydrocephalus)

■ Testing children younger than age two, especially infants

■ Testing that must be done at the bedside

■ Testing agitated patients who cannot be sedated or kept from moving

Select any correct statements.

A. As compared to CT and MRI, echoencephalography is less effective for detecting intracranial tumors.

B. Displaying shifts in midline cerebral structures is an area where echoencephalography is quite effective.

C. Echoencephalography is more likely to be used for older patients than for younger patients.

D. As far as diagnosis related to traumative injuries is concerned, echoencephalography has little use.

E. Echoencephalography is capable of indicating that bleeding or swelling is present in the brain.

CHECKYOURANSWERHERECHECKYOURANSWERHERECHECKYOURANSWERHERE
CHECKYOURANSWERHERECHECKYOURANSWERHERECHECKYOURANSWERHERE
CHECKYOURANSWERHERECHECKYOURANSWERHERECHECKYOURANSWERHERE
CHECKYOURANSWERHERECHECKYOURANSWERHERECHECKYOURANSWERHERE

40. To review what you've just learned about diagnostic tests used in relation to the skull and the brain, match the term in the left-hand column with its correct description in the right-hand column.

1. X-ray

2. CT scan

3. MRI

4. EEG

5. Echoencephalography

___2___ A. Combines existing x-ray procedures with computer technology

___5___ B. Uses sound waves to produce an image of a particular area of the body

___4___ C. Records the electrical activity occurring in the brain

___1___ D. Although more definitive testing procedures exist, this testing procedure is still used to detect skull fractures, cerebral hemorrhaging, and increases in intracranial pressure.

___3___ E. One of the primary uses for this sophisticated testing procedure is neurology.

CHECKYOURANSWERHERECHECKYOURANSWERHERECHECKYOURANSWERHERE
CHECKYOURANSWERHERECHECKYOURANSWERHERECHECKYOURANSWERHERE
CHECKYOURANSWERHERECHECKYOURANSWERHERECHECKYOURANSWERHERE
CHECKYOURANSWERHERECHECKYOURANSWERHERECHECKYOURANSWERHERE

REVIEW

41. Now, review what you've learned about the skull and the brain in this unit by completing these exercises.

   Write in the name of the skull bone described below.

   A. Located at the front of the head _____

   B. Forms the lower back portion of the skull; located between the parietal and temporal bones _____

   C. Upper jaw bone _____

   D. Join on the top of the head and extend part way down the sides, forming a protective covering around a large portion of the brain

   _____

   E. Extend from the occipital bone and terminate at the front of the skull near the temples _____

   F. Lower jaw bone _____

   G. Also called the zygomatic bones _____

   H. Large bone which extends through the skull, but is visible from the sides as a small wedge in front of the temporal bones _____

   _____

CHECKYOURANSWERHERECHECKYOURANSWERHERECHECKYOURANSWERHERE
CHECKYOURANSWERHERECHECKYOURANSWERHERECHECKYOURANSWERHERE
CHECKYOURANSWERHERECHECKYOURANSWERHERECHECKYOURANSWERHERE
CHECKYOURANSWERHERECHECKYOURANSWERHERECHECKYOURANSWERHERE

42. Briefly define the following types of skull fractures.

    A. Linear fracture _____

        _____

    B. Comminuted fracture _____

        _____

    C. Simple fracture _____

        _____

    D. Compound fracture _____

        _____

    E. Basal skull fracture _____

        _____

    F. Depressed skull fracture _____

        _____

CHECKYOURANSWERHERECHECKYOURANSWERHERECHECKYOURANSWERHERE
CHECKYOURANSWERHERECHECKYOURANSWERHERECHECKYOURANSWERHERE
CHECKYOURANSWERHERECHECKYOURANSWERHERECHECKYOURANSWERHERE
CHECKYOURANSWERHERECHECKYOURANSWERHERECHECKYOURANSWERHERE
CHECKYOURANSWERHERECHECKYOURANSWERHERECHECKYOURANSWERHERE
CHECKYOURANSWERHERECHECKYOURANSWERHERECHECKYOURANSWERHERE
CHECKYOURANSWERHERECHECKYOURANSWERHERECHECKYOURANSWERHERE
CHECKYOURANSWERHERECHECKYOURANSWERHERECHECKYOURANSWERHERE
CHECKYOURANSWERHERECHECKYOURANSWERHERECHECKYOURANSWERHERE
CHECKYOURANSWERHERECHECKYOURANSWERHERECHECKYOURANSWERHERE
CHECKYOURANSWERHERECHECKYOURANSWERHERECHECKYOURANSWERHERE
CHECKYOURANSWERHERECHECKYOURANSWERHERECHECKYOURANSWERHERE
CHECKYOURANSWERHERECHECKYOURANSWERHERECHECKYOURANSWERHERE

43. Which of these statements concerning injuries to the brain are correct?

    A. A cerebral hemorrhage is a blood tumor located somewhere within the brain.

    B. Brain contusions usually cause a period of unconsciousness.

    C. A contusion bruises the brain and resembles a bruise anywhere else on the body.

    D. Once an individual has recovered from a cerebral concussion, he or she will never experience any residual symptoms from the injury.

    E. A brain laceration usually is caused by a depressed skull fracture.

    F. A cerebral hematoma puts pressure on the brain, which can cause nerve damage and eventually lead to death.

    G. Cerebral hemorrhages usually result from brain contusions or brain lacerations.

CHECKYOURANSWERHERECHECKYOURANSWERHERECHECKYOURANSWERHERE
CHECKYOURANSWERHERECHECKYOURANSWERHERECHECKYOURANSWERHERE
CHECKYOURANSWERHERECHECKYOURANSWERHERECHECKYOURANSWERHERE
CHECKYOURANSWERHERECHECKYOURANSWERHERECHECKYOURANSWERHERE

44. Answer these questions about diagnostic tests for skull and brain injuries.
    A. Which testing technique would probably be used to detect a skull fracture?
        1. EEG
        2. CT scan
        3. X-ray

    B. Which test is most effective at diagnosing seizure disorders, such as epilepsy?
        1. EEG
        2. MRI
        3. CT scan

    C. The diagnostic test that is particularly effective at diagnosing cerebral hematomas, cerebral contusions, and brainstem abnormalities is
        1. MRI.
        2. X-ray.
        3. EEG.

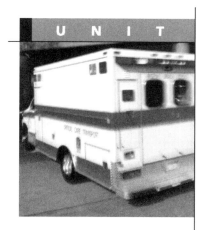

4

The Spine and Spinal Cord

IDENTIFYING THE VERTEBRAE

1. The **spine** is a protective column surrounding the spinal cord. It is formed by 26 **vertebrae** divided into five groups. From the top of the spine, which forms the neck, to the tailbone, the vertebrae are divided into the following groups:

Vertebral Groups

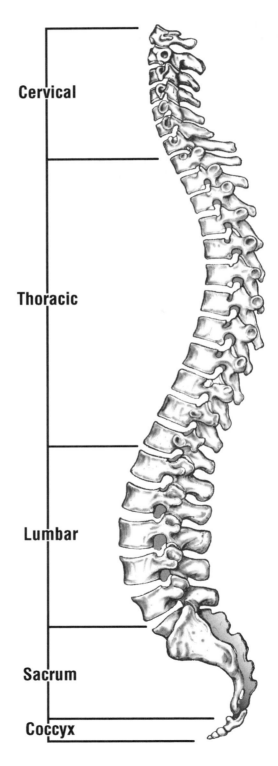

Cervical

Thoracic

Lumbar

Sacrum

Coccyx

■ **Cervical:** First 7 vertebrae in the neck

■ **Dorsal, or thoracic:** Next 12 vertebrae in the upper back

■ **Lumbar:** Next 5 vertebrae in the lower back

■ **Sacrum:** One large bone resulting from five smaller bones which, in adults, have fused; the sacrum forms the back of the pelvis.

■ **Coccyx:** The tailbone which, in adults, results from the fusion of four smaller bones

A. Which vertebral group forms the neck? _____

B. The lumbar vertebral group is located between the _____ vertebral group and the _____.

C. Which vertebral region makes up the tailbone? _____

CHECKYOURANSWERHERECHECKYOURANSWERHERECHECKYOURANSWERHERE
CHECKYOURANSWERHERECHECKYOURANSWERHERECHECKYOURANSWERHERE
CHECKYOURANSWERHERECHECKYOURANSWERHERECHECKYOURANSWERHERE
CHECKYOURANSWERHERECHECKYOURANSWERHERECHECKYOURANSWERHERE

2. Each vertebra is identified by its location within the cervical, dorsal/thoracic or lumbar group. The following system is used to describe a vertebra:

■ The first letter of the vertebral group where the vertebra is located, and

■ The number of that vertebra within the vertebral group, counting downward from the top of the group.

For example, the fifth vertebra in the lumbar region is described as **L-5**, and the second vertebra in the cervical region is described as **C-2**.

Identifying the Vertbrae

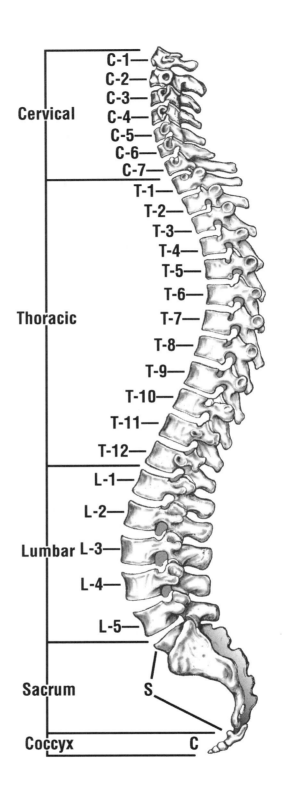

Cervical

- C-1
- C-2
- C-3
- C-4
- C-5
- C-6
- C-7

Thoracic

- T-1
- T-2
- T-3
- T-4
- T-5
- T-6
- T-7
- T-8
- T-9
- T-10
- T-11
- T-12

Lumbar

- L-1
- L-2
- L-3
- L-4
- L-5

Sacrum   S

Coccyx   C

Following are excerpts from medical reports. Identify the vertebra referred to in these reports using the lettering and numbering system we've just discussed.

A. Patient suffered a linear fracture in the fifth vertebra in the cervical group. _____

B. Patient's pain in the lower back was traced to an abnormality in the fourth vertebra in the lumbar group. _____

C. Patient was diagnosed with a simple linear fracture in the second vertebra of the thoracic group. _____

CHECKYOURANSWERHERECHECKYOURANSWERHERECHECKYOURANSWERHERE
CHECKYOURANSWERHERECHECKYOURANSWERHERECHECKYOURANSWERHERE
CHECKYOURANSWERHERECHECKYOURANSWERHERECHECKYOURANSWERHERE
CHECKYOURANSWERHERECHECKYOURANSWERHERECHECKYOURANSWERHERE

3. Which of the following statements are correct?

A. There are five dorsal, or thoracic, vertebrae.

B. The lumbar vertebrae are located at the very top of the spinal column.

C. The sacrum is a large bone which, in adults, is the result of the fusion of five smaller bones.

D. The lumbar vertebrae form the back of the pelvis.

E. There are seven cervical vertebrae.

F. The second vertebra in the lumbar region would be described in a medical report as 2-L.

G. A medical report describing an injury to the sixth cervical vertebra would refer to this vertebra as C-6.

CHECKYOURANSWERHERECHECKYOURANSWERHERECHECKYOURANSWERHERE
CHECKYOURANSWERHERECHECKYOURANSWERHERECHECKYOURANSWERHERE
CHECKYOURANSWERHERECHECKYOURANSWERHERECHECKYOURANSWERHERE
CHECKYOURANSWERHERECHECKYOURANSWERHERECHECKYOURANSWERHERE

UNDERSTANDING JOINT FUNCTION

4. The illustrations we've seen of the spine make it appear to be a long, inflexible stack of bone. We know this isn't true, however, because our backs are capable of many variations in movement. These movements are possible because of the **joints** which are located in between each vertebra.

As you know, a joint is the place where two bones join together. Another term used to describe a joint is **articulation**. In the illustration on the following page, the joints in the vertebral column are circled.

Bone ends are covered with **cartilage**, which is slightly elastic and lubricates the bones so they will move smoothly. Cartilage has no nerves or blood supply, so it is difficult to heal. If a fracture should extend into a joint and disturb the cartilage, the joint may become stiff, and joint movement limited. Fractures which extend into the joints are called **articular fractures**.

Vertebral Joints

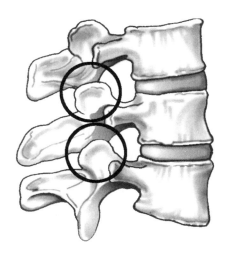

A joint

A. is the place where two bones join together.

B. is the same thing as cartilage.

C. may become stiff if an articular fracture disturbs the cartilage surrounding the bone.

CHECKYOURANSWERHERECHECKYOURANSWERHERECHECKYOURANSWERHERE
CHECKYOURANSWERHERECHECKYOURANSWERHERECHECKYOURANSWERHERE
CHECKYOURANSWERHERECHECKYOURANSWERHERECHECKYOURANSWERHERE
CHECKYOURANSWERHERECHECKYOURANSWERHERECHECKYOURANSWERHERE

Terms of Movement

5. When speaking of joint movements, certain terms are used, depending upon the direction of the movement. The five most common terms and their meanings are:

Joint Movements

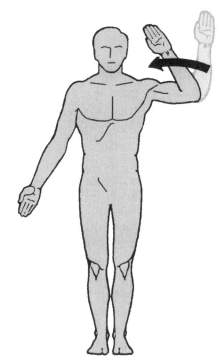

Flexion is the act of bending.

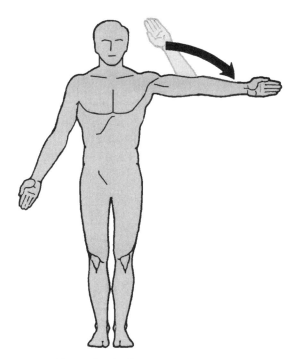

Extension is the act of straightening out.

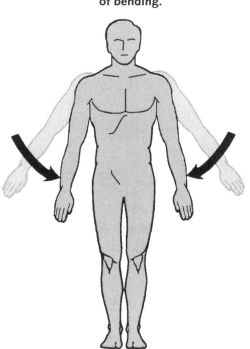

Adduction is the act of bringing a part of the body *toward* the middle of the body, though not necessarily to the middle.

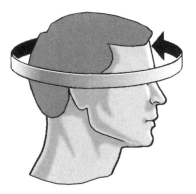

Rotation is the act of turning around on an axis.

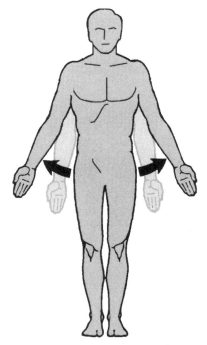

Abduction is the act of moving a part of the body *away* from the middle of the body.

A. When you raise your leg and bend your knee to climb a ladder, this is called _____.

B. When you raise your arm to the side to point at an object, this is called _____.

C. When you shake your head to express a negative response, this is called _____.

CHECKYOURANSWERHERECHECKYOURANSWERHERECHECKYOURANSWERHERE
CHECKYOURANSWERHERECHECKYOURANSWERHERECHECKYOURANSWERHERE
CHECKYOURANSWERHERECHECKYOURANSWERHERECHECKYOURANSWERHERE
CHECKYOURANSWERHERECHECKYOURANSWERHERECHECKYOURANSWERHERE

6. Physicians make reference to these joint movements when tests have been made to determine the results of injuries involving joints. These tests involve various movements, depending upon the area of injury. Movements will be indicated in percentages against what is considered normal for most people, such as "extension 70%, the normal being 90%;" or against the movement ability of a like body part which has not been injured, such as, "abduction of the right extremity is 50% of the capability of the left extremity." Joint movements may also be described in degrees, such as 30° flexion of the neck. Your concern with these movements depends largely on the patient involved. For example, the inability of a football player to flex or extend his leg will have much more significance to him than the same inability would to a typist.

When assessing injuries involving joints, physicians determine the percentage or degree of movement of the joint against

A. what is considered normal for most people.

B. the movement ability of a like body part which has not been injured.

C. both A and B.

CHECKYOURANSWERHERECHECKYOURANSWERHERECHECKYOURANSWERHERE
CHECKYOURANSWERHERECHECKYOURANSWERHERECHECKYOURANSWERHERE
CHECKYOURANSWERHERECHECKYOURANSWERHERECHECKYOURANSWERHERE
CHECKYOURANSWERHERECHECKYOURANSWERHERECHECKYOURANSWERHERE

7. Review what you've learned about joint function by matching the term in the left-hand column with its correct description in the right-hand column.

1. Articulation

2. Articular fracture

3. Cartilage

4. Straightening out of a body part

5. Bending of a body part

__2__ A. Fracture that extends into the joint between bones

__5__ B. Flexion

__3__ C. Substance that lubricates the ends of bones

__1__ D. Another name for a joint

__4__ E. Extension

CONSTRUCTION AND FUNCTION OF THE SPINE

Articular Processes

8. Now that you're familiar with joint function, including terms of movement related to the joints, let's consider the construction and function of the spine.

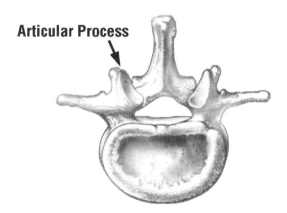

Articular Process

Each vertebra has protrusions called **articular processes** which allow movement in the spine. A vertebra's articular processes *articulate* with the articular processes of the vertebrae above and below. This means that joints are formed between the vertebrae, making movement possible. This illustration shows a top view of a lumbar vertebra, with one of the articular processes identified.

Which component of the vertebra allows movement in the spine?

Intervertebral Discs

9. **Intervertebral discs** are little cushions of fibrous cartilage located between vertebrae. Their purpose is to prevent the vertebrae from damaging each other during movement.

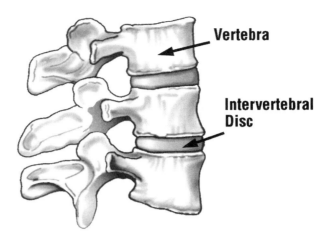

What is the purpose of an intervertebral disc?

A. To prevent the vertebrae from damaging each other during movement

B. To allow movement in the back

C. To join the vertebrae together to prevent excessive movement in the back

CHECKYOURANSWERHERECHECKYOURANSWERHERECHECKYOURANSWERHERE
CHECKYOURANSWERHERECHECKYOURANSWERHERECHECKYOURANSWERHERE
CHECKYOURANSWERHERECHECKYOURANSWERHERECHECKYOURANSWERHERE
CHECKYOURANSWERHERECHECKYOURANSWERHERECHECKYOURANSWERHERE

Location Terms

10. Before we continue with our discussion of the construction and function of the spine, you need to learn the meanings of some of the **location terms** used to describe relative positions of the body.

    In a previous unit, we discussed two of these terms in connection with the jaw bones. The two terms you learned were **inferior** and **superior**. To review, the *upper* jawbone is called the *superior* maxilla, and the *lower* jawbone is called the *inferior* maxilla. These location terms also apply to other parts of the body. When the body is standing upright, any part above another is *superior*. The part below is *inferior*.

    Following are three pairings of vertebral groups. For each pair, label the superior group with an **S** and the inferior group with an **I**.

    A. Lumbar _____   Coccyx _____

    B. Sacrum _____   Cervical _____

    C. Dorsal/thoracic _____   Lumbar _____

CHECKYOURANSWERHERECHECKYOURANSWERHERECHECKYOURANSWERHERE
CHECKYOURANSWERHERECHECKYOURANSWERHERECHECKYOURANSWERHERE
CHECKYOURANSWERHERECHECKYOURANSWERHERECHECKYOURANSWERHERE
CHECKYOURANSWERHERECHECKYOURANSWERHERECHECKYOURANSWERHERE

11. Two other location terms you need to be familiar with are **anterior** and **posterior**. Anterior means *in the front*; posterior means *in the back*. Each part of the body has an anterior and a posterior aspect.

In discussions of certain parts of the body, the terms inferior/superior and anterior/posterior are used together to clarify a description. This is often true when the vertebrae are discussed.

The lines on this illustration point to one vertebra. Let's say a medical report you're studying refers to the **anterior inferior aspect** of this one vertebra.

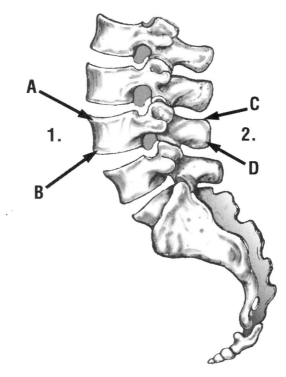

A. Which side is the anterior side? (Side 1/ Side 2) _____

B. The anterior inferior aspect is shown as point (A/B/C/D) _____.

CHECKYOURANSWERHERECHECKYOURANSWERHERECHECKYOURANSWERHERE
CHECKYOURANSWERHERECHECKYOURANSWERHERECHECKYOURANSWERHERE
CHECKYOURANSWERHERECHECKYOURANSWERHERECHECKYOURANSWERHERE
CHECKYOURANSWERHERECHECKYOURANSWERHERECHECKYOURANSWERHERE

Construction of the Vertebrae

12. While varying slightly in size and shape, all vertebrae are constructed basically the same way. For the illustrations in this frame, we've shown the top view of a lumbar vertebra.

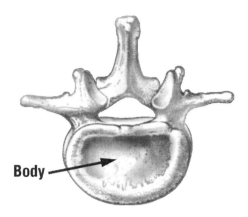

Body

The anterior portion of the vertebra is an oval-shaped, solid segment of bone called the *body* of the vertebra.

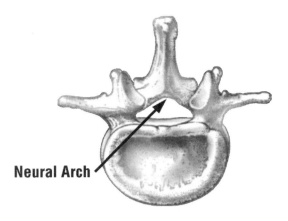

Neural Arch

In the posterior portion, two laminae and two roots join together to form the *neural arch*, leaving an opening between the vertebral body and the neural arch.

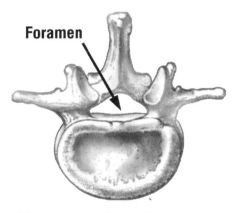

Foramen

The opening between the vertebral body and the neural arch is called the *foramen* (plural is *foramina*). The spinal cord passes through this opening.

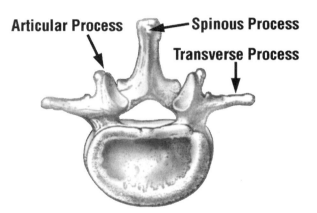

Articular Process   **Spinous Process**

Transverse Process

Outside the neural arch are seven protrusions, or *processes*. Four of these are the articular processes, discussed earlier in this unit. There are also two transverse processes and one spinous process.

Which one of the following is NOT a component of an individual vertebra?

A. Foramen

B. Neural arch

C. Processes

D. Coccyx

E. Body

CHECKYOURANSWERHERECHECKYOURANSWERHERECHECKYOURANSWERHERE
CHECKYOURANSWERHERECHECKYOURANSWERHERECHECKYOURANSWERHERE
CHECKYOURANSWERHERECHECKYOURANSWERHERECHECKYOURANSWERHERE
CHECKYOURANSWERHERECHECKYOURANSWERHERECHECKYOURANSWERHERE

13. Since the bodies of the vertebrae are stacked together, they provide the main support to the trunk of the human body. In addition, each of the 12 vertebral bodies in the thoracic, or dorsal, region has cup-shaped depressions on the sides called **costal pits**. The ribs fit into these costal pits.

    Where are the costal pits located?
    A. Anterior portion of the lumbar vertebrae
    B. Sides of the thoracic/dorsal vertebrae
    C. Posterior portion of the cervical articular processes

CHECKYOURANSWERHERECHECKYOURANSWERHERECHECKYOURANSWERHERE
CHECKYOURANSWERHERECHECKYOURANSWERHERECHECKYOURANSWERHERE
CHECKYOURANSWERHERECHECKYOURANSWERHERECHECKYOURANSWERHERE
CHECKYOURANSWERHERECHECKYOURANSWERHERECHECKYOURANSWERHERE

14. To review your knowledge of the construction and function of the spine, match the term in the column on the left with its correct description in the column on the right.

    1. Articular processes
    2. Intevertebral discs
    3. Inferior and superior
    4. Anterior and posterior
    5. Costal pits
    6. Foramen

    _6_ A. Opening between the body of the vertebra and the neural arch through which the spinal cord passes

    _4_ B. Location terms used to describe front and back, respectively

    _1_ C. Part of the vertebra that allows movement in the spine

    _2_ D. Cushion of fibrous cartilage located between vertebrae

    _3_ E. Location terms used to describe lower and upper, respectively

    _5_ F. Cup-shaped depressions on the sides of the thoracic vertebrae where the ribs fit

CHECKYOURANSWERHERECHECKYOURANSWERHERECHECKYOURANSWERHERE
CHECKYOURANSWERHERECHECKYOURANSWERHERECHECKYOURANSWERHERE
CHECKYOURANSWERHERECHECKYOURANSWERHERECHECKYOURANSWERHERE
CHECKYOURANSWERHERECHECKYOURANSWERHERECHECKYOURANSWERHERE

THE SPINAL CORD

15. The **spinal cord** extends from the lower portion of the brain stem, the **medulla oblongata**, to approximately the second lumbar vertebra. It is a thin column of nerve-enriched tissue. Every nerve to the trunk and limbs of the body issues from the spinal cord.

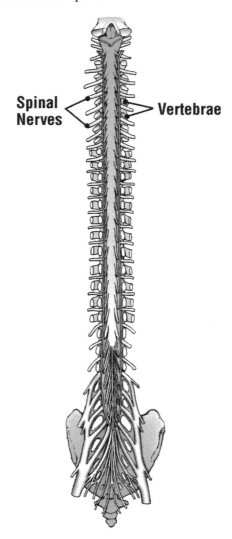

Spinal Nerves   **Vertebrae**

The illustration to the left shows the spinal cord lying within the vertebral column. The vertebral processes and laminae and the top coverings of the spinal cord have been removed.

The spinal cord does not completely fill the vertebral foramina. The remainder of the space is taken up by the **meninges** of the cord, as you can see in the illustration at the right. The meninges of the spinal cord function like the meninges of the brain by providing a padding between the spinal cord and the vertebrae. They also have the same names as the meninges of the brain: the **pia mater**, **arachnoid**, and **dura mater**. The pia mater is located closest to the spinal cord, the arachnoid is the middle membrane, and the dura mater is the furthest from the spinal cord.

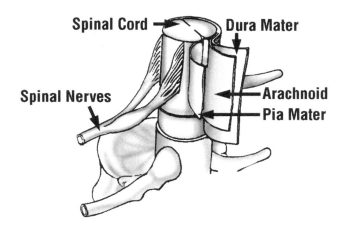

In addition to the three membranes, there is a protective fluid surrounding the spinal cord called **cerebrospinal fluid**. This fluid is also present in the brain, but in claim work, references to this fluid are most often found in connection with a **cerebrospinal puncture**, or "spinal tap," when taken from the spinal cord for diagnostic purposes.

A. Where does the spinal cord begin, and how far does it extend?

_____

_____

_____

B. Name the four elements, besides the spinal cord, that are located in the vertebral foramina.

1. _____

2. _____

3. _____

4. _____

16. The spinal cord is responsible for all nerve impulses that occur in the body, with the exception of the head. In addition, the spinal cord is the center of all *reflex* action in the body. For example, when you touch a hot pan on the stove, your immediate reaction is to jerk your hand away from the heat. This action takes place in a split second, without conscious thought.

   Any injury to the spine is considerably more serious if it involves the spinal cord in any way. We'll talk more about the effect of spinal cord injuries in the next section.

The spinal cord

A. has no role in the body's nerve impulses or reflex actions.

B. is responsible for all nerve impulses in the body (with the exception of the head), but has no part in the body's reflex actions.

C. is responsible for both the body's nerve impulses and reflex actions.

CHECKYOURANSWERHERECHECKYOURANSWERHERECHECKYOURANSWERHERE
CHECKYOURANSWERHERECHECKYOURANSWERHERECHECKYOURANSWERHERE
CHECKYOURANSWERHERECHECKYOURANSWERHERECHECKYOURANSWERHERE
CHECKYOURANSWERHERECHECKYOURANSWERHERECHECKYOURANSWERHERE

17. Which of the following statements concerning the spinal cord are correct?

A. The spinal cord begins at the lower portion of the brain stem, or the medulla oblongata, and ends at approximately the second lumbar vertebra.

B. The vertebral foramina contains only the spinal cord.

C. Unlike the brain, the spinal cord has no protective coverings.

D. The protective fluid surrounding the spinal cord is called cerebrospinal fluid.

E. Any injury to the spine is considerably more serious if it involves the spinal cord in any way.

CHECKYOURANSWERHERECHECKYOURANSWERHERECHECKYOURANSWERHERE
CHECKYOURANSWERHERECHECKYOURANSWERHERECHECKYOURANSWERHERE
CHECKYOURANSWERHERECHECKYOURANSWERHERECHECKYOURANSWERHERE
CHECKYOURANSWERHERECHECKYOURANSWERHERECHECKYOURANSWERHERE

INJURIES TO THE SPINE AND SPINAL CORD

Fractures and Dislocations

18. A fracture in the spinal column can range in disabling effect from no disability to complete disability. A fracture of one of the spinal processes without displacement of the bone can heal quickly without surgery. If the bone fragment is displaced, surgery may be necessary to insure proper alignment, and an extended period of temporary disability may result from the need to immobilize the back.

You're studying a medical report involving a patient with a fracture in her spinal column. Which of the following statements could apply to her condition?

A. The patient's condition can only be corrected by surgery.

B. The patient's condition always results in complete disability.

C. The patient's condition may be treated with or without surgery, depending on the type and location of the fracture.

CHECKYOURANSWERHERECHECKYOURANSWERHERECHECKYOURANSWERHERE
CHECKYOURANSWERHERECHECKYOURANSWERHERECHECKYOURANSWERHERE
CHECKYOURANSWERHERECHECKYOURANSWERHERECHECKYOURANSWERHERE
CHECKYOURANSWERHERECHECKYOURANSWERHERECHECKYOURANSWERHERE

19. The laminae are rarely fractured, but when a fracture does occur it usually heals naturally, much like the processes. On rare occasions, because of the lamina's proximity to the spinal cord, a fracture may cause injury to the cord or nerves. Then the condition becomes quite serious, with the possibility of paralysis in one or more parts of the body.

    What is the biggest danger that arises with a fractured lamina?

    A. If the fracture injures the spinal cord or nerves, paralysis in one or more parts of the body may result.

    B. The fracture may also cause an intervertebral disc to rupture.

    CHECKYOURANSWERHERECHECKYOURANSWERHERECHECKYOURANSWERHERE
    CHECKYOURANSWERHERECHECKYOURANSWERHERECHECKYOURANSWERHERE
    CHECKYOURANSWERHERECHECKYOURANSWERHERECHECKYOURANSWERHERE
    CHECKYOURANSWERHERECHECKYOURANSWERHERECHECKYOURANSWERHERE

20. A fractured vertebral body is a serious injury. The vertebral bodies are fairly easily fractured. These fractures range from minor linear fractures, which are painful and temporarily disabling but heal quickly, to seriously disabling fractures involving spinal cord damage. However, fractures to vertebral bodies rarely involve the spinal cord.

Fractured Vertebral Body

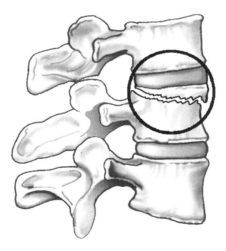

    Which one of the following statements concerning fractures to vertebral bodies is correct?

    A. Fractures to vertebral bodies are rare.

    B. Fractures to vertebral bodies are always seriously disabling.

    C. Fractures to vertebral bodies can range from minor linear fractures to seriously disabling fractures involving spinal cord damage.

    CHECKYOURANSWERHERECHECKYOURANSWERHERECHECKYOURANSWERHERE
    CHECKYOURANSWERHERECHECKYOURANSWERHERECHECKYOURANSWERHERE
    CHECKYOURANSWERHERECHECKYOURANSWERHERECHECKYOURANSWERHERE
    CHECKYOURANSWERHERECHECKYOURANSWERHERECHECKYOURANSWERHERE

Cervical Vertebrae Injuries

21. Damage to the spinal cord is always a possibility, however remote, with any type of vertebral fracture. The location in the spinal column of the fractured vertebra is very significant regarding permanent disability. Fractures in the **cervical vertebrae** are potentially the most dangerous from the standpoint of permanent total disability, since spinal cord damage in this area can easily result in permanent, total paralysis of the patient's trunk and limbs.

    Which one of the following excerpts from medical reports describes a situation where permanent, total paralysis of the patient's trunk and limbs may result?

    A. Comminuted fractures to C-3 and C-4, dislocated posteriorly, fragments compressed into vertebral foramina.

    B. Linear fracture to L-5, no injury to spinal cord or nerves.

    C. Compression fracture of T-12, no injury to spinal cord or nerves.

CHECKYOURANSWERHERECHECKYOURANSWERHERECHECKYOURANSWERHERE
CHECKYOURANSWERHERECHECKYOURANSWERHERECHECKYOURANSWERHERE
CHECKYOURANSWERHERECHECKYOURANSWERHERECHECKYOURANSWERHERE
CHECKYOURANSWERHERECHECKYOURANSWERHERECHECKYOURANSWERHERE

Subjective Complaints and Objective Findings

22. Even when permanent total paralysis or other disability does not result, a cervical spinal cord injury can cause any number of **subjective complaints** and **objective findings**, from headaches to loss of motion. Let's take a quick look at the meaning of these two terms.

    A *subjective complaint* is one that cannot be observed or perceived by another person. For example, a physician cannot actually see a patient's headache or stomach pain. This does not mean that the patient is not actually suffering from pain, only that the physician cannot observe or perceive it.

    While *subjective* refers to complaints that cannot be seen by another, *objective* means that the physician has actually found some abnormalities in the patient. These are called objective *findings*, as opposed to subjective complaints.

    Note that subjective complaints and objective findings may be seen with all types of injuries, not just those involving the cervical area of the spinal cord.

    In front of each medical report excerpt below, write in an **S** if the example is a subjective complaint or an **O** for an objective finding.

    _____ A. The pain that Mr. Seitz complains of in his lower back is no doubt a result of the fractured vertebra he suffered in an auto accident.

    _____ B. Although all tests were negative, Mr. Billings continues to complain of pain in his lower back upon movement.

    _____ C. Ms. Parsons' neck pain was determined to be the result of a simple linear fracture to C-5.

    _____ D. Mrs. James complains of severe pain in the coccyx. All tests were negative.

Dislocation and Subluxation

23. Fractures in the cervical area do not occur often. Far more common is a **dislocation** of a vertebra, in the cervical and other areas. Dislocation occurs when some force pushes the vertebra out of its proper location. When this happens, the vertebra is rarely completely dislocated, but only partially pushed away from the other vertebrae. Such a partial dislocation is called a **subluxation**.

    A dislocation can cause as much damage to the spinal cord as a fracture. When the dislocated vertebra slips forward or backward, it may pull muscles, nerve roots, or blood vessels along with it. Hemorrhaging may result, causing pressure on the nerve roots.

    A. What happens when a vertebra is dislocated? _____
    _____

    B. What term is used to describe a vertebra that is only partially pushed away from the other vertebrae? _____

Thoracic/Dorsal Vertebrae Injuries

24. Injuries of any sort to the dorsal, or thoracic, vertebrae are less common than in other areas. One reason for this is the rib attachments which help anchor these vertebrae in front as well as in the spinal column. Another reason is that this portion of the back is subjected to less strain and movement than the other vertebral regions.

    The most common type of fracture in this area is a **compression fracture of the spine**, where a vertebra is crushed between the vertebrae above and below it. Compression fractures can result from trauma, but are more likely to be caused by **osteoporosis**, a condition that causes bone mass to decrease. This loss of bone mass can cause the vertebrae to collapse, resulting in compression fractures.

The dorsal vertebrae are

A. not often fractured, but if a fracture occurs it is likely to be a compression fracture.

B. very susceptible to any type of fracture.

C. subjected to more strain and motion than the other vertebral regions.

D. protected from injury in part by the ribs attached to them.

CHECKYOURANSWERHERECHECKYOURANSWERHERECHECKYOURANSWERHERE
CHECKYOURANSWERHERECHECKYOURANSWERHERECHECKYOURANSWERHERE
CHECKYOURANSWERHERECHECKYOURANSWERHERECHECKYOURANSWERHERE
CHECKYOURANSWERHERECHECKYOURANSWERHERECHECKYOURANSWERHERE

Lumbar Vertebrae Injuries

25. Fractures, dislocations, and other types of injuries probably occur more often in the lumbar or sacral region of the spine than in any other location. These areas, particularly the lumbar area, are subjected to many extremes of motion and bear the strain of most of the lifting and carrying we do.

   The lumbar vertebrae are susceptible to compression fractures, but a compression fracture in the lumbar area is less likely to damage the spinal cord because the spinal cord ends at the second lumbar vertebra.

   One type of condition that often affects the lumbar vertebrae is **spondylolisthesis**. Spondylolisthesis is the forward displacement of one vertebra over another, usually the fifth lumbar over the sacrum, or pelvis. This results in a pelvic deformity which causes pain and discomfort and may make movement difficult.

   Why do fractures, dislocations, and other types of injuries occur more often in the lumbar or sacral region of the spine? _____
   _____
   _____

CHECKYOURANSWERHERECHECKYOURANSWERHERECHECKYOURANSWERHERE
CHECKYOURANSWERHERECHECKYOURANSWERHERECHECKYOURANSWERHERE
CHECKYOURANSWERHERECHECKYOURANSWERHERECHECKYOURANSWERHERE
CHECKYOURANSWERHERECHECKYOURANSWERHERECHECKYOURANSWERHERE
CHECKYOURANSWERHERECHECKYOURANSWERHERECHECKYOURANSWERHERE
CHECKYOURANSWERHERECHECKYOURANSWERHERECHECKYOURANSWERHERE

Intervertebral Disc Herniation

26. Earlier, we described the intervertebral disc and its function in cushioning the impact of one vertebra during movement. Discs are subjected to a great deal of pressure during a lifetime, and begin to deteriorate from constant wear and tear at an early age, probably about age 30. Because there is no nerve or blood supply to the disc, it is unable to regenerate itself or reverse degeneration. Eventually, if sufficient pressure is applied, the disc may rupture, and the result is called a **herniated disc**. Here's a detailed look at what happens when a disc herniates or ruptures:

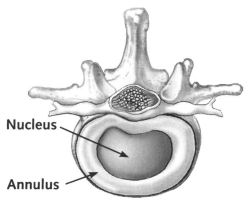

Nucleus

Annulus

An intervertebral disc is made up of a strong outer lining, which is attached to the vertebral bodies above and below the disc, and a fluid, jelly-like center, which is primarily water, at the center of the disc. The purpose of the outer lining, or *annulus*, is to hold the fluid center of the disc in place. The fluid center is called the *nucleus*.

An intervertebral disc is made up of a strong outer lining, which is attached to the vertebral bodies above and below the disc, and a fluid, jelly-like center, which is primarily water, at the center of the disc. The purpose of the outer lining, or *annulus*, is to hold the fluid center of the disc in place. The fluid center is called the *nucleus*.

Movement of Intervertebral Disc

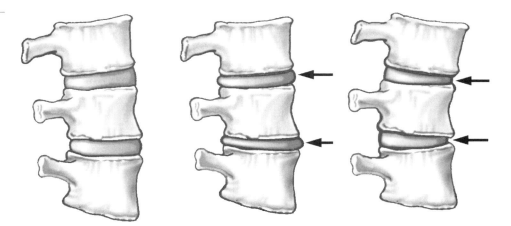

Various types of body movements and positions put pressure on the nucleus of the disc, and when this happens, the nucleus tends to move around. But if the annulus is strong and the disc is healthy, the nucleus stays in its proper place.

Bulging Disc   Herniated Disc

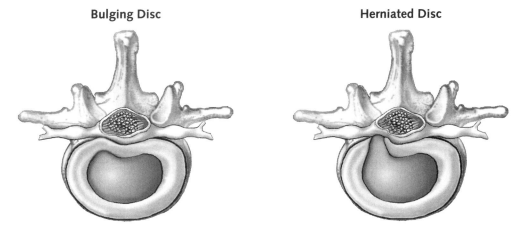

The nucleus can create a *bulge* in the annulus if it is weak. In severe cases, the annulus breaks, and the nucleus leaks out of its normal position. This is called a *herniated* or *ruptured disc*.

True or false?

A. Normal wear and tear can put enough pressure on a disc to cause disc herniation.   ( ) True   ( ) False

B. The outer lining of a disc is called the nucleus.   ( ) True   ( ) False

C. The fluid, jelly-like center of a disc is called the annulus.
( ) True   ( ) False

D. A herniated disc occurs when the annulus breaks and the nucleus leaks out of its normal position.   ( ) True   ( ) False

CHECKYOURANSWERHERECHECKYOURANSWERHERECHECKYOURANSWERHERE
CHECKYOURANSWERHERECHECKYOURANSWERHERECHECKYOURANSWERHERE
CHECKYOURANSWERHERECHECKYOURANSWERHERECHECKYOURANSWERHERE
CHECKYOURANSWERHERECHECKYOURANSWERHERECHECKYOURANSWERHERE

27. A bulging or herniated disc often puts pressure on the nerve roots which exit the spinal column. This pressure can cause pain, numbness, tingling, or a loss of sensation in the patient's arms or legs. It can also affect the patient's reflexes. However, if the bulging or herniated disc is not pressing on nerve roots, the patient may not experience any symptoms at all, because the disc itself has no nerves.

As a general rule, a disc deteriorates gradually and eventually ruptures in the normal course of activities, without symptoms to the patient. However, trauma can either cause a healthy disc to herniate or aggravate an already herniated disc and cause symptoms to appear.

Which of the following statements concerning herniated discs are true?

A. A herniated disc can be caused by trauma.

B. A herniated disc may or may not produce symptoms in the patient, depending on whether the disc is pressing on spinal nerve roots.

C. A herniated disc often is the result of normal deterioration during the patient's lifetime.

D. All of the above are true.

CHECKYOURANSWERHERECHECKYOURANSWERHERECHECKYOURANSWERHERE
CHECKYOURANSWERHERECHECKYOURANSWERHERECHECKYOURANSWERHERE
CHECKYOURANSWERHERECHECKYOURANSWERHERECHECKYOURANSWERHERE
CHECKYOURANSWERHERECHECKYOURANSWERHERECHECKYOURANSWERHERE

28. Herniated discs are more common in the lumbar region, especially between the fourth and fifth vertebrae. This is probably due to the extremes of stress and motion that the lumbar vertebrae must undergo. When a disc ruptures in the lumbar area, it may compress the nerve roots that make up the **sciatic nerve**, which is the large nerve that runs down the back of the leg. This compression causes pain or muscle spasms in the lower extremities. Occasionally, the disc between the fifth and sixth cervical vertebrae ruptures, which causes similar symptoms in the upper extremities.

Treatment for herniated discs varies depending on the location and severity of the herniated disc and the patient's symptoms. Some of the more common treatment methods include:

- Medications such as muscle relaxers, anti-inflammatories, and steroids

- Complete bed rest/restricted physical activity

- Physical therapy

- Surgery

Traction may be used to treat a herniated disc in the cervical region.

A. Herniated discs are most common in the

    1. lumbar region.

    2. dorsal, or thoracic, region.

B. Which one of the following statements concerning treatment of herniated discs is correct?

    1. Herniated discs must be treated surgically.

    2. Herniated discs are never treated with physical therapy.

    3. Treatment of herniated discs varies depending on the location and severity of the herniated disc and the patient's symptoms.

CHECKYOURANSWERHERECHECKYOURANSWERHERECHECKYOURANSWERHERE
CHECKYOURANSWERHERECHECKYOURANSWERHERECHECKYOURANSWERHERE
CHECKYOURANSWERHERECHECKYOURANSWERHERECHECKYOURANSWERHERE
CHECKYOURANSWERHERECHECKYOURANSWERHERECHECKYOURANSWERHERE

Strains and Sprains

29. Strains and sprains are the most common injuries to the back. As you learned in an earlier unit, a strain is a minor injury involving stretching of muscles or tendons beyond their usual limits. A sprain is an extension of a strain, in which a part of a muscle or ligament is torn away from its normal location.

    A strain or a sprain can cause the same symptoms and the same amount of pain as a fracture, dislocation, or herniated disc. Often, a diagnostic test such as an X-ray, MRI, or CT scan is the only way to determine the nature of the patient's complaint. Sprains and strains are usually treated by medication, such as muscle relaxers and anti-inflammatories, and bed rest.

Bob sprained his lower back lifting a heavy carton. Mary strained hers lifting weights at the gym. Which of the following statements about their injuries are true?

A. They are the most common injuries to the back.

B. Their symptoms are very different from those of fractures, dislocations, and herniated discs.

C. They are never painful.

D. A doctor may run diagnostic tests to determine the exact nature of Bob and Mary's injuries.

CHECKYOURANSWERHERECHECKYOURANSWERHERECHECKYOURANSWERHERE
CHECKYOURANSWERHERECHECKYOURANSWERHERECHECKYOURANSWERHERE
CHECKYOURANSWERHERECHECKYOURANSWERHERE
CHECKYOURANSWERHERECHECKYOURANSWERHERECHECKYOURANSWERHERE

Hyperextension-Hyperflexion Injury

30. A **hyperextension-hyperflexion injury** is a descriptive term used to describe an injury that occurs when the neck is first extended excessively backward, then thrown forward with extreme bending of the neck.

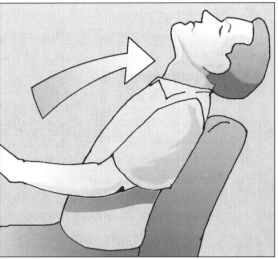

This type of injury is sometimes described as **whiplash**. You may see this nontechnical term used to describe a great variety of injuries to the neck, running the gamut from baseless subjective complaints to very seriously disabling objective symptoms.

When a hyperextension-hyperflexion type of injury occurs, it usually results in a strain or sprain of muscles or ligaments in the neck. Damage to vertebral nerves or blood vessels or nerves in the occipital area of the brain may also occur, although this is rare.

A hyperextension-hyperflexion injury

A. describes the type of injury where the neck is first extended excessively backward, then thrown forward with extreme bending of the neck.

B. usually causes strained muscles or ligaments or sprained ligaments.

C. is always an extremely serious injury.

CHECKYOURANSWERHERECHECKYOURANSWERHERECHECKYOURANSWERHERE
CHECKYOURANSWERHERECHECKYOURANSWERHERECHECKYOURANSWERHERE
CHECKYOURANSWERHERECHECKYOURANSWERHERECHECKYOURANSWERHERE
CHECKYOURANSWERHERECHECKYOURANSWERHERECHECKYOURANSWERHERE

Common Congenital Anomalies

31. A **congenital anomaly** is a malformation of an organ or structure that was present at birth. Congenital anomalies in the spine are of interest to a claim examiner because these anomalies may remain unnoticed until an injury or disease calls for a diagnostic test, which then reveals the anomaly. Also, anomalies are frequently misread as injuries. In the lumbar area of the spine, there are three common anomalies you may encounter in claimants' medical reports:

■ Failure of the transverse process of the first lumbar vertebra to fuse to the vertebra

■ Abnormal fusion of the fourth and fifth lumbar vertebrae (especially common with achondroplasia, or dwarfism)

■ Absence of one lumbar vertebra, resulting in four lumbar vertebrae rather than five

Name two reasons why a congenital anomaly of the spine is of interest to claim examiners.

A. _____

_____

B. _____

_____

CHECKYOURANSWERHERECHECKYOURANSWERHERECHECKYOURANSWERHERE
CHECKYOURANSWERHERECHECKYOURANSWERHERECHECKYOURANSWERHERE
CHECKYOURANSWERHERECHECKYOURANSWERHERECHECKYOURANSWERHERE
CHECKYOURANSWERHERECHECKYOURANSWERHERECHECKYOURANSWERHERE

32. Review what you've learned about injuries to the spine and spinal cord by matching the term in the left-hand column with its correct definition in the right-hand column.

1. Fracture in the spinal column

2. Dislocation of a vertebra

3. Subluxation of a vertebra

4. Spondylolisthesis

5. Herniated intervertebral disc

6. Strain/Sprain

7. Hyperextension-hyperflexion injury

8. Congenital anomaly

_____ A. Condition where the inner portion of the intervertebral disc leaks out of position and breaks through the wall of the disc

_____ B. Involves stretching of muscles or tendons beyond their usual limits or tearing a part of a muscle or ligament away from its normal location

_____ C. Malformation of an organ or structure that was present at birth

_____ D. May affect a spinal process, vertebral body, or lamina

_____ E. Some force completely pushes a vertebra out of its proper location

_____ F. Forward displacement of one vertebra over another, usually the fifth lumbar over the sacrum

_____ G. Some force partially pushes a vertebra out of its proper location

_____ H. Describes an injury to the neck area where the neck is first extended excessively backward, then thrown forward with extreme bending of the neck

DIAGNOSTIC TESTS AND SIGNS

33. Many types of diagnostic tests and signs are used to determine the nature of injuries to the spine and spinal cord. You already learned about two of these tests in a previous unit: the MRI and the CT scan.

    Both the MRI and the CT scan are used frequently to diagnose back conditions. Either may be used to diagnose:

    ■ Nerve root compression

    ■ Herniated discs

    ■ Tumors

    Another test you have learned about, the x-ray, has been largely replaced in favor of more advanced testing procedures. However, x-rays are still used to diagnose fractures or congenital deformities in the spine.

    Answer the following true/false questions to review your knowledge of the MRI and CT scan.

    A. The CT scan does not use x-rays.   ( ) True   (x) False

    B. With the CT scan, many different views of the body part being examined are made, rather than just one or two different angles.
       (x) True   ( ) False

    C. The CT scan is a safe, noninvasive procedure.   (x) True   ( ) False

    D. The CT scan combines x-rays and computer technology.   (x) True
       ( ) False

    E. MRI is especially effective for examining soft tissues with high fluid content.   (x) True   ( ) False

    F. MRI combines x-rays and contrast agents.   ( ) True   (x) False

    G. MRI is a dangerous, invasive procedure which should only be used as a last resort when other diagnostic tests have failed to diagnose the patient's condition.   ( ) True   (x) False

Myelography

34. **Myelography** combines a fluorescent screen called a fluoroscope with x-ray equipment and a contrast agent to produce x-ray images of the interior of the vertebrae.

Myelography

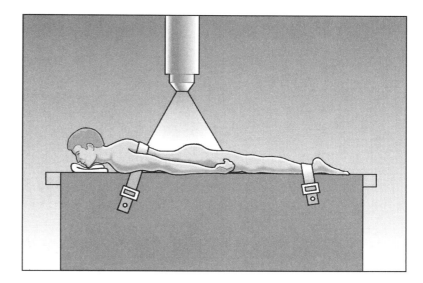

The patient is positioned between the x-ray tube and the fluoroscope, which is part of the x-ray table. A contrast agent is injected into the spine, the table is tilted to permit the agent to flow, and the flow is observed with the fluoroscope.

Visualization occurs by means of the fluoroscope, and x-ray images are taken to make a permanent record.

Myelography is particularly effective for diagnosing herniated intervertebral discs. Because a disc is not a bone, it cannot be distinguished by x-ray. With myelography, the contrast agent flows *around* a herniated disc and produces an outline; this outline shows up on the x-ray.

Myelography is also effective for diagnosing various types of tumors in spinal structures, certain inflammations of the spinal structures, and congenital anomalies.

You read in a medical report that myelography was used to diagnose a patient's back injury. You know that myelography

A. combines x-ray techniques and computer technology to produce three-dimensional images of the spine.

B. combines a fluorescent screen called a fluoroscope with x-ray equipment and a contrast agent to produce x-ray images of the interior of the vertebrae.

C. is particularly effective for diagnosing herniated intervertebral discs.

D. is not used to diagnose herniated intervertebral discs, because this condition can be detected with x-rays.

Electromyography (EMG)

35. **Electromyography**, or **EMG**, measures the electrical activity in skeletal muscles. Here is how EMG works:

Electromyography

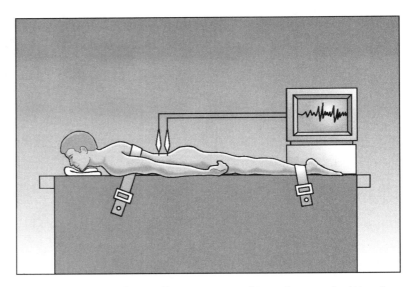

Electrodes, which are actually needles, are inserted into the muscle. Waveforms are displayed on an oscilloscope screen. Audio amplification is used since voltage fluctuations in muscle are audible, and the sounds provide diagnostic information.

The graphics produced on the oscilloscope are temporary, so photographs are taken of the EMG on-screen image and retained for permanent records.

Typically, the EMG monitors activity both when the muscle is at rest and during voluntary contractions made by the patient. At rest, very little electrical activity occurs in normal muscle tissue. It is during contraction that abnormalities can be observed.

EMG is usually not diagnostic without confirmation from other tests or sources such as the patient's medical history, but is useful to help in diagnosing:

■ Tumors

■ Nerve root irritation from an extruded disc

■ Source of back pain

Electromyography

A. measures electrical activity in muscles.

B. can usually confirm a diagnosis without confirmation from other tests or sources.

C. is used to diagnose nerve root irritation from an extruded disc and the source of back pain.

CHECKYOURANSWERHERECHECKYOURANSWERHERECHECKYOURANSWERHERE
CHECKYOURANSWERHERECHECKYOURANSWERHERECHECKYOURANSWERHERE
CHECKYOURANSWERHERECHECKYOURANSWERHERECHECKYOURANSWERHERE
CHECKYOURANSWERHERECHECKYOURANSWERHERECHECKYOURANSWERHERE

Nerve Conduction Studies

36. **Nerve conduction studies** are often performed simultaneously with EMG. Nerve conduction tests are typically performed only in this context, not separately.

    Conduction refers to a nerve's impulse in response to a stimulus at one point, which then causes a reaction at another point. Conduction occurs not only in nerve fibers but also in muscle fibers. For example, conduction through your nervous system allows this familiar sequence of events:

Here's what happens in a nerve conduction study:

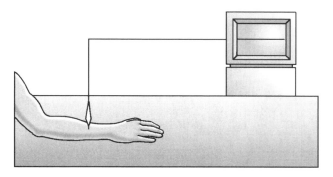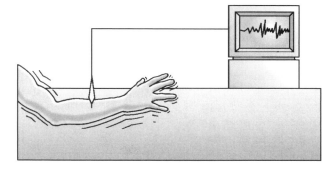

A needle electrically stimulates a nerve, giving the patient a mild electrical shock. At an established distance from the stimulated nerve, the nerve's response is recorded on the oscilloscope.

The oscilloscope then measures the time from stimulation to recorded response—the conduction. The speed of conduction is measured, and the time is compared to established norms. Using the time differentials, a physician can identify the presence of certain nerve injuries and diseases.

Complete the following sentences.

A. Nerve conduction studies are usually performed (in conjunction with/ separately from) _____ EMG.

B. Nerve conduction studies measure the (speed of/presence or lack of) _____ nerve conduction.

CHECKYOURANSWERHERECHECKYOURANSWERHERECHECKYOURANSWERHERE
CHECKYOURANSWERHERECHECKYOURANSWERHERECHECKYOURANSWERHERE
CHECKYOURANSWERHERECHECKYOURANSWERHERECHECKYOURANSWERHERE
CHECKYOURANSWERHERECHECKYOURANSWERHERECHECKYOURANSWERHERE

Straight Leg-Raising Test

37. The **straight leg-raising test (SLR)** is used to distinguish between **sciatica**, which is pain along the sciatic nerve that runs down the back of the leg that may be caused by a number of conditions, and **hip joint disease**. Here is how the straight leg-raising test is performed:

Straight Leg-Raising Test

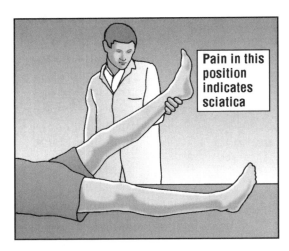

Pain in this position indicates sciatica

With the patient supine (face up), the physician gently raises the patient's extended leg. If there is pain when the leg is lifted in extension, this is sciatica caused by a condition involving the sciatic nerve. If there is no pain, the physician continues the procedure as shown in the next illustration.

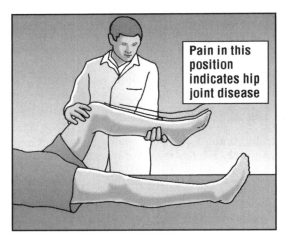

Pain in this position indicates hip joint disease

The physician then bends the knee while the leg is still raised, which flexes the hip joint. If pain occurs when the knee is bent as illustrated, this is an indication of hip joint disease.

Occasionally, an optional SLR is used. This involves the patient sitting with the leg extended, then bending the leg, applying the same type of sciatic nerve stress and the same results.

A. The straight leg-raising test is used to differentiate between _____ _____ and _____.

B. With the straight leg-raising test, sciatic nerve involvement is indicated when pain is felt when the leg is (extended/bent) _____.

38. In the last few frames, we've been discussing various types of **tests** used to diagnose injuries to the spine and spinal cord. In the next couple of frames, we'll focus on two common **signs** that may be mentioned in medical reports in connection with claims for back injuries.

    A **sign** is **objective evidence or manifestation of a disorder**, such as a positive result of a physical examination test. A sign is *objective* because it can be **seen, heard, felt**, and/or **measured** by someone other than the patient, whereas symptoms are often *subjective* since they are perceptible only to the patient.

    Objective signs are important diagnostic aids because they cannot be faked. Whether or not a sign is present is beyond the patient's control. On the other hand, a patient can fake a symptom, such as complaining of back pain when there is no medical evidence of a back problem. But remember, pain may actually exist even when there is no objective evidence of a disorder.

    Objective signs

    A. can be faked by the patient.

    B. are objective evidence or manifestations of a disorder.

    C. can be seen, heard, felt, or measured by someone other than the patient.

    D. are not considered important diagnostic tools.

Babinski's Reflex

39. **Babinski's reflex** indicates damage to the nervous system. Here is how it is elicited:

Babinski's Reflex

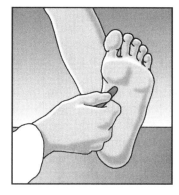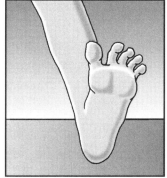

The physician strokes the lateral side of the sole of the foot. Babinski's reflex is the backward flexion of the great toe, often accompanied by fanning out of the other toes.

When Babinski's is negative, rather than positive as indicated in the previous illustrations, the stroking causes all toes to flex forward, rather than backward and fanning out. This response means there is no damage to the nervous system. The particular type of nervous system damage indicated by a positive Babinski's reflex might be caused by a number of different conditions, including spinal cord injury or a spinal cord tumor.

A. A positive Babinski's reflex results in
    1. backward flexion of the great toe.
    2. forward flexion of the great toe.
    3. flexion of all of the toes.

B. When Babinski's reflex is positive, what often occurs to the other toes?
    1. The other toes also flex backward.
    2. The other toes also flex forward.
    3. The other toes may fan out.

CHECKYOURANSWERHERECHECKYOURANSWERHERECHECKYOURANSWERHERE
CHECKYOURANSWERHERECHECKYOURANSWERHERECHECKYOURANSWERHERE
CHECKYOURANSWERHERECHECKYOURANSWERHERECHECKYOURANSWERHERE
CHECKYOURANSWERHERECHECKYOURANSWERHERECHECKYOURANSWERHERE

Romberg's Sign

40. Nerve damage is indicated by a positive **Romberg's sign**, which occurs like this:

Romberg's Sign

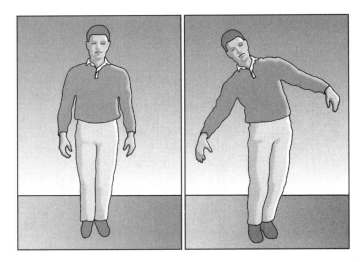

The patient stands with feet close together and closes eyes. Swaying or other indication of inability to maintain balance with eyes closed is Romberg's sign.

While Romberg's sign *indicates* nerve damage, it does not specifically *diagnose* the cause of the damage. There are many causes of nerve damage, including injury, disease, or degeneration of the spinal cord. Typically, a physician might use Romberg's sign to confirm nerve damage, then perform appropriate additional tests to pinpoint the diagnosis based on the patient's other symptoms.

A. Romberg's sign is positive when, standing with feet close together, the patient

1. is unable to maintain balance after closing the eyes.

2. is unable to maintain balance after opening the eyes.

3. falls down.

B. What would be a typical procedure for a physician to follow after eliciting a positive Romberg's sign?_____

_____

CHECKYOURANSWERHERECHECKYOURANSWERHERECHECKYOURANSWERHERE
CHECKYOURANSWERHERECHECKYOURANSWERHERECHECKYOURANSWERHERE
CHECKYOURANSWERHERECHECKYOURANSWERHERECHECKYOURANSWERHERE
CHECKYOURANSWERHERECHECKYOURANSWERHERECHECKYOURANSWERHERE

41. Following are illustrations of all the diagnostic tests and signs we've discussed in this unit. Write in the name of the test or sign being depicted under each illustration.

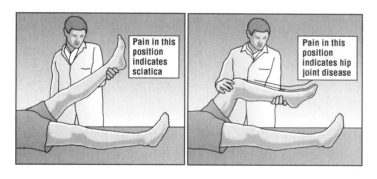

A. _____

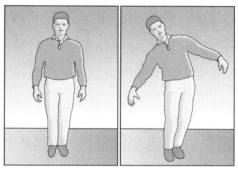

B. _____

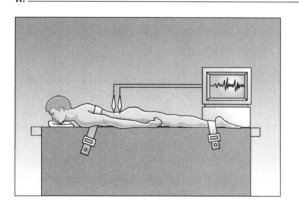

C. _____

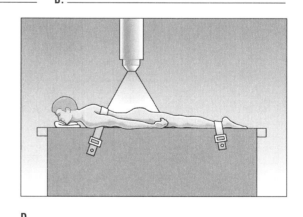

D. _____

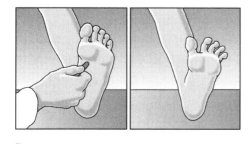

E. _____

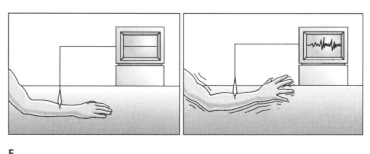

F. _____

REVIEW

42. Review what you've learned about the spine and spinal cord by answering the following questions.

    Which one of the following is NOT one of the five vertebral groups?

    A. Dorsal/thoracic
    B. Lumbar
    C. Cervical
    D. Coccyx
    E. Foramen
    F. Sacrum

43. The opening in the spinal column which the spinal cord passes through is called the

    A. laminae.
    B. neural arch.
    C. foramen.
    D. coccyx.

44. Which of the following statements concerning the spinal cord are true?

    A. It extends from the lower portion of the brain stem to approximately the second lumbar vertebra.
    B. It is surrounded by protective coverings and cerebrospinal fluid.
    C. It has no role in the body's nerve impulses or reflex actions.
    D. It controls all nerve impulses in the body, with the exception of the head.
    E. It is the center of all reflex action in the body.
    F. An injury to the spine is more serious when the spinal cord is also damaged.

45. Fractures, dislocations, and other types of injuries usually occur more frequently in which region of the spine?

   A. Cervical

   B. Lumbar

   C. Dorsal/thoracic

   D. Coccyx

46. Which of the following statements concerning herniated intervertebral discs are correct?

   A. Herniated discs are never caused or aggravated by trauma.

   B. Because a disc contains a complex system of nerves, a herniated intervertebral disc always causes pain, even if the disc is not pressing on spinal nerve roots.

   C. Normal wear and tear can put enough pressure on a disc to cause disc herniation.

   D. Symptoms of a herniated disc can include pain, numbness, tingling, or a loss of sensation in the arms or legs.

   E. Herniated discs are most common in the dorsal/thoracic region.

   F. Treatment of herniated discs varies depending on the location and severity of the herniated disc and the patient's symptoms.

47. Match the name of the diagnostic test in the left-hand column with its correct description in the right-hand column.

1. Myelography
2. Electromyography
3. Nerve conduction studies
4. Straight leg-raising
5. Babinski's reflex
6. Romberg's sign

_____ A. Used to distinguish between sciatica and hip joint disease

_____ B. Combines a contrast agent and a fluoroscope to produce x-ray images of the interior of the vertebrae

_____ C. Performed by having the patient close the eyes while standing with feet close together

_____ D. Elicited by stroking the lateral side of the sole of the foot

_____ E. Measures electrical activity in skeletal muscles

_____ F. Measures the time from nerve stimulation to response

CHECKYOURANSWERHERECHECKYOURANSWERHERECHECKYOURANSWERHERE
CHECKYOURANSWERHERECHECKYOURANSWERHERECHECKYOURANSWERHERE
CHECKYOURANSWERHERECHECKYOURANSWERHERECHECKYOURANSWERHERE
CHECKYOURANSWERHERECHECKYOURANSWERHERECHECKYOURANSWERHERE

5

The Upper Body and Upper Extremities

SHOULDER BONES

Clavicles

1. You have moved in your study from the skull and brain down through the spine and now you're ready to learn about the shoulder, arms and hands, and the chest.

    The bones we usually refer to as **collar bones** are called the **clavicles**. One of these long, slender bones extends from each side of the breastbone in the mid-chest to the far edges of the shoulder where the arms begin.
    In the following illustration, the clavicles are indicated by arrows

    A. A and B.
    B. B and C.
    C. C and D.
    D. A and D.

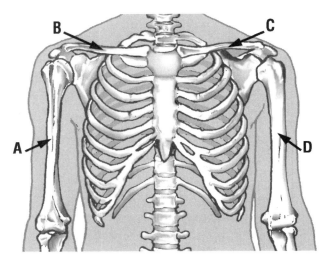

CHECKYOURANSWERHERECHECKYOURANSWERHERECHECKYOURANSWERHERE
CHECKYOURANSWERHERECHECKYOURANSWERHERECHECKYOURANSWERHERE
CHECKYOURANSWERHERECHECKYOURANSWERHERECHECKYOURANSWERHERE
CHECKYOURANSWERHERECHECKYOURANSWERHERECHECKYOURANSWERHERE

Scapulas

2. The **scapulas**, or **scapulae**, are the large, flat, triangular bones that form the back part of the shoulder. The scapulas are commonly known as the **shoulder blades**. The scapulas join the clavicles at the far edge of the shoulders where the arms begin.

Front and Back Views of the
Scapulas

Front

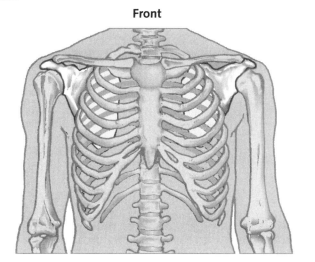

Back

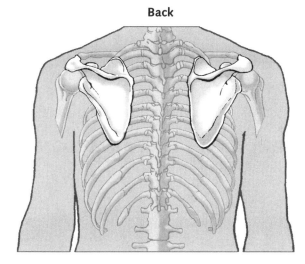

The scapulas are highlighted in each illustration.

Which of the following describe the scapulas?

A. Long, slender bones

B. Commonly called shoulder blades

C. Join the clavicles at the far edge of the shoulders where the arms begin

D. Extend from the breastbone

E. Large, flat, triangular bones

CHECKYOURANSWERHERECHECKYOURANSWERHERECHECKYOURANSWERHERE
CHECKYOURANSWERHERECHECKYOURANSWERHERECHECKYOURANSWERHERE
CHECKYOURANSWERHERECHECKYOURANSWERHERECHECKYOURANSWERHERE
CHECKYOURANSWERHERECHECKYOURANSWERHERECHECKYOURANSWERHERE

3. Refer to the following illustration to answer these questions.

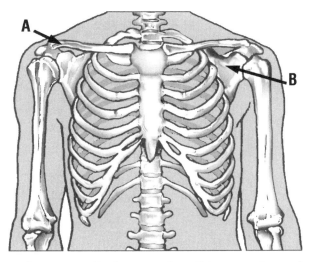

A. You're studying a medical report describing a patient who has suffered a simple linear fracture to the right clavicle. You know that the patient has suffered a fracture to the bone indicated by (Arrow A/ Arrow B) _____.

B. You receive a claim from an individual whose left scapula was fractured in an auto accident. This fracture occurred to the bone indicated by (Arrow A/Arrow B) _____.

ARM AND FOREARM BONES

Humerus

4. In anatomy terms, the word **arm** refers to what we might call the upper arm, which extends from the shoulder to the elbow. The arm has one long bone called the **humerus**. The humerus is highlighted in the illustration on the right.

Humerus

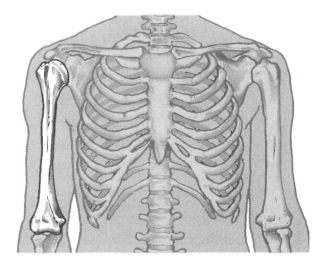

The long bone in a claimant's upper arm is fractured. The term for this bone is

A. scapula.

B. clavicle.

C. humerus.

D. vertebra.

Radius and Ulna

5. While the area from the shoulder to the elbow is called the arm, anatomically, the portion from the elbow to the wrist is called the **forearm**. The forearm is composed of two bones called the **radius** and the **ulna**.

Which of the fractures described below affect the forearm?

A. Compound fracture of the left humerus

B. Simple linear fracture of the left radius

C. Simple linear fracture of the right clavicle

D. Compound, comminuted fracture of the left radius and ulna

CHECKYOURANSWERHERECHECKYOURANSWERHERECHECKYOURANSWERHERE
CHECKYOURANSWERHERECHECKYOURANSWERHERECHECKYOURANSWERHERE
CHECKYOURANSWERHERECHECKYOURANSWERHERECHECKYOURANSWERHERE
CHECKYOURANSWERHERECHECKYOURANSWERHERECHECKYOURANSWERHERE

6. The *ulna* is the *inner bone* of the forearm, and the *radius* is the *outer bone* of the forearm. To help you determine which bone is which, study the illustration on your left. Take a careful look at the left hand and forearm in the illustration. Ignore the arrows on the illustration for now.

   Note how the skeleton's left thumb is pointing *away* from the body. This means the hand is turned so it is held with the palm forward. Standing at ease with the palms of the hand forward is known as the normal anatomical position. It is with the body in this position that all references are made to its parts—references such as an inner bone and an outer bone, or the radius and ulna of the forearm.

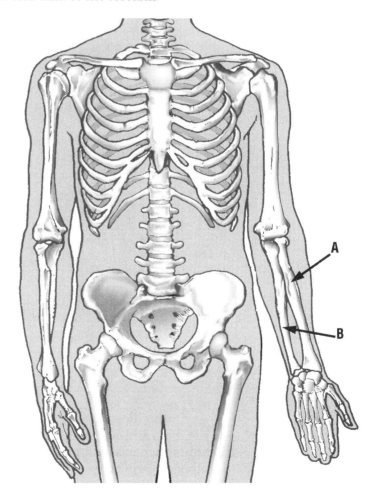

Now, look at the two arrows marked A and B which point to two bones in the left forearm of the illustration. Remember, the ulna is the *inner bone* of the forearm.

A. Which arrow is pointing to the ulna? (Arrow A/Arrow B) _____
    _____

B. Which arrow is pointing to the radius? (Arrow A/Arrow B) _____
    _____

7. Now study the illustration to your left, paying careful attention to the right hand and forearm.

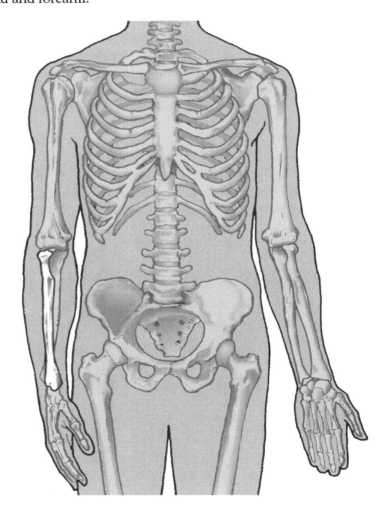

In this illustration, the right thumb is positioned *toward* the body. With the hand in this position, you can see that one of the bones in the forearm, which has been highlighted for emphasis, *revolves* partially around the other forearm bone.

What is the name of the bone that slightly crosses over the other bone near the wrist? (Radius/Ulna) _____

8. Briefly review the bones of the arm and forearm by matching the term in the left-hand column with its correct description in the right-hand column.

    1. Radius   _____ A. Long bone in the upper arm

    2. Humerus   _____ B. Inner bone in the forearm

    3. Ulna   _____ C. Outer bone in the forearm

HAND AND WRIST BONES

9. The bones of the hand are divided into the following categories, as noted in the highlighted areas of the next three illustrations:

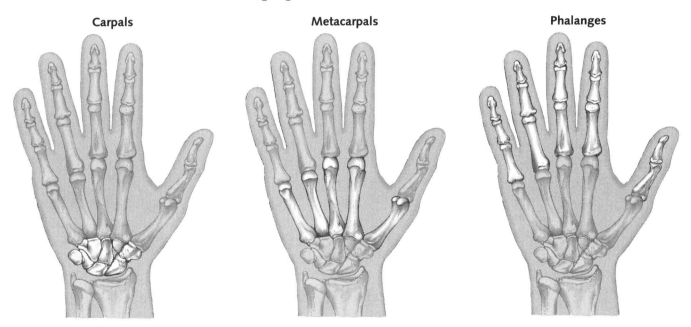

Carpals   Metacarpals   Phalanges

The **carpals** form the **wrist**. There are eight carpal bones, which vary slightly in size and shape, in each wrist. They form two uneven rows of four bones each.

The **metacarpals** make up the **body of the hand**. There is one metacarpal bone for each finger, five for each hand. These bones do not have names, but are referred to as the first metacarpal (thumb), second metacarpal (index finger), and so on. Occasionally they are referred to by the adjoining finger, such as the little finger metacarpal. (You'll learn the proper names of the fingers a little later on.)

The **phalanges** form the **fingers**. One finger bone is called a **phalanx**. With the exception of the thumbs, each finger has three phalanges; the thumbs have two.

A. The finger bones are called the _____.

B. The bones that make up the body of the hand are called the

_____.

C. What is the name of the group of bones that form the wrist?

_____

CHECKYOURANSWERHERECHECKYOURANSWERHERECHECKYOURANSWERHERE
CHECKYOURANSWERHERECHECKYOURANSWERHERECHECKYOURANSWERHERE
CHECKYOURANSWERHERECHECKYOURANSWERHERECHECKYOURANSWERHERE
CHECKYOURANSWERHERECHECKYOURANSWERHERECHECKYOURANSWERHERE

Location Terms

10. Each phalanx is referred to in **location terms** with respect to the point of attachment of the body part:

Proximal Phalanx   **Middle Phalanx**   **Distal Phalanx**

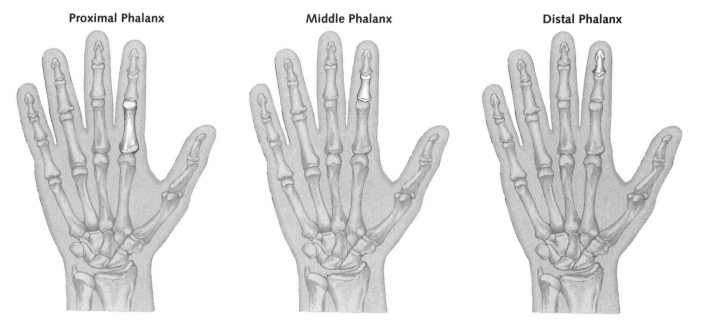

The part **nearest the point of attachment to the body** is called **proximal**. A proximal phalanx, then, is the finger bone nearest to the wrist, which is the point of attachment of the hand to the forearm.

The **middle** phalanx is simply known as the **middle** phalanx.

The phalanx **furthest from the point of attachment to the body** is called the **distal** phalanx.

Two other location terms you should be familiar with are **medial** and **lateral**. Medial means **toward the median or center line of the body**; lateral means **away from the median of the body**.

True or false?

A. The phalanx located furthest from the point of attachment to the body is called the middle phalanx. ( ) True ( ) False

B. The phalanx located closest to the point of attachment to the body is called the proximal phalanx. ( ) True ( ) False

C. The phalanx located between the proximal and distal phalanges is called the middle phalanx. ( ) True ( ) False

D. Medial means away from the median or center line of the body. ( ) True ( ) False

E. Lateral means toward the median or center line of the body. ( ) True ( ) False

CHECKYOURANSWERHERECHECKYOURANSWERHERECHECKYOURANSWERHERE
CHECKYOURANSWERHERECHECKYOURANSWERHERECHECKYOURANSWERHERE
CHECKYOURANSWERHERECHECKYOURANSWERHERECHECKYOURANSWERHERE
CHECKYOURANSWERHERECHECKYOURANSWERHERECHECKYOURANSWERHERE

11. Medical reports will refer to the name of the **finger** with the injured phalanx. The fingers are, beginning with the thumb, the index, middle, ring, and little.

Which arrow in the following illustration is pointing to the proximal phalanx of the index finger? (A/B/C/D) _____

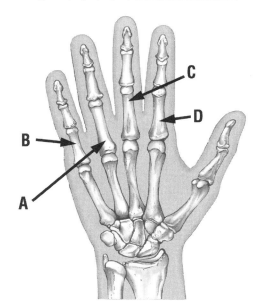

CHECKYOURANSWERHERECHECKYOURANSWERHERECHECKYOURANSWERHERE
CHECKYOURANSWERHERECHECKYOURANSWERHERECHECKYOURANSWERHERE
CHECKYOURANSWERHERECHECKYOURANSWERHERECHECKYOURANSWERHERE
CHECKYOURANSWERHERECHECKYOURANSWERHERECHECKYOURANSWERHERE

12. Briefly review what you've learned about the hand bones by matching the name of the bone in the left-hand column with its correct description in the right-hand column.

1. Carpals	____ A.	Bones that make up the body of the hand
2. Middle phalanx		
3. Phalanges	____ B.	Phalanx located closest to the point of attachment to the body
4. Metacarpals		
5. Distal phalanx	____ C.	Phalanx located between the proximal and distal phalanges
6. Proximal phalanx	____ D.	Bones that make up the wrist
7. Medial	____ E.	Bones that form the fingers
8. Lateral	____ F.	Phalanx located furthest away from the body
	____ G.	Location term meaning to the side
	____ H.	Location term meaning to the middle

CHECKYOURANSWERHERECHECKYOURANSWERHERECHECKYOURANSWERHERE
CHECKYOURANSWERHERECHECKYOURANSWERHERECHECKYOURANSWERHERE
CHECKYOURANSWERHERECHECKYOURANSWERHERECHECKYOURANSWERHERE
CHECKYOURANSWERHERECHECKYOURANSWERHERECHECKYOURANSWERHERE

THORACIC SKELETAL STRUCTURES

Sternum

13. Earlier in this unit, you learned that the clavicles extend from each side of the **breastbone** in the mid-chest. The technical name for the breastbone is the **sternum**. The sternum is highlighted in the illustration at the right.

Sternum

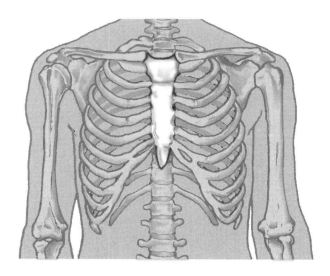

The clavicles are attached to which skeletal structure?

A. Radius

B. Ulna

C. Sternum

D. Sphenoid

True, False, and Floating Ribs

14. You can see from the illustration in the previous frame that the **ribs** are attached to the sternum. However, not all of the 24 rib bones (12 on each side of the body) are attached to the sternum. There are three types of ribs.

True Ribs

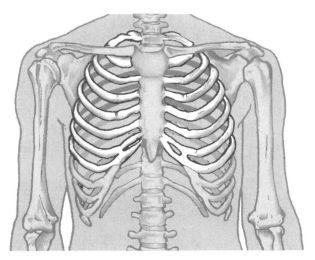

The top 14 ribs (7 on each side) attach directly to the sternum. These are called *true ribs*.

False Ribs

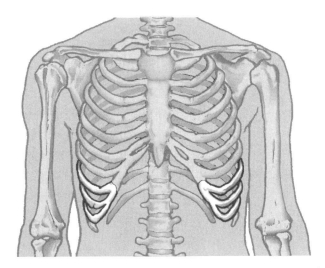

The 14 true ribs are followed by 6 (3 on each side) ribs that, instead of being attached to the sternum, are each attached to the rib above it. These are the *false ribs*.

Floating Ribs

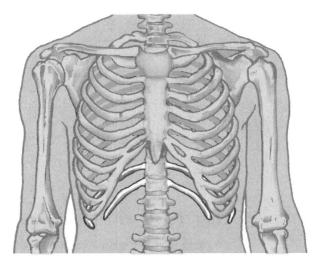

Finally, the four bottom ribs (two on each side) are not attached to anything in front. These are called *floating ribs*.

The ribs provide protection for the organs within the chest, which is also called the **thorax**. For this reason, the entire rib cage area is often referred to as the *thorax* or **thoracic region**.

In front of each item below, write in a **T** for true ribs, an **F** for false ribs, or an **FL** for floating ribs.

_____ A. Six bones, each attached to the one above it.

_____ B. Fourteen ribs attached directly to the sternum.

_____ C. Four ribs that are not attached to anything in front.

CHECKYOURANSWERHERECHECKYOURANSWERHERECHECKYOURANSWERHERE
CHECKYOURANSWERHERECHECKYOURANSWERHERECHECKYOURANSWERHERE
CHECKYOURANSWERHERECHECKYOURANSWERHERECHECKYOURANSWERHERE
CHECKYOURANSWERHERECHECKYOURANSWERHERECHECKYOURANSWERHERE

15. Answer the following questions to review your knowledge of the thoracic skeletal structures.

A. The technical name for the breastbone is the

1. sternum.

2. rib.

3. humerus.

4. mandible.

B. How many false ribs are there, per side? _____

C. How many true ribs are there, per side? _____

D. The floating ribs

1. attach directly to the sternum.

2. are each attached to the rib above it.

3. are not attached to anything in front.

CHECKYOURANSWERHERECHECKYOURANSWERHERECHECKYOURANSWERHERE
CHECKYOURANSWERHERECHECKYOURANSWERHERECHECKYOURANSWERHERE
CHECKYOURANSWERHERECHECKYOURANSWERHERECHECKYOURANSWERHERE
CHECKYOURANSWERHERECHECKYOURANSWERHERECHECKYOURANSWERHERE

SHOULDER INJURIES

Clavicle Fractures

16. The clavicle is one of the most frequently fractured bones. Its long, slender shape and location make it especially vulnerable to injury, both from direct force to the bone and from indirect force. The most common cause of a clavicle fracture by indirect force is falling on an outstretched hand or arm, or falling on the shoulder; the shock of the fall is transmitted through the other bones and breaks the clavicle.

Clavicle Fracture

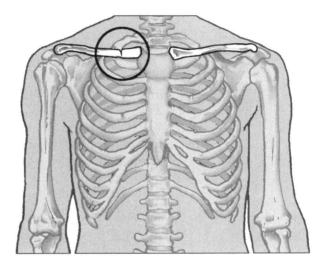

Fractured clavicle bones are usually treated by immobilizing the clavicle with a sling, although the bone fragments may reunite on their own even if they are not aligned. Sometimes the fragments overlap, causing a lump when healed. These clavicle lumps are usually tender and are considered unsightly by many people. There is no way of knowing whether a clavicle lump will appear until after the bone has healed.

Clavicle fractures

A. are a common injury.

B. may be caused by direct force, but never by indirect force.

C. are usually treated by immobilizing the clavicle with a sling.

D. sometimes produce a clavicle lump after they have healed.

Scapula Fractures

17. A fracture to the scapula is a rare occurrence, possibly because the bone is broad and flat and well protected by muscles.

Scapula Fracture

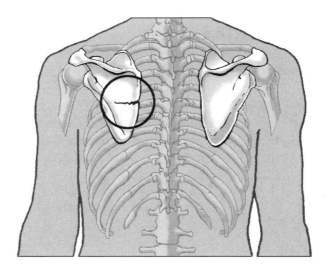

The presence of these muscles, however, may cause another problem involving the junction where the scapula articulates with the humerus. In the vicinity of joints, small sacs, each called a **bursa**, are present to reduce friction between the bone and another structure, such as a muscle. If an injury occurs, the bursa often becomes inflamed. An inflammation of a bursa is called **bursitis**. If not properly and promptly treated, bursitis can result in loss of motion at the shoulder joint. Since bursae are present at all joints, bursitis can occur at any joint; however, in claim work, it is seen most often in the shoulder.

A. A fractured scapula is a (rare/common) _____ injury seen in claims work.

B. A fractured scapula may cause (bursitis/arthritis) _____.

CHECKYOURANSWERHERECHECKYOURANSWERHERECHECKYOURANSWERHERE
CHECKYOURANSWERHERECHECKYOURANSWERHERECHECKYOURANSWERHERE
CHECKYOURANSWERHERECHECKYOURANSWERHERECHECKYOURANSWERHERE
CHECKYOURANSWERHERECHECKYOURANSWERHERECHECKYOURANSWERHERE

18. Mark each statement below with a **C** if it refers to a clavicle fracture or an **S** if it refers to a scapula fracture.

_____ A. One of the most frequently fractured bones in the body.

_____ B. A fracture to this bone often causes bursitis.

_____ C. This bone is sometimes fractured indirectly when a person falls on an outstretched arm or hand.

_____ D. Improper healing of a fracture to this bone may cause a bone lump.

_____ E. This bone is rarely fractured, possibly because it is broad and flat and well protected by muscles.

CHECKYOURANSWERHERECHECKYOURANSWERHERECHECKYOURANSWERHERE
CHECKYOURANSWERHERECHECKYOURANSWERHERECHECKYOURANSWERHERE
CHECKYOURANSWERHERECHECKYOURANSWERHERECHECKYOURANSWERHERE
CHECKYOURANSWERHERECHECKYOURANSWERHERECHECKYOURANSWERHERE

ARM AND FOREARM INJURIES—HUMERUS

Long Bone Construction

19. In order to understand the effect of injuries to the humerus, you must first understand how it is constructed. The humerus is highlighted in the illustration below.

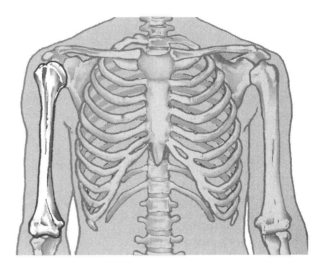

The humerus belongs to a group of bones called **long bones,** which are found only in the upper and lower extremities (you'll learn about the long bones of the lower extremities in a later unit). Long bones are theoretically divided into thirds for ease in discussing injuries to them. Each third is referred to in connection with its point of attachment to the body. You'll recall from our discussion of the phalanges that these location terms are proximal, middle, and distal. Other parts of long bones include:

Parts of a Humerus

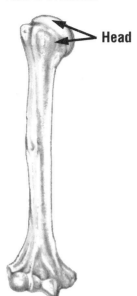 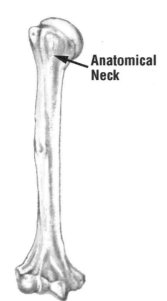 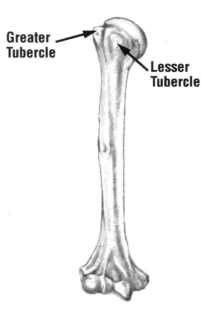 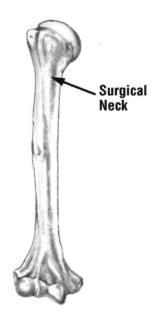

The round part of a bone at its proximal end, which fits into the socket of the joint, is called the *head* of the bone.

The *anatomical neck* of the bone joins the head to the rest of the bone, which, for long bones, is called the *shaft.*

Below the neck are several rounded, elevated projections called *tuberosities.*

Directly below the tuberosities of the humerus is a part of the bone known as the *surgical neck.*

Match the part of the long bone in the left-hand column with its correct description in the right-hand column.

1. Head
2. Anatomical neck
3. Tuberosities
4. Surgical neck

_____ A. Rounded projections at the proximal end of the shaft

_____ B. Joins the head to the rest of the bone

_____ C. Round part of the bone at its proximal end which fits into the socket of the joint

_____ D. Located directly below the tuberosities of the humerus

CHECKYOURANSWERHERECHECKYOURANSWERHERECHECKYOURANSWERHERE
CHECKYOURANSWERHERECHECKYOURANSWERHERECHECKYOURANSWERHERE
CHECKYOURANSWERHERECHECKYOURANSWERHERECHECKYOURANSWERHERE
CHECKYOURANSWERHERECHECKYOURANSWERHERECHECKYOURANSWERHERE

Radial Nerve Injuries

20. Fractures of the surgical neck of the humerus are common, but not particularly serious because they do not involve a joint, are easily repaired, and seldom are complicated by other injuries.

Equally common, but much more serious, are fractures to the middle third of the humerus. An injury in this area is serious because of the **radial nerve**, which winds around the humerus at this point. The radial nerve controls sensation and movement of the entire arm. A bone fragment can easily lacerate this nerve, or the nerve may be pinched as the bone heals.

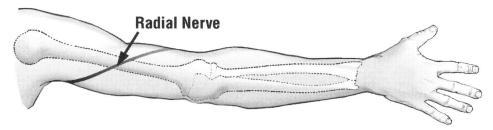

Radial Nerve

Why is a fracture to the middle third of the humerus considered more serious than a fracture to the proximal end of the humerus?

A. Such a fracture is likely to involve a joint, causing loss of motion.

B. This part of the bone is responsible for movement of the entire arm.

C. The presence of the important radial nerve in this area poses the possibility of nerve damage.

D. The middle third of the humerus generally requires a longer healing period than the proximal third.

21. It's easy to see how the radial nerve may be lacerated by a fragment of a broken bone. But we also said that the nerve may be pinched as the bone heals. To understand why this happens, we need to know how a bone mends:

   ■ Bones are surrounded by a membrane containing bone-forming cells which are dormant until a bone has been fractured. When this occurs, the cells are activated to create new bone.

   ■ When the fracture occurs, blood vessels are broken and form clots around the fracture site. The bone-forming cells begin to grow in the clots, forming what is called **fibrous tissue**.

   ■ Blood vessels surrounding the fracture site feed the fibrous tissue and **callus** begins to form. Callus is a bony material which will eventually harden and become part of the bone.

If the radial nerve should become involved with the callus while it is hardening, it may be pinched, resulting in a loss of sensation or movement.

Describe how the radial nerve might become pinched while a bone fracture heals. _____
_____

22. Answer the following questions to test your knowledge of the humerus.

    A. The humerus is a member of what group of bones that are found only in the upper and lower extremities?
       1. Long
       2. Short
       3. Distal
       4. Proximal

    B. What is the name of the round part of the humerus at the proximal end which fits into the socket of the joint?
       1. Anatomical neck
       2. Tuberosity
       3. Head
       4. Surgical neck

    C. You're reading a medical report on a patient who has suffered a fracture in the middle third of the humerus. You know that a fracture in this area may be serious because of the possibility that the _____ may be lacerated or pinched.
       1. shoulder joint
       2. bursa
       3. callus
       4. radial nerve

Bony Unions

23. It would be easy to dismiss fractures as no more troublesome than a small cut. After all, if the fracture causes bone-forming cells to go to work, bone union must always occur, either with or without help from a physician. Unfortunately, nature does let us down from time to time. Normally, good, firm union of the bones does occur, usually within three months after the fracture. Depending on the individual, however, several things may happen instead, including:

    ■ **Partial union**, where the callus does not grow over the entire fractured area, leaving portions of the fragments ununited.

    ■ **Fibrous union**, when the callus does not harden.

    ■ **Malunion**, where the fragments unite in a position which renders the bone useless, or when fragments unite with another bone.

■ **Nonunion,** when new bone is not created, and the fragments are held together only by tissue.

Surgery is sometimes required to repair an incorrect union.

A. Describe a malunion._____

_____

_____

B. Describe a nonunion. _____

_____

_____

24. Following are excerpts from medical reports describing bone fractures which have not healed properly. Label the type of union described in each excerpt with a **P** for partial union, an **F** for fibrous union, an **M** for malunion, or an **N** if there has been no union.

_____ A. X-rays taken two weeks after the fracture occurred demonstrated that one fragment of the ulna was being connected by callus formation to the radius.

_____ B. Because the patient was unconscious and his other injuries required immediate attention, it was nearly five days after the accident before it was discovered that the humerus was fractured. By that time, healing had begun and callus formed at the site held the bone fragments in such a position that the extremity was not useful.

_____ C. The x-rays showed a fragment of the fractured humerus extending at an approximate 45 degree angle from the position where callus had partially bridged the fracture.

_____ D. The patient's inability to stand can be attributed to the absence of bony reformation in the fragmented leg bone.

_____ E. Although the fracture had apparently begun to heal, the bone cells had not hardened after three months.

Reduction of Fractures

25. It's apparent that if bone fragments are not properly aligned, they can heal in a position that is less than functional to the patient. We've learned that in some cases, such as fractured clavicles or ribs, perfect alignment is not always necessary. However, in bones that are very important to everyday

activity, such as the arms and legs, proper alignment is of utmost importance if we are to go on functioning as before.

When a fracture leaves the bone fragments out of alignment, it is said to be a **displaced fracture**. A displaced fracture in the arm requires the attention of a physician to realign the bones. Realignment of a fracture is called **reduction**. There are two types of reductions:

- A **closed reduction**, where the broken bone is manipulated into proper alignment by the physician's hands. Another type of closed reduction is **traction**, where weights are used to hold the fragments in place.

- An **open reduction**, where the fracture site is opened surgically to move the bones back into position. The physician may insert something into the fragments to ensure that they stay together, such as plates or pins.

With a closed reduction,

A. fragments are manipulated into proper position by the physician's hands, without opening the fracture site surgically.

B. pins or plates may be inserted into the fragments to hold them together.

C. weights may be used to hold the bone fragments in place.

D. bone fragments are manipulated by surgical means.

CHECKYOURANSWERHERECHECKYOURANSWERHERECHECKYOURANSWERHERE
CHECKYOURANSWERHERECHECKYOURANSWERHERECHECKYOURANSWERHERE
CHECKYOURANSWERHERECHECKYOURANSWERHERECHECKYOURANSWERHERE
CHECKYOURANSWERHERECHECKYOURANSWERHERECHECKYOURANSWERHERE

26. Mark each example below with a **C** if it describes a closed reduction or an **O** if it describes an open reduction.

_____ A. X-rays of the left arm demonstrated a comminuted displaced fracture of the proximal left humerus. The patient was admitted to the hospital for surgical repair of the fracture, which was performed under general anesthetic.

_____ B. Diagnosis was a fracture of the first metacarpal, right thumb. Reduction was carried out with a wooden splint.

_____ C. Miss Darnell had a compound, displaced fracture of the distal third, right humerus. She was taken to surgery, where her right humerus was reduced and put into a cast while she was under general anesthetic.

CHECKYOURANSWERHERECHECKYOURANSWERHERECHECKYOURANSWERHERE
CHECKYOURANSWERHERECHECKYOURANSWERHERECHECKYOURANSWERHERE
CHECKYOURANSWERHERECHECKYOURANSWERHERECHECKYOURANSWERHERE
CHECKYOURANSWERHERECHECKYOURANSWERHERECHECKYOURANSWERHERE

Types of Fractures

27. After the broken bone has been reduced, the healing period begins. One of the complications in healing a fractured humerus may result from the *type* of fracture.

Because the humerus hangs down, its weight will tend to pull the fragments apart when they should be held closely together for good healing.

A fracture that still has bone-to-bone contact remaining will heal better and more quickly. If the humerus is broken completely through—which is known as a **complete fracture**—there is no bone contact until the fracture is reduced. Even after reduction, the fracture is constantly subjected to gravity wanting to separate the fragments.

Which one of these illustrations shows a complete fracture?
(A/B/C) _____

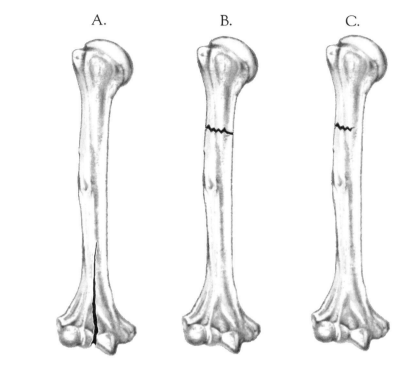

A.   B.   C.

Transverse, Longitudinal, Oblique, and Spiral Fractures

28. Four other fairly common fracture types heal more quickly in the humerus because the broken parts remain in close contact and the bone is not broken through. They are:

Transverse Fracture	**Longitudinal Fracture**	**Oblique Fracture**	**Spiral Fracture**
		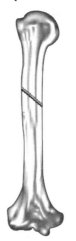	

Transverse fractures, where the break is more or less at right angles to the bone

Longitudinal fractures, where the break extends in a longitudinal direction, paralleling the length of the bone

Oblique fractures, where the fracture line slants across the bone

Spiral fractures, where the fracture line winds around the bone

Match the fracture type in the left-hand column with its correct definition in the right-hand column.

1. Spiral fracture
2. Longitudinal fracture
3. Transverse fracture
4. Oblique fracture

____ A. Fracture line winds around the bone

____ B. Fracture line slants across the bone

____ C. Fracture line is lengthwise on the bone

____ D. Fracture line is more or less at right angles to the bone

CHECKYOURANSWERHERECHECKYOURANSWERHERECHECKYOURANSWERHERE
CHECKYOURANSWERHERECHECKYOURANSWERHERECHECKYOURANSWERHERE
CHECKYOURANSWERHERECHECKYOURANSWERHERECHECKYOURANSWERHERE
CHECKYOURANSWERHERECHECKYOURANSWERHERECHECKYOURANSWERHERE

Other Types of Fractures

29. Before we conclude our discussion of fracture types, you should familiarize yourself with some other common fracture types that you may see in medical reports. These are:

Incomplete Fracture

Incomplete fractures, where the break has not completely severed the bone

Undisplaced Fracture

Undisplaced fractures, where the bone fragments are still in alignment

Greenstick Fracture

Greenstick fractures, where the bone is partially bent and partially broken

Impacted Fracture

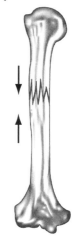

Impacted fractures, where one fragment of bone is wedged into the interior of the other

Mark all correct statements.

A. An impacted fracture is one where the bone is partially bent and partially broken.

B. With an undisplaced fracture, the bone fragments are out of alignment.

C. A greenstick fracture means that the bone is partially bent and partially broken.

D. A fracture that does not completely sever the bone is called an incomplete fracture.

CHECKYOURANSWERHERECHECKYOURANSWERHERECHECKYOURANSWERHERE
CHECKYOURANSWERHERECHECKYOURANSWERHERECHECKYOURANSWERHERE
CHECKYOURANSWERHERECHECKYOURANSWERHERECHECKYOURANSWERHERE
CHECKYOURANSWERHERECHECKYOURANSWERHERECHECKYOURANSWERHERE

30. Identify the following fractures.

A. Fracture has completely severed the bone _____

B. Bone is partially broken and partially bent _____

C. Fracture line is at right angles to the bone _____

D. Fracture line parallels the length of the bone _____

E. Fracture has not completely severed the bone _____

F. Fracture line winds around the bone _____

G. Fracture line slants across the bone _____

H. Bone fragments are aligned _____

I. One fragment of bone is wedged into the interior of the other

_____

CHECKYOURANSWERHERECHECKYOURANSWERHERECHECKYOURANSWERHERE
CHECKYOURANSWERHERECHECKYOURANSWERHERECHECKYOURANSWERHERE
CHECKYOURANSWERHERECHECKYOURANSWERHERECHECKYOURANSWERHERE
CHECKYOURANSWERHERECHECKYOURANSWERHERECHECKYOURANSWERHERE

Epiphyses Injuries

31. Greenstick fractures occur in children because their bones are not as brittle as adults' bones. This is because children's bones are composed of a great deal of cartilage, which is gradually replaced by hard bone. At both ends of each long bone in a child is a "growth center" which is separated from the remainder of the bone by cartilage. This growth center is called the **epiphysis**, and it becomes part of the bone as the child grows.

    If an epiphysis is damaged by a fracture, the damage may cause the bone to stop growing. This condition may be minor to a teenager who is almost fully grown, but of major significance to a younger child.

    The epiphysis
    A. disappears when growth is complete.
    B. never becomes real, hard bone.
    C. remains a growth center until death.
    D. is a very brittle part of the bone.

32. In which of the following situations is damage to the epiphysis consideration?
    A. Boyd Lester, age 27, fractures his distal left humerus.
    B. Eric Martin, age 6, suffers a fracture to the proximal right humerus.
    C. Kyle Isenbarger, age 12, fractures his distal right humerus.
    D. Elsie Jackson, age 75, fractures her proximal right humerus.

Olecranon Process Injuries

33. Most of the elbow is made up of a round, protruding portion of the ulna called the **olecranon process.** This process forms a socket which articulates with the lower end of the humerus, allowing flexion and extension of the forearm. In the next illustration, the arrow is pointing to the olecranon process.

Olecranon Process

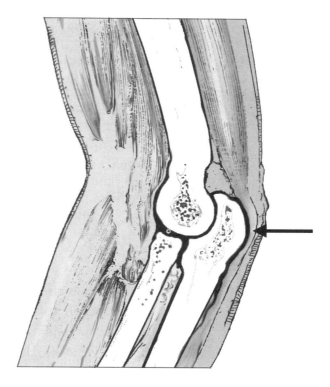

The olecranon process and the humerus form the elbow joint. This is a very important joint, considering the number of things we do which require bending at the elbow. Unfortunately, fractures to the olecranon process are common, and the means by which fractures heal themselves is itself a source of trouble to the joint function.

As callus forms to heal the fracture, it may build up in the joint and impair free movement. An easy way to visualize this result is to imagine an open door. If an object, such as a stick, is placed in the opening of the door near the hinge, the door cannot be completely closed. Excessive callus in the elbow joint will produce a similar result.

A. The olecranon process is a portion of the (radius/ulna) _____.

B. The elbow joint is formed by the articulation of the olecranon process and the (humerus/radius) _____.

CHECKYOURANSWERHERECHECKYOURANSWERHERECHECKYOURANSWERHERE
CHECKYOURANSWERHERECHECKYOURANSWERHERECHECKYOURANSWERHERE
CHECKYOURANSWERHERECHECKYOURANSWERHERECHECKYOURANSWERHERE
CHECKYOURANSWERHERECHECKYOURANSWERHERECHECKYOURANSWERHERE

34. Check all correct statements.

A. The olecranon process forms most of the elbow.

B. The elbow joint is formed by the olecranon process and the ulna.

C. A buildup of callus in the elbow joint complicates the healing of a fracture to the olecranon process.

D. When excessive callus forms in the elbow joint, movement may be impaired.

E. Flexion and extension are not affected by fractures to the olecranon process.

ARM AND FOREARM INJURIES—RADIUS AND ULNA

35. With the exception of fractures to the olecranon process, the ulna is not broken as frequently as the radius, although both bones may be fractured at the same time. If only one bone is broken, reduction is easier since the other bone helps hold the fractured bone in position. When both are fractured, however, there can be four fragments at odds with gravity, with no natural opposing force to offset the pull. Reduction of such fractures is difficult since functional healing depends a great deal on keeping each bone in proper position.

Regarding fractures to the forearm,

A. the radius and ulna are rarely broken at the same time.

B. reduction is more difficult when only the radius is fractured.

C. if one bone is broken, the other tends to hold the fractured bone in position.

D. reduction is more difficult when only the ulna is fractured.

Colles Fracture

36. The most common type of fracture to the radius is a **Colles fracture,** named for the nineteenth-century surgeon who first described its characteristics:

■ The fracture occurs at the **distal end of the radius**

■ It is a **transverse** fracture

■ The **lower fragment of the radius is displaced backward and outward**, causing the hand to be displaced in the same manner

Colles Fracture

A Colles fracture is also known as a **silver-fork deformity,** because the resulting shape resembles the curve on the back of a fork.

A Colles fracture may be treated by either open or closed reduction. A cast is applied to hold the fragments in place. Good, bony union is usually established quickly. However, because of the function of the radius with the wrist joint, the usual joint movements of the wrist may be limited or impaired. With a Colles fracture, joint movement generally returns, although it may be a very slow process, and any limitation is usually slight.

A claimant has suffered a Colles fracture. Which of the following statements are true concerning this claimant's condition?

A. This fracture is sometimes called a silver fork deformity.

B. The fracture has occurred at the distal end of the radius.

C. It is an oblique fracture.

D. The lower fragment of the radius is undisplaced.

E. This fracture may impair joint movement in the patient's wrist.

37. Label each statement below with an **F** if it applies to fractures to the forearm in general or a **C** if it refers specifically to a Colles fracture.

_____ A. This type of fracture is also called a silver fork deformity.

_____ B. Reduction is simpler if only one bone in this area is broken.

_____ C. One characteristic of this type of fracture is that it is a transverse fracture.

_____ D. Both bones in this area are often broken together.

HAND AND WRIST INJURIES

Functions of the Hand and Thumb

38. From the standpoint of mechanical ability, the hands and fingers have the most complicated construction of any bones in the body. They are also subjected to more frequent movement than any other bones. Just think of the actions they perform every day—from the time you snap off the alarm in the morning to the time you pull up the covers at night.

    The numerous uses to which we put our hands fall into one of four primary categories of functions:

- Grasping
- Pinching
- Hooking
- Touching (including sensation)

The loss of the ability to perform any of the primary hand functions can affect our self-sufficiency. For example, the loss of a leg may be compensated with an artificial limb or a wheelchair, but we could still move about independently. However, we become very dependent upon others if we can't comb our own hair, write a letter, or tie our shoes.

Of all the functions of the hand, pinching is probably the most important, and it involves the use of the thumb. The ability to touch the thumb to the other fingertips is considered 50% of the use of the hand. This means that the loss of this ability leaves the hand only 50% functional. On the other hand, if the thumb and at least two of the other four fingers are usable, nearly all use of the hand is maintained, or can be relearned (such as learning to write with a pen held by the thumb and ring finger).

Which one of the following hand injuries presents the greatest possibility for loss of use of the hand?

A. Compound fracture of the first right metacarpal

B. Amputation of the right index finger through the proximal phalanx

C. Simple fracture of the distal and middle phalanges of the left ring finger

D. Total amputation of the left thumb

CHECKYOURANSWERHERECHECKYOURANSWERHERECHECKYOURANSWERHERE
CHECKYOURANSWERHERECHECKYOURANSWERHERECHECKYOURANSWERHERE
CHECKYOURANSWERHERECHECKYOURANSWERHERECHECKYOURANSWERHERE
CHECKYOURANSWERHERECHECKYOURANSWERHERECHECKYOURANSWERHERE

Carpal Tunnel Syndrome

39. A very common wrist condition seen in claim work is **carpal tunnel syndrome**. Carpal tunnel syndrome is a nerve compression disorder involving compression of the *median nerve* at the wrist.

     As the median nerve passes from the forearm into the hand, it travels through the **carpal tunnel**. The carpal tunnel is a narrow space that contains both tendons and the median nerve. It is covered by the **transverse carpal ligament**. An injury or disease which causes this tunnel to narrow, or which enlarges the structures within the tunnel, will compress the median nerve beneath the transverse carpal ligament.

The Carpal Tunnel

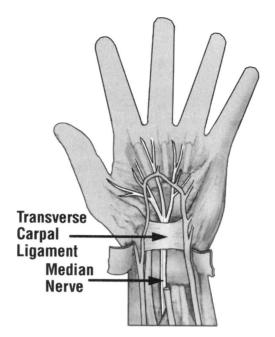

Transverse Carpal Ligament

Median Nerve

In this illustration, the palm is facing up.

Describe carpal tunnel syndrome. _____

_____

_____

Symptoms

40. Symptoms of carpal tunnel syndrome include numbness, pain, and a tingling, "pins and needles" sensation in the wrist, palm, or fingers. For some patients, the pain is worse at night. Weakness and atrophy in the muscles of the thumb may also occur.

    Two conditions that produce the same symptoms as carpal tunnel syndrome, and so are frequently misdiagnosed as carpal tunnel syndrome, are **cervical disc herniation** and **thoracic outlet syndromes.** Cervical disc herniation was discussed in a previous chapter; you'll learn more about thoracic outlet syndromes later in this unit.

    All of the following are common symptoms of carpal tunnel syndrome EXCEPT

    A. pain in the wrist, hand, and fingers.

    B. numbness or a "pins and needles" type of sensation in the affected area.

    C. weakness and atrophy in the muscles of the thumb.

    D. total, permanent paralysis of the affected hand.

Causes

41. Carpal tunnel syndrome has many causes, including:

    ■ Work-related or other activities involving repetitive use of the wrist, hand, or fingers

    ■ Trauma, such as a blow to the wrist, fracture or dislocation of one of the carpal bones, or hyperextension of the wrist

    ■ Inflammation of the transverse carpal ligament, which is often caused by an infection in the hand

    ■ Diseases such as rheumatoid arthritis, diabetes mellitus, and hypothyroidism

    ■ Lesions, such as cysts or tumors, in the carpal tunnel

    True or false?

    A. The only cause of carpal tunnel syndrome is repetitive use of the wrist, hand, or fingers.   ( ) True   ( ) False

    B. Trauma can cause carpal tunnel syndrome.   ( ) True   ( ) False

CHECKYOURANSWERHERECHECKYOURANSWERHERECHECKYOURANSWERHERE
CHECKYOURANSWERHERECHECKYOURANSWERHERECHECKYOURANSWERHERE
CHECKYOURANSWERHERECHECKYOURANSWERHERECHECKYOURANSWERHERE
CHECKYOURANSWERHERECHECKYOURANSWERHERECHECKYOURANSWERHERE

Treatments

42. Nerve conduction studies may be used to diagnose carpal tunnel syndrome. Treatment methods vary depending on the cause of the condition and the severity of the symptoms. If the cause is traced to repetitive use of the hand, wrist, or fingers, the patient may find relief simply by modifying his or her activities. Often, the affected hand is immobilized in a splint. Anti-inflammatory drugs and steroids may also be prescribed. When conservative treatments fail, surgery may be required.

    Which of the following may be used to treat carpal tunnel syndrome?

    A. Modification of activity

    B. Surgery

    C. Anti-inflammatory drugs and steroids

    D. Immobilizing splint

    E. All of the above

CHECKYOURANSWERHERECHECKYOURANSWERHERECHECKYOURANSWERHERE
CHECKYOURANSWERHERECHECKYOURANSWERHERECHECKYOURANSWERHERE
CHECKYOURANSWERHERECHECKYOURANSWERHERECHECKYOURANSWERHERE
CHECKYOURANSWERHERECHECKYOURANSWERHERECHECKYOURANSWERHERE

Thoracic Outlet Syndromes

43. A common group of complaints involving pain, tingling, or numbness in the neck, shoulders, arms, or hands results from conditions called **thoracic outlet compression syndromes** or **thoracic outlet syndromes (TOS).**

    The term **thoracic outlet** refers to various places originating from the thorax. The **compression** portion of the term derives from the believed cause of the symptoms, which is compression of the blood vessels or nerves indicated in this illustration:

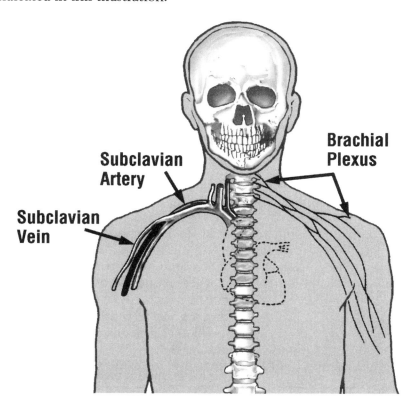

    Usually, the vessels or nerves are compressed by another body part, such as:

    ■ The first rib (which is in the thoracic area) pressing the vessels or nerves against the clavicle

    ■ An extra rib on a cervical vertebra (where no rib usually exists) pressing vessels or nerves against the clavicle

    ■ Certain muscles in an abnormal position pressing against surrounding vessels or nerves

    In many cases, the cause of the compression is not known. There is some speculation that TOS can be caused by trauma to the head or neck or by poor posture.

Thoracic outlet syndromes

A. are caused by compression of a nerve or blood vessel in the thoracic region.

B. involve pain, tingling, or numbness in the shoulder, neck, arm, or hand.

C. could be caused by trauma to the head or neck.

D. cannot be caused by poor posture.

CHECKYOURANSWERHERECHECKYOURANSWERHERECHECKYOURANSWERHERE
CHECKYOURANSWERHERECHECKYOURANSWERHERECHECKYOURANSWERHERE
CHECKYOURANSWERHERECHECKYOURANSWERHERECHECKYOURANSWERHERE
CHECKYOURANSWERHERECHECKYOURANSWERHERECHECKYOURANSWERHERE

Symptoms

44. Symptoms of thoracic outlet syndromes include:

- Pain, tingling, and a loss of sensation along the inner side of the arm, forearm, or hand

- Progressive weakness in the hand, particularly the thumb

- Muscle fatigue with normal use of the arm

In some cases, compression of a vessel will cause a **thrombosis** (a blood clot) or an **aneurysm** (an abnormal dilation) to develop within the vessel. Patients with either a thrombosis or aneurysm in a vessel may complain that the arm feels cold. The skin of the hand may turn gray or blue because the blood cannot carry enough oxygen to the skin. This condition is called **cyanosis**.

You're studying a medical report on a patient who has been diagnosed with a TOS affecting his right arm. In addition to the usual symptoms of pain, loss of sensation in the arm, and muscle weakness, the patient complains that the arm feels cold. This probably means that

A. compression of a vessel has caused a thrombosis or aneurysm to develop.

B. cyanosis has developed in the arm.

CHECKYOURANSWERHERECHECKYOURANSWERHERECHECKYOURANSWERHERE
CHECKYOURANSWERHERECHECKYOURANSWERHERECHECKYOURANSWERHERE
CHECKYOURANSWERHERECHECKYOURANSWERHERECHECKYOURANSWERHERE
CHECKYOURANSWERHERECHECKYOURANSWERHERECHECKYOURANSWERHERE

Treatments

45. Treatment for TOS can be difficult if the cause of the compression is not known. Exercise or a shoulder brace may be prescribed if poor posture is the suspected culprit. Surgery may be required if conservative treatment methods fail.

Treatment methods for TOS may include

A. hot or cold packs.

B. exercise.

C. shoulder brace.

D. surgery.

CHECKYOURANSWERHERECHECKYOURANSWERHERECHECKYOURANSWERHERE
CHECKYOURANSWERHERECHECKYOURANSWERHERECHECKYOURANSWERHERE
CHECKYOURANSWERHERECHECKYOURANSWERHERECHECKYOURANSWERHERE
CHECKYOURANSWERHERECHECKYOURANSWERHERECHECKYOURANSWERHERE

46. Answer the following true/false questions to review what you've learned about hand and wrist injuries.

   A. Herniated cervical discs and thoracic outlet syndromes are sometimes misdiagnosed as carpal tunnel syndrome. ( ) True ( ) False

   B. The hand injury which poses the greatest possibility for loss of use of the hand is amputation of an index finger. ( ) True ( ) False

   C. Carpal tunnel syndrome is a nerve compression disorder involving compression of a vessel or nerve in the thoracic region.
   ( ) True ( ) False

   D. Thoracic outlet syndromes involve compression of the median nerve at the wrist. ( ) True ( ) False

   E. Carpal tunnel syndrome may be caused by repetitive use of the wrist, hand, or fingers, trauma, and certain diseases. ( ) True ( ) False

   F. Thoracic outlet syndromes may be caused by the presence of an extra rib on a cervical vertebra. ( ) True ( ) False

CHECKYOURANSWERHERECHECKYOURANSWERHERECHECKYOURANSWERHERE
CHECKYOURANSWERHERECHECKYOURANSWERHERECHECKYOURANSWERHERE
CHECKYOURANSWERHERECHECKYOURANSWERHERECHECKYOURANSWERHERE
CHECKYOURANSWERHERECHECKYOURANSWERHERECHECKYOURANSWERHERE
CHECKYOURANSWERHERECHECKYOURANSWERHERECHECKYOURANSWERHERE
CHECKYOURANSWERHERECHECKYOURANSWERHERECHECKYOURANSWERHERE

THORACIC INJURIES

Sternal Fractures

47. Sternal fractures are rare, but when they do occur, they often involve one or more of the following complications:

Sternal Fracture

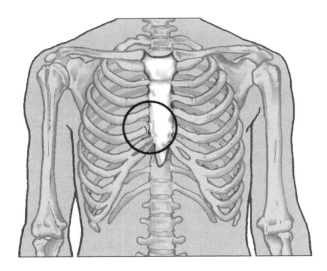

■ Detachment of the ribs from the sternum

■ Fractured spine

■ Bruising of the heart

Of course, the presence of any of these complications greatly increases the seriousness of the injury. A patient with a sternal fracture may be given a rib belt, but it is more common to simply allow the fracture to heal on its own if no complications are involved.

You receive a claim for a patient who has suffered a fractured sternum. List three possible complications of this patient's injury.

A. _____

B. _____

C. _____

CHECKYOURANSWERHERECHECKYOURANSWERHERECHECKYOURANSWERHERE
CHECKYOURANSWERHERECHECKYOURANSWERHERECHECKYOURANSWERHERE
CHECKYOURANSWERHERECHECKYOURANSWERHERECHECKYOURANSWERHERE
CHECKYOURANSWERHERECHECKYOURANSWERHERECHECKYOURANSWERHERE

Rib Fractures

48. A rib fracture is probably one of the least serious types of fractures when no other injury accompanies it. Most rib fractures are simple linear cracks which do not break the rib entirely into two pieces. Even though rib fractures are not serious, they are painful for the patient because of the constant in-out movement of the ribs resulting from breathing. Rib fractures usually heal on their own. The patient may be given a **rib belt,** a device which resembles a corset, to support the area and make him or her more comfortable.

Rib Fracture

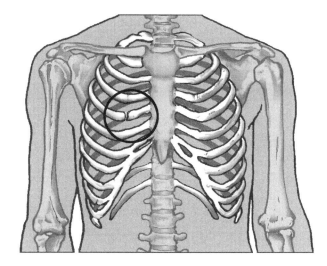

Rib fractures

A. are always serious, even when no other injuries are involved.

B. are never painful for the patient.

C. are painful for the patient because of the movement of the ribs during breathing.

49. Even when a rib is broken into two pieces, it usually heals well because the bone pieces are held closely together by the muscles surrounding the ribs. When broken bones reunite, it is called **union**. If the bones fail to unite, this is known as **nonunion**. Nonunion of a fractured rib is rare.

    The inherent danger of a fractured rib is that a bone fragment may puncture a lung. Any type of fracture like this that causes damage to an internal organ is called a **complicated fracture**.

    You're reviewing a medical report on a patient who has suffered a rib fracture which broke the rib into two pieces. You know that

    A. the fracture will probably heal well because the bone pieces will be held together by the muscles surrounding the ribs.

    B. the patient also could have suffered a punctured lung.

    C. both A and B are correct.

50. Answer the following questions about rib and sternal fractures.

A. Which of the following statements concerning rib fractures are true?

1. Rib fractures are never serious.

2. Rib fractures are never painful for the patient.

3. Rib fractures usually heal well because the bone pieces are held closely together by the muscles surrounding the ribs.

4. The greatest danger of a broken rib is that a bone fragment may puncture a lung.

B. Which of the following statements concerning sternal fractures are true?

1. Sternal fractures may be treated by giving the patient a rib belt.

2. There are no possible complications with a sternal fracture.

3. There are three possible complications with a fractured sternum: the ribs have been detached from the sternum, the spine may also be fractured, or the heart may be bruised.

4. Fractures to the sternum are very common.

CHECKYOURANSWERHERECHECKYOURANSWERHERECHECKYOURANSWERHERE
CHECKYOURANSWERHERECHECKYOURANSWERHERECHECKYOURANSWERHERE
CHECKYOURANSWERHERECHECKYOURANSWERHERECHECKYOURANSWERHERE
CHECKYOURANSWERHERECHECKYOURANSWERHERECHECKYOURANSWERHERE

UNDERSTANDING DISABILITY TERMINOLOGY

Common Classifications of Disability

51. Earlier in this unit, we discussed loss of use of the hand, and throughout the course we've talked about permanent and temporary damage to the body, loss of joint movement, and severity of injuries. All of these considerations must be used by a claim handler when estimating whether or not an injury will **disable** a patient and if so, for how long and to what extent.

When we say a person is *disabled,* we mean that person has lost all or some ability to use a part of the body in the same manner as in the past. This use may involve employment as well as other activities. Disabilities are classified as one of four types:

■ Temporary total disability

■ Temporary partial disability

■ Permanent partial disability

■ Permanent total disability

We'll define each of these four types of disability in the next few frames.

Define the term *disability.* _____

_____

_____

Temporary Total Disability

52. A **temporary total disability** means that, for a *temporary* period of time, the patient will be *totally* unable to perform *any* activity, either at work or anywhere else. Temporary total disability usually refers to the disability during the recovery period after an accident.

    Which of the following situations indicate temporary total disability?

    A. For five months following his accident, Sidney was confined to bed: two months in the hospital and three at his home.

    B. Shirley's leg injury prevented her from returning to her regular job for several months, but she was able to care for herself at home.

    C. While both her arms were in casts, Teresa was unable to carry on any of the activities she had participated in prior to her accident.

Temporary Partial Disability

53. With a **temporary partial disability**, the patient is, for a *temporary* period, only *partially* able to perform usual activities; however, it is expected that the patient will eventually be completely able to perform these activities.

    This disability classification usually applies to the patient's occupation. For example, suppose a waiter fractures his radius. While in the cast, he can perform all of his usual duties except carrying trays, so the disability is temporary and partial. In addition, he might be only partially able to perform his usual personal activities, such as driving or cleaning his house.

    Label each example below with a **TT** if it describes a temporary total disability or a **TP** if it describes a temporary partial disability.

    ____ A. For six months, an accident victim is unable to get out of bed without assistance.

    ____ B. A social worker is able to return to work immediately after an accident, but cannot service field cases for several weeks because of two broken legs.

    ____ C. Following an auto accident, a typist/file clerk's left arm is immobilized, preventing the use of a typewriter for three months. However, she is able to perform her usual filing duties.

Permanent Partial Disability

54. The third type of disability is **permanent partial disability**, the type which is most often found in lawsuits. This means a person is *partially* able to perform usual activities, but is *not expected to ever be completely able to resume pre-injury activities*. Permanent partial disability usually involves the patient's job, but not necessarily. Consider the following example.

    Millie is an accountant. A knee injury does not deter her from returning to work; however, Millie is a stellar tennis player and has made a name for herself in amateur tournaments throughout the country. Unfortunately, Millie's knee is permanently damaged, and her tennis game will never be the same. So, while her job is not affected, a very important part of Millie's life is over.

    On the other hand, the patient's job may be partially affected. An example is an assembly line worker who may still be able to perform the duties of the job, but whose speed in performing those duties is reduced by joint stiffness.

    Which of the following is an example of permanent partial disability?

    A. With the help of a wheelchair, Myra is able to care for herself at home after an accident, but it is several months before she can resume her usual activities.

    B. Ten months after his leg was broken, Fred was back at work as a truck mechanic. However, his job duties are limited because his leg permanently lost its mobility and he is no longer able to work underneath the trucks.

CHECKYOURANSWERHERECHECKYOURANSWERHERECHECKYOURANSWERHERE
CHECKYOURANSWERHERECHECKYOURANSWERHERECHECKYOURANSWERHERE
CHECKYOURANSWERHERECHECKYOURANSWERHERECHECKYOURANSWERHERE
CHECKYOURANSWERHERECHECKYOURANSWERHERECHECKYOURANSWERHERE

Permanent Total Disability

55. The final type of disability is **permanent total disability**, in which the patient will *never* be able to perform his or her pre-injury vocation. This type of disability might also involve activities in other areas of the person's life in addition to pursuing a livelihood. An injury that results in a permanent total disability must be extremely severe and will probably involve several parts of the body.

    Which of the following would probably be classified as permanent total disabilities?

    A. A newspaper editor whose legs are badly scarred from burns.

    B. A waitress whose left leg has been amputated.

    C. A brain surgeon whose finger joints are permanently immobilized.

    D. A plumber who has permanently lost the use of both arms.

CHECKYOURANSWERHERECHECKYOURANSWERHERECHECKYOURANSWERHERE
CHECKYOURANSWERHERECHECKYOURANSWERHERECHECKYOURANSWERHERE
CHECKYOURANSWERHERECHECKYOURANSWERHERECHECKYOURANSWERHERE
CHECKYOURANSWERHERECHECKYOURANSWERHERECHECKYOURANSWERHERE

Medical Vs. Industrial Disability

56. Determining whether a person's disability is total or partial is not as simple in workers compensation claims, since individual states may use different factors to define total and partial disabilities. Depending on the state, the determination is made by deciding, first, whether the worker is:

- **Industrially disabled**, which refers to the individual's *loss of earnings*

- **Medically disabled**, which refers to the *physical condition* that affects functioning

For each situation described, decide whether the first consideration about total or partial disability is industrial **(I)** or medical **(M)** disability.

_____ A.   In this jurisdiction, the first consideration is how the injury has affected the patient's body.

_____ B.   In this jurisdiction, the first consideration is how the patient's ability to earn a living has been affected.

CHECKYOURANSWERHERECHECKYOURANSWERHERECHECKYOURANSWERHERE
CHECKYOURANSWERHERECHECKYOURANSWERHERECHECKYOURANSWERHERE
CHECKYOURANSWERHERECHECKYOURANSWERHERECHECKYOURANSWERHERE
CHECKYOURANSWERHERECHECKYOURANSWERHERECHECKYOURANSWERHERE

57. Where **industrial disability** is the standard, the difference between partial and total disability depends upon whether the individual is able to earn at least some money by working, or has completely lost the ability to work for a living. In this case, the injured person's earning capacity does not necessarily refer to earning wages at the same type of employment pursued prior to the disability. The following illustration indicates partial and total industrial disability.

Industrial Disability

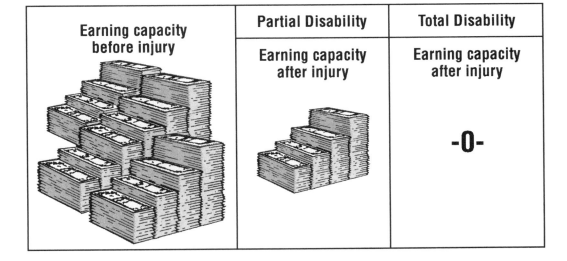

Earning capacity before injury	Partial Disability	Total Disability
	Earning capacity after injury	Earning capacity after injury
		-0-

Similarly, when **medical disability** is the standard, partial or total disability depends upon the individual's physical functioning, as indicated in this illustration.

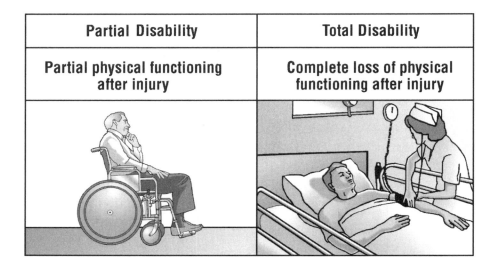

Partial Disability	Total Disability
Partial physical functioning after injury	Complete loss of physical functioning after injury

A. A disabled person capable of performing at least some gainful work is considered to be (totally/partially) _____ disabled in states where workers compensation laws take into account (industrial/medical) _____ disability.

B. In the same type of state described in A above, a disabled person who has lost all earning capability is considered (totally/partially) _____ _____ disabled.

Impairment

58. Factors that are taken into consideration when determining whether or not a person is disabled include age, sex, and occupation. Obviously, these are **nonmedical factors**. The medical factor that is included as part of the disability evaluation is the **impairment**. This distinction is important in evaluating permanent disability, so it is important to know the difference between permanent *disability* and permanent *impairment*.

While permanent disability is not strictly a medical condition, permanent impairment is. Impairment is any abnormality which remains after treatment is completed and which is not expected to improve in the future. Permanent impairment is the medical factor that is considered along with the nonmedical factors in determining permanent disability.

Define a permanent impairment. _____
_____
_____

59. Rating permanent **impairment** is *solely the responsibility of the physician*. On the other hand, it is not the physician's job to evaluate the nonmedical considerations in conjunction with the impairment for the purpose of determining whether there is permanent **disability**. This is an *administrative function* that has to do with the type of settlement the patient will receive.

    To help make the administrative decision about any type of disability, charts are frequently used for claim handling purposes. These charts help to estimate the length of a disability according to the type of injury. These charts are for estimates only, and do not consider complications that may arise in an individual's recovery. A sample of the type of chart which may be used is included at the end of the text.

    A. Determining permanent impairment is
        1. a physician's responsibility.
        2. an administrative responsibility.
        3. both a physician's and an administrative responsibility.

    B. Determining permanent disability is
        1. a physician's responsibility.
        2. an administrative responsibility.
        3. both a physician's and an administrative responsibility.

60. There is a tear-out Temporary Disability Estimate Chart at the end of the course. The chart lists disability time estimates for common medical conditions seen in bodily injury claims.

To review what you've learned about disability terminology, match the term in the left-hand column with its correct definition in the right-hand column.

1. Temporary total disability
2. Temporary partial disability
3. Impairment
4. Permanent partial disability
5. Permanent total disability
6. Industrial disability
7. Medical disability

____ A. Medical factor used in disability evaluation

____ B. Patient is only partially able to perform his or her usual activities for a temporary period of time

____ C. Patient is not expected to ever be completely able to resume his or her pre-injury activities

____ D. Individual's loss of earnings is used to determine whether disability is partial or total

____ E. Patient is totally unable to perform his or her usual activities for a temporary period of time

____ F. Individual's physical condition is used to determine whether disability is partial or total

____ G. Patient will never be able to perform his or her pre-injury activities

CHECKYOURANSWERHERECHECKYOURANSWERHERECHECKYOURANSWERHERE
CHECKYOURANSWERHERECHECKYOURANSWERHERECHECKYOURANSWERHERE
CHECKYOURANSWERHERECHECKYOURANSWERHERECHECKYOURANSWERHERE
CHECKYOURANSWERHERECHECKYOURANSWERHERECHECKYOURANSWERHERE

REVIEW

61. Answer the following questions to review what you've learned about the upper body and upper extremities.

Write in the name of the bone on the line extending from it in the following illustration.

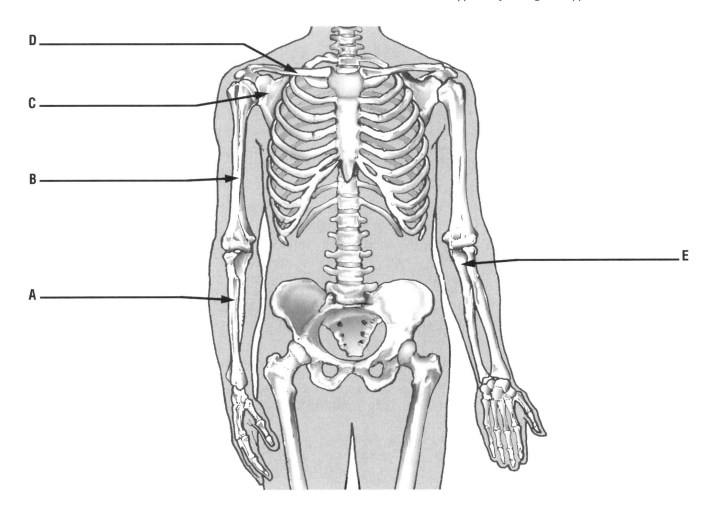

62. Which of the following statements concerning the hand bones are correct?

    A. The carpals make up the body of the hand.
    B. The finger bones are called phalanges.
    C. The metacarpals form the wrist.
    D. With the exception of the thumb, each finger has three phalanges.
    E. The phalanx closest to the point of attachment at the body is called the proximal phalanx.
    F. The phalanx furthest from the point of attachment at the body is called the middle phalanx.

63. True or false?

   A. There are 14 true ribs. ( ) True ( ) False

   B. The floating ribs are each attached to the rib above it.
      ( ) True ( ) False

   C. The clavicles are attached directly to the sternum. ( ) True ( ) False

   D. The biggest danger with a rib fracture is that a bone fragment may
      puncture a lung. ( ) True ( ) False

   E. The sternum is one of the most frequently fractured bones in the body.
      ( ) True ( ) False

   F. The clavicle is often fractured by an indirect force, such as falling on
      an outstretched hand or arm. ( ) True ( ) False

   G. Arthritis often results from a fractured scapula. ( ) True ( ) False

CHECKYOURANSWERHERECHECKYOURANSWERHERECHECKYOURANSWERHERE
CHECKYOURANSWERHERECHECKYOURANSWERHERECHECKYOURANSWERHERE
CHECKYOURANSWERHERECHECKYOURANSWERHERECHECKYOURANSWERHERE
CHECKYOURANSWERHERECHECKYOURANSWERHERECHECKYOURANSWERHERE
CHECKYOURANSWERHERECHECKYOURANSWERHERECHECKYOURANSWERHERE
CHECKYOURANSWERHERECHECKYOURANSWERHERECHECKYOURANSWERHERE

64. Match the description of the injury or condition in the left-hand column
with its correct definition in the right-hand column.

1. Fracture to the humerus bone	____ A. Nerve compression disorder involving the median nerve at the wrist
2. Epiphyses injuries	____ B. Fractures in this area may involve injury to or compression of the radial nerve
3. Carpal tunnel syndrome	____ C. A transverse fracture at the distal end of the radius where the lower fragment of the radius is displaced backward and outward
4. Thoracic outlet syndromes	____ D. Compression of vessels or nerves in the thoracic region
5. Colles fracture	____ E. Damage to this area of the bone may cause the bone to stop growing

CHECKYOURANSWERHERECHECKYOURANSWERHERECHECKYOURANSWERHERE
CHECKYOURANSWERHERECHECKYOURANSWERHERECHECKYOURANSWERHERE
CHECKYOURANSWERHERECHECKYOURANSWERHERECHECKYOURANSWERHERE
CHECKYOURANSWERHERECHECKYOURANSWERHERECHECKYOURANSWERHERE

65. Following are illustrations of some of the fracture types we discussed in this unit. Write in the name of the fracture type under each illustration.

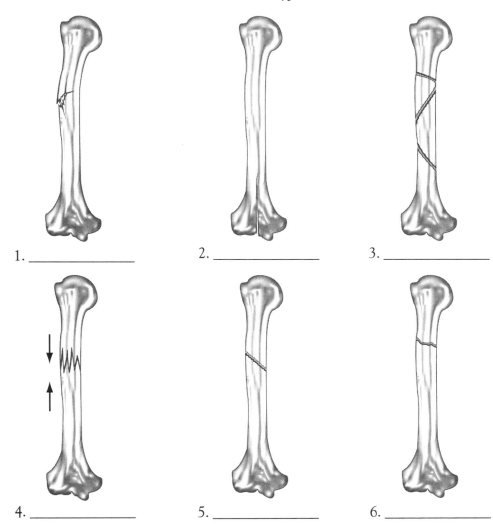

1. _____

2. _____

3. _____

4. _____

5. _____

6. _____

66. Answer the following questions about disability terminology.

    A. Describe temporary total disability._____
    _____

    B. Describe permanent partial disability._____
    _____

    C. The term industrial disability describes the individual's_____
    _____.

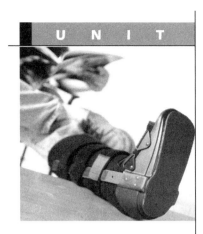

6

The Lower Body and Lower Extremities

PELVIC BONES

1. The **pelvis**, or **pelvic area**, protects the bladder, some reproductive organs, the lower colon, and the rectum. It is composed of five bones. Three of these form the sides and front of the pelvis, and on an adult skeleton, it's difficult to determine where one stops and the other begins. In children, these bones are divided by cartilage, which gradually fuses into solid bone in adulthood. Nevertheless, the bones are still referred to by separate names.

   In the female, the pelvis is broad and roomy, whereas a male's pelvis is much more narrow, as depicted in the following illustrations:

Female Pelvis *male*   *female* **Male Pelvis**

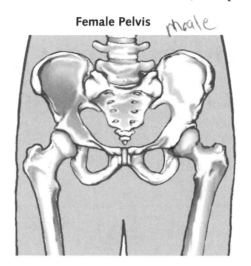 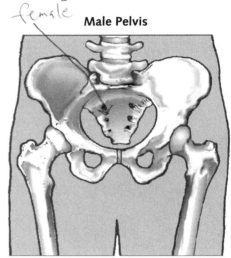

   The pelvis
   A. is composed of five bones.
   B. is shaped exactly the same way in men and women.
   C. protects the bladder, some reproductive organs, the lower colon, and the rectum.

CHECKYOURANSWERHERECHECKYOURANSWERHERECHECKYOURANSWERHERE
CHECKYOURANSWERHERECHECKYOURANSWERHERECHECKYOURANSWERHERE
CHECKYOURANSWERHERECHECKYOURANSWERHERECHECKYOURANSWERHERE
CHECKYOURANSWERHERECHECKYOURANSWERHERECHECKYOURANSWERHERE

Ilium

2. The broad, butterfly-shaped bone at the top and sides of the pelvis is the **ilium**, or **hip bone**. You may also see this bone described as the **innominate bone**. Which arrow in the illustration is pointing to the ilium? (A/B/C) _____

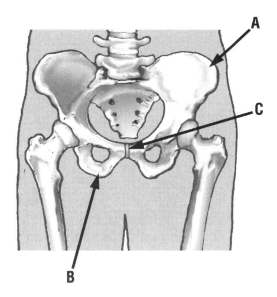

Ischium

3. The pelvic bone that we sit on is called the **ischium**. The arrow on the illustration which indicates the ischium is arrow (A/B/C) _____.

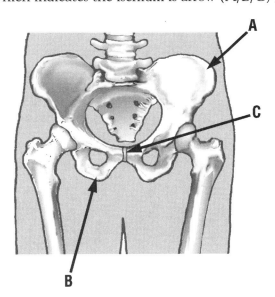

Pubic Bone

4. Above the ischium is a bone that forms a rim in front. This is the **pubic bone**, indicated by the arrow on the illustration.

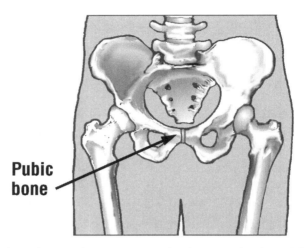

Pubic bone

Name the three bones that compose the front and sides of the pelvis.

A. _____

B. _____

C. _____

Sacrum and Coccyx

5. The last two of the five pelvic bones, the **sacrum** and the **coccyx**, make up the back of the pelvis. These two bones are the lower portions of the spine and, along with the ilium, ischium, and pubic bones, support the entire spinal column.

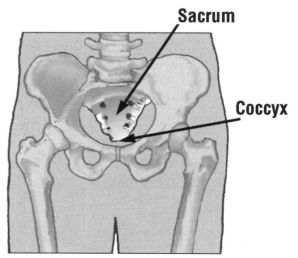

Sacrum

Coccyx

The sacrum is the back of the pelvis. It is shaped roughly like an inverted triangle—wide at the top, and tapering at the bottom. At the bottom, the sacrum is joined by the coccyx, which forms the tip of the sacrum.

Which two pelvic bones are a part of the spine?

A. Ilium and ischium

B. Ischium and pubic bone

C. Sacrum and coccyx

CHECKYOURANSWERHERECHECKYOURANSWERHERECHECKYOURANSWERHERE
CHECKYOURANSWERHERECHECKYOURANSWERHERECHECKYOURANSWERHERE
CHECKYOURANSWERHERECHECKYOURANSWERHERECHECKYOURANSWERHERE
CHECKYOURANSWERHERECHECKYOURANSWERHERECHECKYOURANSWERHERE

6. Write in the name of each bone indicated on the following illustration.

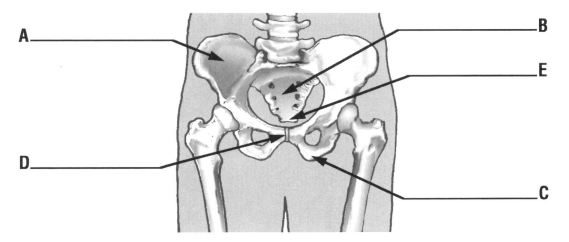

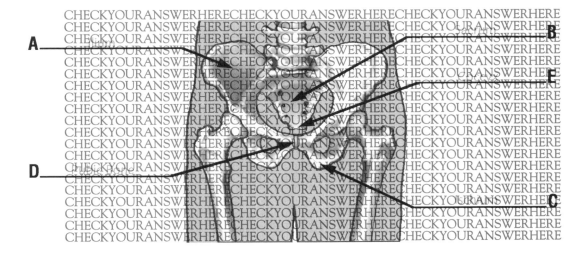

LEG BONES

Femur

7. The longest bone in the body is the thigh bone, which is called the **femur**. It is highlighted in the illustration at the left. The head of the femur sits at an angle to the pelvis, forming a joint which makes a large variety of movements and body positions possible. You'll learn more about this important joint later in this unit. The femur extends from the pelvis to the knee.

Femur

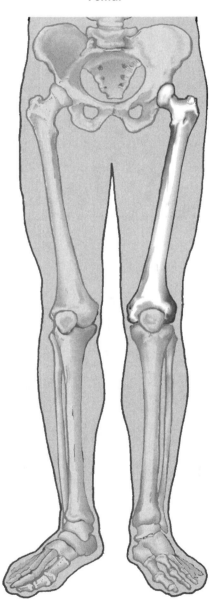

The femur

A. is the longest bone in the body.

B. is also known as the shin bone.

C. extends from the pelvis to the foot.

D. articulates with the pelvis.

Patella

8. The kneecap is called the **patella**, which means, literally, a small pan. This bone is slightly curved and shaped something like a small washpan. On the illustration on the right, the patella is indicated by arrow (A/B/C) _____.

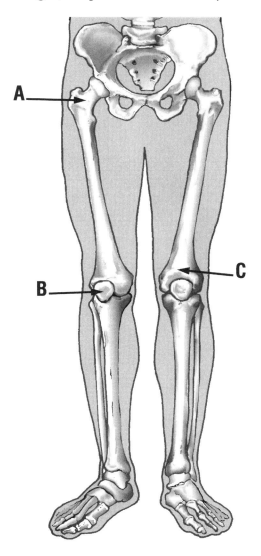

Tibia and Fibula

9. The lower leg, like the forearm, has two bones. The larger of these two bones is the **tibia**, which is on the **inner side of the lower leg** and slightly in front of the smaller bone. The **fibula** is the small bone on the **outer side of the lower leg**.

Tibia and Fibula

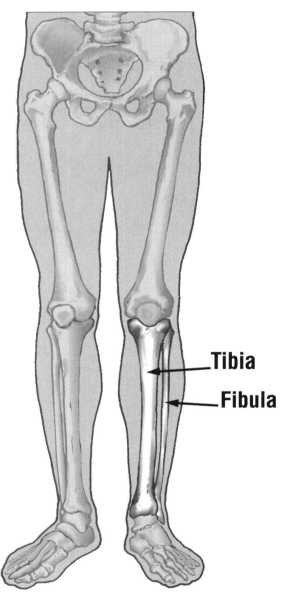

A. The (tibia/fibula) _____ is the small bone on the outer side of the lower leg.

B. The (tibia/fibula) _____ is the large bone on the inner side of the lower leg.

CHECKYOURANSWERHERECHECKYOURANSWERHERECHECKYOURANSWERHERE
CHECKYOURANSWERHERECHECKYOURANSWERHERECHECKYOURANSWERHERE
CHECKYOURANSWERHERECHECKYOURANSWERHERECHECKYOURANSWERHERE
CHECKYOURANSWERHERECHECKYOURANSWERHERECHECKYOURANSWERHERE

Malleoli

10. The four protuberances on the sides of the lower leg which we call **ankle bones** are not actually separate bones, but the lower portions of the tibia and fibula. The name given to these protuberances is **malleoli** (singular is *malleolus*). The malleoli are designated as **medial malleoli** and **lateral malleoli**.

Medial Malleoli

Lateral Malleoli

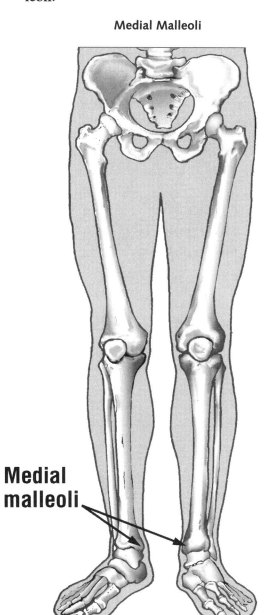
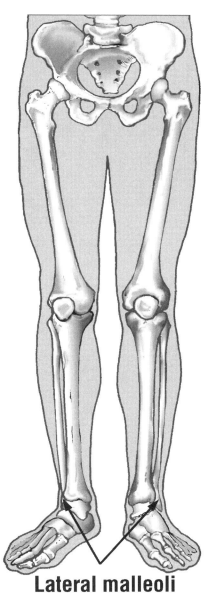

Medial malleoli

Lateral malleoli

The *medial malleoli* are the two malleoli located closest to the *middle of the body*. They are the lower ends of the tibia bones.

The *lateral malleoli* are the two malleoli located *to the side of, or furthest from the body*. They are the lower ends of the fibula bones.

A. A claimant has fractured the two malleoli located closest to the middle of the body. These are the (lateral/medial) _____ malleoli.

B. You're studying a medical report on a patient who has a fracture located at the end of the fibula. This fracture has occurred to a (lateral/medial) _____ malleoulus.

CHECKYOURANSWERHERECHECKYOURANSWERHERECHECKYOURANSWERHERE
CHECKYOURANSWERHEREGHECKYOURANSWERHERECHECKYOURANSWERHERE
CHECKYOURANSWERHERECHECKYOURANSWERHERECHECKYOURANSWERHERE
CHECKYOURANSWERHERECHECKYOURANSWERHERECHECKYOURANSWERHERE

11. Match the name of the bone in the left-hand column with its correct description in the right-hand column.

1. Femur	____ A.	Large bone on the inner side of the lower leg
2. Patella	____ B.	Commonly referred to as the kneecap
3. Tibia	____ C.	Lower end of the tibia
4. Fibula	____ D.	Extends from the pelvis to the knee
5. Medial malleolus	____ E.	Small bone on the outer side of the lower leg
6. Lateral malleolus	____ F.	Lower end of the fibula

CHECKYOURANSWERHERECHECKYOURANSWERHERECHECKYOURANSWERHERE
CHECKYOURANSWERHEREGHECKYOURANSWERHERECHECKYOURANSWERHERE
CHECKYOURANSWERHERECHECKYOURANSWERHERECHECKYOURANSWERHERE
CHECKYOURANSWERHERECHECKYOURANSWERHERECHECKYOURANSWERHERE

FOOT BONES

12. The construction of the foot is similar in its division of bones to the hand. The bones of the foot are divided into the following three categories:

| **Tarsals** | **Metatarsals** | **Phalanges** |

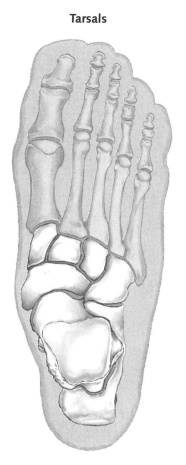 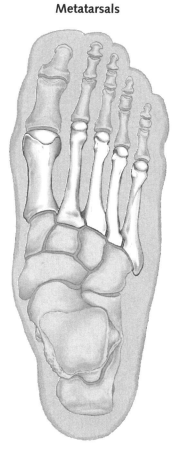 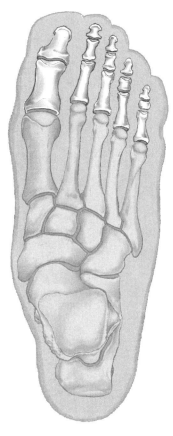

The bones of the ankle are called the *tarsals*. There are seven tarsal bones, one less than the carpals.

The *metatarsals* form the body of the foot. There are five metatarsals in each foot—one for each toe.

Like the fingers, the toes, with the exception of the big toe, are made up of three phalanges. The big toe has two phalanges.

True or false?

A.   The metatarsals form the toes.   ( ) True   ( ) False

B.   Each toe has three phalanges, with the exception of the big toe, which has two.   ( ) True   ( ) False

C.   The bones of the ankle are called the tarsals.   ( ) True   ( ) False

CHECKYOURANSWERHERECHECKYOURANSWERHERECHECKYOURANSWERHERE
CHECKYOURANSWERHERECHECKYOURANSWERHERECHECKYOURANSWERHERE
CHECKYOURANSWERHERECHECKYOURANSWERHERECHECKYOURANSWERHERE
CHECKYOURANSWERHERECHECKYOURANSWERHERECHECKYOURANSWERHERE

13. Write in the name of the foot bone highlighted in each of the following illustrations.

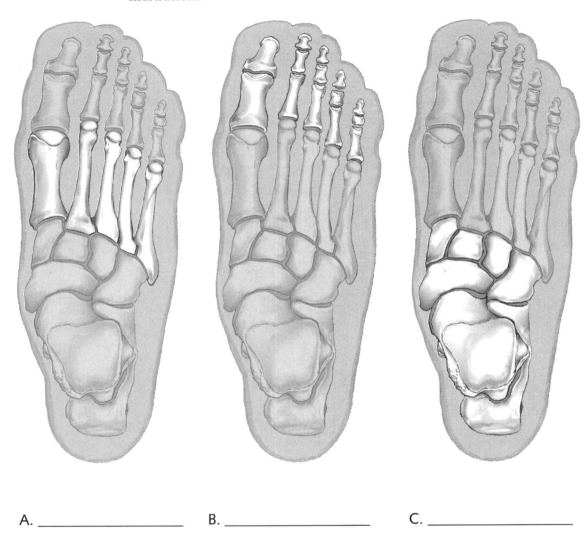

A. _____   B. _____   C. _____

INJURIES TO THE PELVIC BONES AND LOWER SPINE

Injuries to the Pelvic Bones

14. Fractures to the pelvic bones are rare, but when they do occur, they can be serious and very painful since the pelvic bones provide support for both the abdomen and lower spine.

    The most commonly fractured pelvic bone is the pubic bone. A fracture in this area may tear the urethra, which carries urine from the bladder. This complication usually occurs to men.

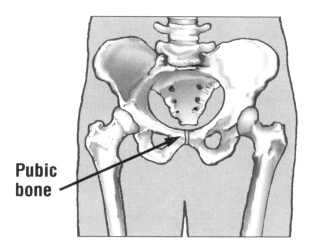

Pubic
bone

For women, there is a remote possibility that a pelvic fracture may interfere with the birth canal in some way, making normal childbirth difficult or impossible.

You receive a claim from a patient who has suffered a pelvic fracture. Name two possible complications of a fracture in this area.

A. _____

B. _____

Injuries to the Lower Spine

15. Injuries to the sacrum are also uncommon. The sacrum is joined to the ilium with the **sacroiliac joint**. You may see a number of claims for injuries to this joint although, in reality, injuries to the sacroiliac joint are rare. This is because the joint is nearly immobile and protected by plenty of muscle. Claims for injuries to the sacroiliac joint should be backed up by x-rays or other diagnostic tests.

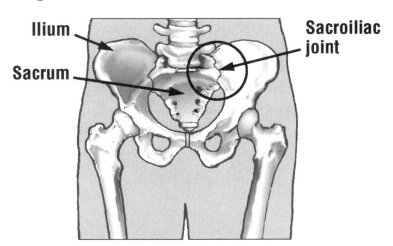

Ilium

Sacrum

Sacroiliac
joint

The sacroiliac joint

A. joins the sacrum and the coccyx.

B. is often injured.

C. joins the ilium and the sacrum.

D. is rarely injured.

CHECKYOURANSWERHERECHECKYOURANSWERHERECHECKYOURANSWERHERE
CHECKYOURANSWERHERECHECKYOURANSWERHERECHECKYOURANSWERHERE
CHECKYOURANSWERHERECHECKYOURANSWERHERECHECKYOURANSWERHERE
CHECKYOURANSWERHERECHECKYOURANSWERHERECHECKYOURANSWERHERE

16. Fractures to the coccyx are rare, but very painful for the patient. While this type of fracture is usually easy to reduce, it often slips out of place again. This dislocation causes even more pain, and the bone fragment may have to be surgically removed. Sometimes, the patient still has subjective complaints of pain even after the bone fragment is removed.

    A claimant has suffered a fractured coccyx. Which of the following statements are true about this claimant's injury?

    A. Bone fragments may slip out of place after the fracture has been reduced.

    B. Dislocated bone fragments may have to be surgically removed.

    C. If a dislocated bone fragment is removed, the claimant will never have subjective complaints of pain in this area.

CHECKYOURANSWERHERECHECKYOURANSWERHERECHECKYOURANSWERHERE
CHECKYOURANSWERHERECHECKYOURANSWERHERECHECKYOURANSWERHERE
CHECKYOURANSWERHERECHECKYOURANSWERHERECHECKYOURANSWERHERE
CHECKYOURANSWERHERECHECKYOURANSWERHERECHECKYOURANSWERHERE

17. Answer the following true/false questions to review what you've learned about pelvic and lower spine injuries.

    A. Fractures to the pelvic bones are very common. ( ) True ( ) False

    B. A fracture to the pubic bone may tear the urethra.
       ( ) True ( ) False

    C. Pelvic fractures in women never interfere with the birth canal.
       ( ) True ( ) False

    D. The sacroiliac joint is one of the most commonly injured joints in the body. ( ) True ( ) False

    E. Fractures to the coccyx are rare. ( ) True ( ) False

CHECKYOURANSWERHERECHECKYOURANSWERHERECHECKYOURANSWERHERE
CHECKYOURANSWERHERECHECKYOURANSWERHERECHECKYOURANSWERHERE
CHECKYOURANSWERHERECHECKYOURANSWERHERECHECKYOURANSWERHERE
CHECKYOURANSWERHERECHECKYOURANSWERHERECHECKYOURANSWERHERE

INJURIES TO THE LEG BONES—ACETABULUM AND FEMUR

Injuries to the Acetabulum

18. One of the most serious types of fractures involving the pelvis is a fracture through the head of the femur where it angles into a socket in the pelvis and forms the joint. The part of the pelvis which receives the head of the femur is called the **acetabulum**, and it is one of the most important joints in the body.

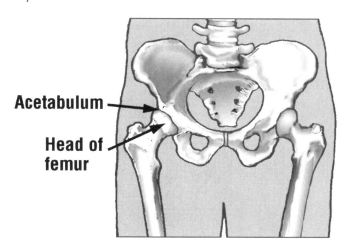

Through the acetabulum, the weight of the body is supported by the femur. In addition, this joint plays a major role in our ability to walk. Like any fracture involving a joint, a fracture to the acetabulum is potentially disabling and can have an adverse effect on many aspects of living.

Check all correct statements.

A. The head of the femur fits into a socket in the pelvis called the acetabulum.

B. The acetabulum joint has no role in providing support for the body.

C. The ability to walk and move is directly related to the acetabulum joint.

D. Like any joint fracture, a fracture into the acetabulum is potentially disabling.

19. A fractured acetabulum is considered a hip fracture. This type of fracture involves a long healing period for several reasons:

■ The angle of the bone as it joins the acetabulum makes it difficult to reduce the fracture

■ The downward pull of the muscles makes it difficult to keep the bone fragments in place during healing

■ Poor blood circulation in this area hinders bone growth and healing

Beulah Livingston slipped on a wet floor in a grocery and fractured her hip. Name three reasons why Beulah's injury will take a long time to heal.

A. _____
   _____

B. _____
   _____

C. _____
   _____

CHECKYOURANSWERHERECHECKYOURANSWERHERECHECKYOURANSWERHERE
CHECKYOURANSWERHERECHECKYOURANSWERHERECHECKYOURANSWERHERE
CHECKYOURANSWERHERECHECKYOURANSWERHERECHECKYOURANSWERHERE
CHECKYOURANSWERHERECHECKYOURANSWERHERECHECKYOURANSWERHERE
CHECKYOURANSWERHERECHECKYOURANSWERHERECHECKYOURANSWERHERE
CHECKYOURANSWERHERECHECKYOURANSWERHERECHECKYOURANSWERHERE
CHECKYOURANSWERHERECHECKYOURANSWERHERECHECKYOURANSWERHERE

20. In addition to the temporary disability that results from the lengthy recovery period, the patient may also have slight to moderate loss of hip motion, and the thigh muscles may atrophy because they are not used. Other serious complications that may arise are:

■ **Osteoarthritis**, which involves degeneration of the joints

■ **Avascular necrosis**, where poor blood circulation to the injured area causes tissue in both the head of the femur and the acetabulum to die

Avascular necrosis may not be diagnosed for up to a year after the injury. Patients who suffer from avascular necrosis must have the hip joint surgically removed and replaced with an artificial joint.

Beulah Livingston, our claimant from the preceding frame, may develop which of the following complications as a result of her fractured hip?

A. Osteoarthritis

B. Atrophy of thigh muscles

C. Slight to moderate loss of hip motion

D. Avascular necrosis

E. Need for replacement of the hip joint with an artificial hip

F. All of the above are potential complications of a fractured acetabulum

CHECKYOURANSWERHERECHECKYOURANSWERHERECHECKYOURANSWERHERE
CHECKYOURANSWERHERECHECKYOURANSWERHERECHECKYOURANSWERHERE
CHECKYOURANSWERHERECHECKYOURANSWERHERECHECKYOURANSWERHERE
CHECKYOURANSWERHERECHECKYOURANSWERHERECHECKYOURANSWERHERE

Injuries to the Femur

21. The femur (the highlighted bone in the illustration) is the most important weight-bearing bone in the body, because it is not only the longest bone, but also the strongest. However, its size makes it difficult to heal when fractured because of poor blood circulation in the area. In relation to the size of the femur, its blood vessels are very small.

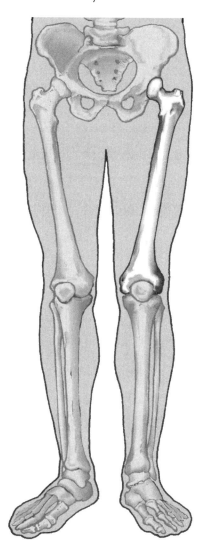

Complete fractures to the femur are especially difficult to heal because there is less bone-to-bone contact than with other types of fractures that do not completely sever the bone. And, just like the humerus, the weight of the femur can complicate healing by pulling the bone fragments apart.

Why are fractures to the femur difficult to heal?

A. Poor blood circulation in the area

B. Weight of the femur sometimes pulls the bone fragments apart

C. Both A and B are correct

CHECKYOURANSWERHERECHECKYOURANSWERHERECHECKYOURANSWERHERE
CHECKYOURANSWERHERECHECKYOURANSWERHERECHECKYOURANSWERHERE
CHECKYOURANSWERHERECHECKYOURANSWERHERECHECKYOURANSWERHERE
CHECKYOURANSWERHERECHECKYOURANSWERHERECHECKYOURANSWERHERE

22. Because of its weight-bearing role, good bony union of the femur is important but, as we've learned, difficult to achieve. Too often, a fibrous union results instead. Since the callus does not harden with a fibrous union, the femur will be unable to bear weight as it's supposed to.

    Most femur fractures are repaired by open reduction, including the use of metal plates, pins, or rods to help hold the fragments together and speed up healing time. Even so, it takes a long time to recover from a fractured femur. Permanent effects that can result include loss of hip motion, partial loss of knee motion, and atrophy of the thigh muscles (which may be corrected with physical therapy). If the fracture occurs to the distal end of the femur of a child, there is the possibility that the epiphysis will be damaged, causing the bone to stop growing. A comminuted fracture to the femur may result in discrepancies in leg length.

    True or false?

    A. A fractured femur should heal with a fibrous union to ensure that the femur will be able to bear weight as it's supposed to.
       ( ) True   ( ) False

    B. Femur fractures are usually repaired by open reduction, and metal plates, pins, or rods are often used to help hold the bone fragments together.   ( ) True   ( ) False

    C. Permanent effects of a fractured femur may include loss of hip motion, partial loss of knee motion, and atrophy of the thigh muscles.
       ( ) True   ( ) False

CHECKYOURANSWERHERECHECKYOURANSWERHERECHECKYOURANSWERHERE
CHECKYOURANSWERHERECHECKYOURANSWERHERECHECKYOURANSWERHERE
CHECKYOURANSWERHERECHECKYOURANSWERHERECHECKYOURANSWERHERE
CHECKYOURANSWERHERECHECKYOURANSWERHERECHECKYOURANSWERHERE

23. Label each statement below with an **A** if it refers to a fracture to the acetabulum, an **F** if it describes a fracture to the femur, or a **B** if it describes both types of fractures.

    _____ A. Involves a fracture to the joint formed by the femur and the pelvis.

    _____ B. Fracture to this area may cause both partial loss of knee motion and atrophy of the thigh muscles.

    _____ C. Considered a hip fracture.

    _____ D. Difficult to heal because poor blood circulation in the area hinders bone growth and healing.

    _____ E. Formation of good bony union with this type of fracture is critical so the bone can continue to bear the body's weight.

    _____ F. Fracture to this area may cause both osteoarthritis and slight to moderate loss of hip motion.

CHECKYOURANSWERHERECHECKYOURANSWERHERECHECKYOURANSWERHERE
CHECKYOURANSWERHERECHECKYOURANSWERHERECHECKYOURANSWERHERE
CHECKYOURANSWERHERECHECKYOURANSWERHERECHECKYOURANSWERHERE
CHECKYOURANSWERHERECHECKYOURANSWERHERECHECKYOURANSWERHERE

INJURIES TO THE KNEE

Injuries to the Knee Joint

24. Fractures into the knee joint, like any other joint, may result in loss of movement. A fractured knee joint is also susceptible to developing **arthritis**, which is an inflammation of a joint. Either with or without arthritis, a fractured knee joint can result in the patient being unstable when walking or standing.

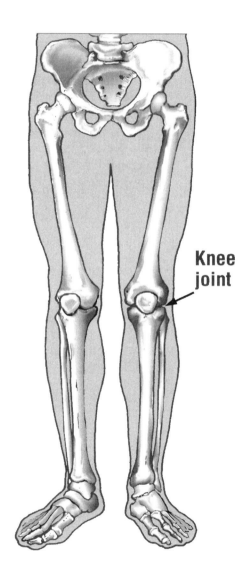

Knee joint

List three common results of a fracture into a knee joint.

A. _____

B. _____

C. _____

Injuries to the Patella

25. The patella, or kneecap, is very susceptible to injuries, and easily fractured in a fall or if it is hit. A fractured patella is difficult to reduce because of its mobility and the pull of its large muscles. The bone fragments may have to be wired together, and even then they may not remain in position. In some cases, the patella has to be removed surgically.

    A fracture to the patella may result in the problems common to fractures involving joints: instability and loss of mobility of the joint. Even though it is not a joint, an injury to the patella affects the knee because of its proximity to that joint.

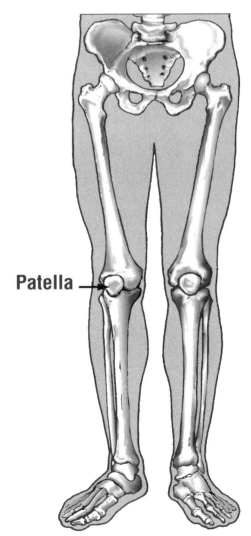

Patella

Check all correct statements.

A. The patella is rarely fractured or injured.

B. A fractured patella is difficult to reduce because of its mobility and the pull of its large muscles.

C. A fractured patella usually heals successfully with no instability or loss of mobility of the knee.

D. An injury to the patella affects the knee because of its proximity to that joint.

Injuries to the Menisci

26. One of the most common knee injuries is a tear in the **meniscus** (plural is *menisci*), which is cartilage found inside joints. The knee joint has both lateral and medial menisci, as indicated in this illustration:

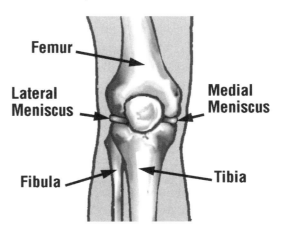

A. What is meniscus? _____

B. Name the two types of meniscus found in the knee joint.

1. _____

2. _____

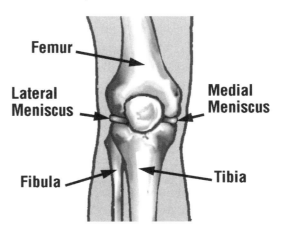

27. Menisci tears frequently occur to young athletes when they fall in a way that strains their legs beneath them. However, menisci tears can happen to anyone, including older adults. Beginning at around age 40, the menisci begin to stiffen and become less flexible, which makes them more susceptible to injury. There are two common types of menisci tears.

Common Types of Menisci Tears

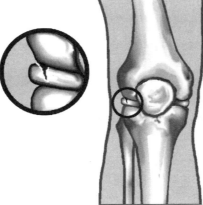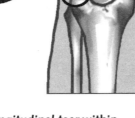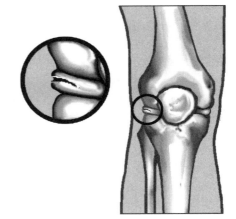

A *longitudinal tear* within the body of the meniscus

A *horizontal tear* from the edge of the meniscus into its body

Longitudinal tears are most common in younger people. They are usually caused by over-twisting the knee. In older persons, horizontal tears are more common. They can be caused by an injury or because the meniscus is degenerating with age. In the latter case, however, the degeneration may have begun and progressed more rapidly because of a previous injury.

Label each statement with an **LT** if it describes a longitudinal meniscus tear or an **HT** if it describes a horizontal meniscus tear.

_____ A. May be caused by degeneration of the meniscus

_____ B. Occurs more frequently in young people

_____ C. Often caused by over-twisting the knee

_____ D. Occurs more frequently in older adults

28. Treatment for torn menisci can involve either surgery to remove the torn tissue or more conservative nonsurgical treatment. Nonsurgical treatment is less successful than surgery, since meniscus tears often occur where there is not an adequate blood supply to promote healing. In addition, if surgery is required, delaying it can lead to rapid arthritic changes in the joint, causing an impairment in knee function.

While it's not customary for a physician to make a quick decision to treat meniscal injuries surgically, surgery is generally indicated when:

■ There has been a previous meniscus injury

■ The tear is located in an area where it cannot heal on its own

■ The knee joint has locked and can't be relieved through conservative measures

In these cases, delaying surgery may cause irreversible damage to the joint.

Meniscus tears

A. cannot be treated surgically.

B. can cause impairment in knee function if necessary surgery is delayed.

C. usually heal well on their own without treatment.

D. may be treated with nonsurgical techniques, although they are usually less effective than surgery.

Arthroscopy

29. Menisci injuries are frequently diagnosed and treated with a technique called **arthroscopy**. Arthroscopy means **examination of the interior of joints**, and it works like this:

Arthroscopy

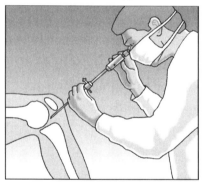

A tube called an *endoscope* is inserted into a surgical incision made in the knee. The endoscope includes an eyepiece and a light to allow viewing inside the knee, and a channel through which various medical tools may pass. After viewing and diagnosing the problem in the joint, surgical instruments or other tools may be inserted through the tube attached to the arthroscope to treat the injury. This requires another surgical incision.

A claimant tore a meniscus while playing soccer. What technique might be used to diagnose and treat this injury?

A. Closed reduction

B. MRI

C. EEG

D. Arthroscopy

30. Label each statement below with a **K** if it describes an injury to the knee joint, a **P** if it describes an injury to the patella, or an **M** if it describes an injury to the menisci.

    _____ A. Fracture to this part of the body is difficult to reduce because of its mobility and the pull of its large muscles.

    _____ B. Patient may develop arthritis after fracturing this area.

    _____ C. This type of injury is often diagnosed and treated with arthroscopy.

    _____ D. This type of injury happens frequently to young athletes who fall in a way that twists the leg.

CHECKYOURANSWERHERECHECKYOURANSWERHERECHECKYOURANSWERHERE
CHECKYOURANSWERHERECHECKYOURANSWERHERECHECKYOURANSWERHERE
CHECKYOURANSWERHERECHECKYOURANSWERHERECHECKYOURANSWERHERE
CHECKYOURANSWERHERECHECKYOURANSWERHERECHECKYOURANSWERHERE

INJURIES TO THE LEG BONES—TIBIA AND FIBULA

Injuries to the Tibia and Fibula

31. Of the two lower leg bones, only the larger bone, the tibia, helps the femur bear the body's weight. This is because the tibia and the femur make up the knee joint.

    The tibia is easily injured because it has very little muscular protection in front. Fractures to the tibia often occur in the middle or distal third of the bone. Blood circulation in these areas is poor, which complicates the healing of fractures since the blood vessels play an important part in callus growth.

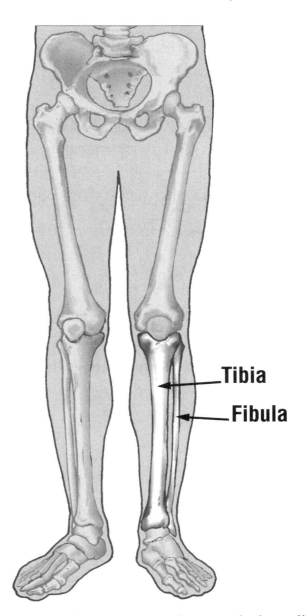

You're reviewing a medical report on a claimant who has suffered a fracture to the middle third of the tibia. Which one of the following statements is true about this injury?

A. Since there is good blood circulation in this area of the body, the fracture should heal quickly without complications.

B. This injury should heal quickly and without complications since blood circulation plays no role in the healing of fractures.

C. Poor blood circulation in this area will probably make this fracture difficult to heal.

CHECKYOURANSWERHERECHECKYOURANSWERHERECHECKYOURANSWERHERE
CHECKYOURANSWERHERECHECKYOURANSWERHERECHECKYOURANSWERHERE
CHECKYOURANSWERHERECHECKYOURANSWERHERECHECKYOURANSWERHERE
CHECKYOURANSWERHERECHECKYOURANSWERHERECHECKYOURANSWERHERE

32. Unlike the tibia, the fibula has no weight-bearing function. Its primary purpose is to hold muscles in place. Fibula fractures are generally not serious and usually do not lead to disability unless the tibia is also fractured at the same time.

   Which of the following statements about the fibula are true?

   A. It helps support the weight of the body.

   B. It anchors muscles.

   C. Fractures to the fibula always result in long-term disabilities.

CHECKYOURANSWERHERECHECKYOURANSWERHERECHECKYOURANSWERHERE
CHECKYOURANSWERHERECHECKYOURANSWERHERECHECKYOURANSWERHERE
CHECKYOURANSWERHERECHECKYOURANSWERHERECHECKYOURANSWERHERE
CHECKYOURANSWERHERECHECKYOURANSWERHERECHECKYOURANSWERHERE

Pott's Fracture

33. We said that a fibula fracture will usually not cause disability unless the tibia is fractured at the same time. Actually, it's more common for both bones to be broken together, in the area of the malleoli. When this occurs, it's called a **Pott's fracture**. The characteristics of a Pott's fracture are:

Pott's Fracture

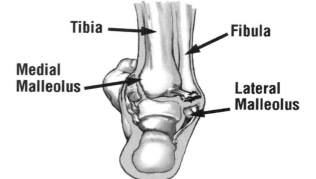

- The tibia and fibula are both fractured at the distal ends

- The foot is dislocated outward and backward

   Because a Pott's fracture involves the ankle joint, there are three potential areas of disability to consider. First, as in any type of fracture involving a joint, there is the danger of loss of ankle motion. Second, reduction must be absolutely perfect so that the foot and ankle do not turn out after healing, and so the weight-bearing function of the ankle is preserved. Third, the patient may develop arthritis in the affected ankle.

   What are the characteristics of a Pott's fracture?

   A. _____

   B. _____

CHECKYOURANSWERHERECHECKYOURANSWERHERECHECKYOURANSWERHERE
CHECKYOURANSWERHERECHECKYOURANSWERHERECHECKYOURANSWERHERE
CHECKYOURANSWERHERECHECKYOURANSWERHERECHECKYOURANSWERHERE
CHECKYOURANSWERHERECHECKYOURANSWERHERECHECKYOURANSWERHERE

34. Which of these statements concerning lower leg injuries are correct?
    A. The fibula is one of the most commonly fractured bones in the body.
    B. Fractures to the middle or distal third of the tibia are difficult to heal because the blood circulation in this area is poor.
    C. With a Pott's fracture, the tibia and fibula are both fractured at the proximal end near the knee, and the ankle and foot are dislocated outward and backward.
    D. Loss of ankle motion and the development of arthritis are possible complications of a Pott's fracture.
    E. Pott's fractures must be perfectly reduced so the foot and ankle do not turn out after healing, and so the weight-bearing function of the ankle is preserved.

CHECKYOURANSWERHERECHECKYOURANSWERHERECHECKYOURANSWERHERE
CHECKYOURANSWERHERECHECKYOURANSWERHERECHECKYOURANSWERHERE
CHECKYOURANSWERHERECHECKYOURANSWERHERECHECKYOURANSWERHERE
CHECKYOURANSWERHERECHECKYOURANSWERHERECHECKYOURANSWERHERE

INJURIES TO THE FOOT BONES

Injuries to the Tarsals

35. Of the tarsal bones, two in particular are frequently broken.

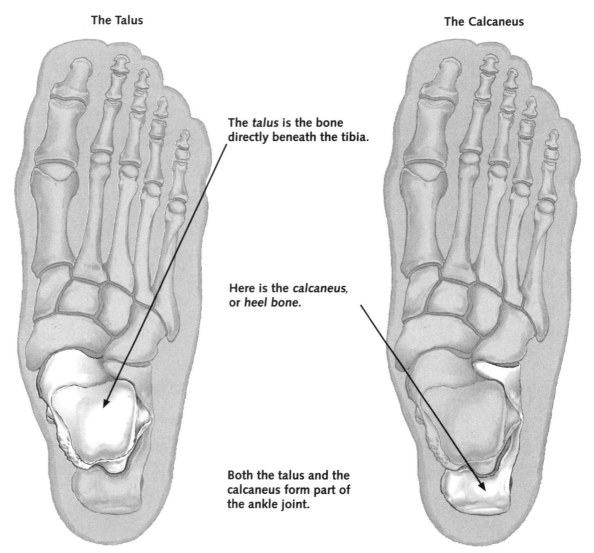

The Talus

The Calcaneus

The *talus* is the bone directly beneath the tibia.

Here is the *calcaneus*, or *heel bone*.

Both the talus and the calcaneus form part of the ankle joint.

The calcaneus is also called the **os calcis**. A fracture to either the talus or calcaneus bones is serious and usually leads to permanent partial disability. Since these bones make up part of the ankle joint, loss of movement in the ankle and the development of arthritis are possible complications.

A. Name the two most commonly fractured tarsal bones.

1. _____

2. _____

B. Why is a fracture to either of these bones considered a serious injury?

_____

_____

_____

36. A fracture to the calcaneus is especially painful. The pain results not only from the body's weight, but also from the involvement of the **Achilles tendon**.

The Achilles tendon has great strength and tends to pull the bone out of place. The most common type of fracture to the calcaneus is an **avulsion fracture**, meaning the calcaneus has been literally torn away from its usual position. The pull from the Achilles tendon contributes to the frequency of this type of fracture.

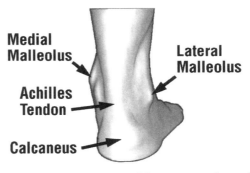

A. What is the most common type of fracture to the calcaneus?

_____

B. Why is this type of fracture common in this area?

_____

_____

Injuries to the Metatarsals and Phalanges

37. Although the metatarsals and phalanges are frequently broken (usually as a result of having objects dropped on them), such fractures are rarely serious. They generally reunite well, and any loss of motion in these bones has little effect on the lives of most people. However, this type of injury might have a great effect on people involved in certain occupations. Which one of the following do you think would be most affected by a fracture to a metatarsal or phalanx?

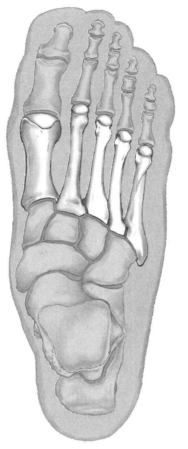
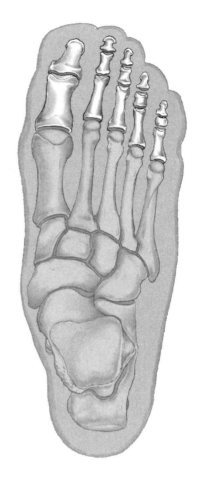

A. Book editor

B. Professional dancer

C. Long-distance telephone operator

D. Air traffic controller

38. For each statement below, write in a **T** if it describes a fracture to the talus, a **C** if it describes a fracture to the calcaneus, or an **MP** if it describes a fracture to the metatarsals or phalanges. **There may be more than one correct answer**.

_____ A. A fracture to one of these bones rarely has any serious lasting effects for most people.

_____ B. The most common type of fracture to this bone is an avulsion fracture.

_____ C. A fracture to one of these bones is serious and usually ends in permanent partial disability.

_____ D. Since these bones make up part of the ankle joint, a fracture in either bone could cause loss of movement in the ankle.

HEALING COMPLICATIONS

Arthritis

39. Many factors enter into the body's ability to recover from an injury or fracture. One of these is the presence or subsequent appearance of a disease which may delay or otherwise complicate healing. Let's study some of the more common diseases that can complicate healing. Remember, these diseases can affect the healing process of injuries in almost all areas of the body.

    We've already mentioned that arthritis often results from joint injuries. This disease, which may result from any number of conditions, is classified in several forms which describe its effect on the body. One of the most common types found in claim work is **osteoarthritis,** which is also known as degenerative arthritis. With this type of arthritis, the cartilage degenerates while the bone tries to compensate by growing over the joint. Osteoarthritis develops slowly over a long period of time and can seriously impair the functioning of a joint.

    Describe osteoarthritis. _____

    _____

    _____

CHECKYOURANSWERHERECHECKYOURANSWERHERECHECKYOURANSWERHERE
CHECKYOURANSWERHERECHECKYOURANSWERHERECHECKYOURANSWERHERE
CHECKYOURANSWERHERECHECKYOURANSWERHERECHECKYOURANSWERHERE
CHECKYOURANSWERHERECHECKYOURANSWERHERECHECKYOURANSWERHERE

40. Osteoarthritis usually does not result from a single injury. However, a claim can be made for *aggravation* of the existing condition as a result of an injury. In order for such a claim to be valid, any increase in symptoms must appear shortly after the incident which is claimed to be the cause of the aggravation. In most cases, two weeks is the maximum.

    When osteoarthritis is aggravated by an injury, the aggravation does not necessarily cause the disease to progress more swiftly. Instead, the aggravation makes the patient more aware of the pain, and will probably cause the pain to remain for a longer period of time. Think of a decaying tooth, where the pain is often intermittent. Drinking hot liquids can cause extreme, increased pain in the tooth, but will not speed up the process of decay.

    Other types of arthritis may be the direct result of a severe injury to a joint. In these cases, the joint is generally one involved with weight-bearing bones, such as the knee, hip, or ankle.

    Osteoarthritis

    A. rarely results from a single injury.

    B. can be aggravated by an injury.

    C. progresses more rapidly when it is aggravated by an injury.

CHECKYOURANSWERHERECHECKYOURANSWERHERECHECKYOURANSWERHERE
CHECKYOURANSWERHERECHECKYOURANSWERHERECHECKYOURANSWERHERE
CHECKYOURANSWERHERECHECKYOURANSWERHERECHECKYOURANSWERHERE
CHECKYOURANSWERHERECHECKYOURANSWERHERECHECKYOURANSWERHERE

Bursitis

41. Another disease we've previously discussed which can complicate healing of an injury or fracture is **bursitis**. To review, bursitis is an inflammation of a *bursa*, which is found near joints and serves to reduce friction between muscle and bone.

    Bursitis tends to affect the shoulder more often than any other joint. Bursitis in the shoulder is usually the most painful for the patient and results in the greatest loss of joint movement. This disability may be severe and permanent. Bursitis of the hip, though not as common, is also very painful and may result in long-term disability.

    On the other hand, bursitis in the knee or elbow may cause only minor discomfort and loss of function, and no disability. However, even if no permanent disability results, complete joint motion may not return for up to a year.

    Bursitis

    A. is an inflammation of the joints.

    B. is most common in the knee or elbow.

    C. is usually the most painful for the patient and produces the greatest loss of joint movement when it occurs in the shoulder.

    D. can be severely disabling when it occurs in the shoulder.

    E. may cause little to no disability when it occurs in the knee or elbow.

CHECKYOURANSWERHERECHECKYOURANSWERHERECHECKYOURANSWERHERE
CHECKYOURANSWERHERECHECKYOURANSWERHERECHECKYOURANSWERHERE
CHECKYOURANSWERHERECHECKYOURANSWERHERECHECKYOURANSWERHERE
CHECKYOURANSWERHERECHECKYOURANSWERHERECHECKYOURANSWERHERE

Osteomyelitis

42. **Osteomyelitis** is an inflammation of the bone marrow, or of both bone and marrow. It often results from infection after a compound fracture when the bone is exposed to the air and its impurities. Osteomyelitis is a persistent disease with a long and difficult recovery period. Surgical treatment is sometimes required to remove the diseased marrow. This complication can prevent settlement of a claim for an extended period of time.

    A claimant has suffered a compound fracture of the left femur. You know that the healing of this fracture may be complicated by the development of

    A. bursitis.

    B. osteomyelitis.

    C. arthritis.

CHECKYOURANSWERHERECHECKYOURANSWERHERECHECKYOURANSWERHERE
CHECKYOURANSWERHERECHECKYOURANSWERHERECHECKYOURANSWERHERE
CHECKYOURANSWERHERECHECKYOURANSWERHERECHECKYOURANSWERHERE
CHECKYOURANSWERHERECHECKYOURANSWERHERECHECKYOURANSWERHERE

Diabetes Mellitus

43. **Diabetes mellitus** is a disorder in which there is excessive sugar in the blood. While this disease cannot be caused by an injury, it is included in this section because:

   ■ it is present in many individuals, and

   ■ its presence delays healing, often leading to further complications.

   The fact that diabetes mellitus affects the blood is significant in the healing of a fracture, because fractures can't heal without blood feeding the bone cells. Healing may be further complicated if a diabetic suffers an injury in a part of the body that has poor blood circulation to begin with, such as the hips, lower legs, or feet.

   Diabetes mellitus

   A. can be caused by an injury.

   B. can delay the healing of injuries.

   C. is likely to cause serious complications in the healing of an injury, especially when the injury occurs in an area where blood circulation is poor.

   D. may lead to other complications in the healing of an injury.

Gangrene

44. Blood circulation is generally poorest in the feet, ankles, and lower legs. Therefore, an injury to any of these parts can cause severe complications, particularly for diabetics. Probably the worst possible complication is **gangrene,** which is the decomposition of soft tissue in the body. There are two types:

   ■ **Dry gangrene,** which is caused by an interruption of the blood supply to the affected area. Diabetes mellitus is a common cause of dry gangrene.

   ■ **Wet gangrene,** which is caused by bacterial infection in the affected area.

   Dry gangrene can be treated by surgically reestablishing blood flow to the affected area. For wet gangrene, massive doses of antibiotics may cure the condition. However, if treatment of either type of gangrene is not successful, it may be necessary to amputate the affected body part to keep the gangrene from spreading to other parts of the body.

Check all correct statements.

A. Gangrene is the decomposition of soft tissue.

B. Dry gangrene is often the result of diabetes mellitus.

C. The only possible treatment for wet gangrene is amputation of the affected body part.

D. Wet gangrene is caused by a bacterial infection in the affected area.

CHECKYOURANSWERHERECHECKYOURANSWERHERECHECKYOURANSWERHERE
CHECKYOURANSWERHERECHECKYOURANSWERHERECHECKYOURANSWERHERE
CHECKYOURANSWERHERECHECKYOURANSWERHERECHECKYOURANSWERHERE
CHECKYOURANSWERHERECHECKYOURANSWERHERECHECKYOURANSWERHERE

45. Match the healing complication in the left-hand column with its correct definition in the right-hand column.

1. Arthritis

2. Bursitis

3. Osteomyelitis

4. Diabetes Mellitus

5. Gangrene

_____ A. Inflammation of bone marrow or both bone and bone marrow

_____ B. Disorder in which there is too much sugar in the blood

_____ C. Inflammation of joints

_____ D. Decomposition of soft tissue in the body

_____ E. Inflammation of the body part that reduces friction between muscle and bone

CHECKYOURANSWERHERECHECKYOURANSWERHERECHECKYOURANSWERHERE
CHECKYOURANSWERHERECHECKYOURANSWERHERECHECKYOURANSWERHERE
CHECKYOURANSWERHERECHECKYOURANSWERHERECHECKYOURANSWERHERE
CHECKYOURANSWERHERECHECKYOURANSWERHERECHECKYOURANSWERHERE

REVIEW

46. Complete the following review exercises before going on to the next unit.

Write in the name of the pelvic bone depicted by each arrow on the following illustration.

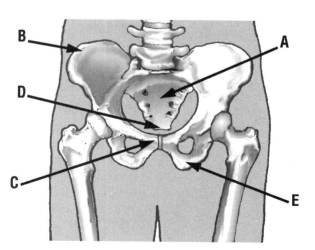

A. Arrow A _____

B. Arrow B _____

C. Arrow C _____

D. Arrow D _____

E. Arrow E _____

47. Write in the name of the leg bone depicted by each arrow on the following illustration.

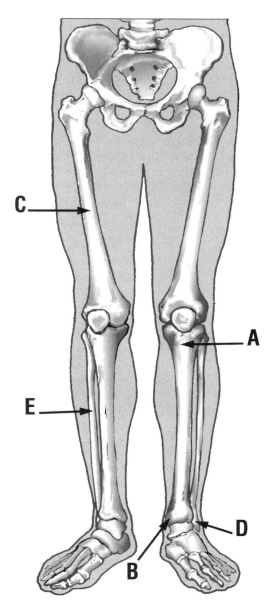

A. Arrow A _____

B. Arrow B _____

C. Arrow C _____

D. Arrow D _____

E. Arrow E _____

CHECKYOURANSWERHERECHECKYOURANSWERHERECHECKYOURANSWERHERE
CHECKYOURANSWERHERECHECKYOURANSWERHERECHECKYOURANSWERHERE
CHECKYOURANSWERHERECHECKYOURANSWERHERECHECKYOURANSWERHERE
CHECKYOURANSWERHERECHECKYOURANSWERHERECHECKYOURANSWERHERE

48. Match the name of each foot bone in the left-hand column with its correct description in the right-hand column.

    1. Tarsals   ____ A. Foot bones
    2. Metatarsals   ____ B. Toes
    3. Phalanges   ____ C. Ankle bones

CHECKYOURANSWERHERECHECKYOURANSWERHERECHECKYOURANSWERHERE
CHECKYOURANSWERHERECHECKYOURANSWERHERECHECKYOURANSWERHERE
CHECKYOURANSWERHERECHECKYOURANSWERHERECHECKYOURANSWERHERE
CHECKYOURANSWERHERECHECKYOURANSWERHERECHECKYOURANSWERHERE

49. Which of the following statements concerning injuries to the pelvis and lower spine are correct?

    A. The sacroiliac joint is one of the most frequently fractured joints in the body.

    B. Pubic bone fractures can also tear the urethra or interfere with the birth canal.

    C. When the coccyx is fractured, the bone fragments may slip out of place after the fracture has been reduced.

    D. In general, fractures in the pelvic area are rare, but they can be serious and very painful for the patient.

CHECKYOURANSWERHERECHECKYOURANSWERHERECHECKYOURANSWERHERE
CHECKYOURANSWERHERECHECKYOURANSWERHERECHECKYOURANSWERHERE
CHECKYOURANSWERHERECHECKYOURANSWERHERECHECKYOURANSWERHERE
CHECKYOURANSWERHERECHECKYOURANSWERHERECHECKYOURANSWERHERE

50. You receive a claim for a patient who has suffered a fractured acetabulum. Which of the following statements concerning this patient's condition are true?

    A. The injury occurred at the joint formed by the femur and the tibia.

    B. This patient's injury is very serious and potentially disabling.

    C. This type of fracture takes a long time to heal for many reasons, including the fact that poor blood circulation in the area hinders bone growth and healing.

D. The patient is at risk of developing avascular necrosis, a condition where poor blood circulation to the injured area causes tissue in both the head of the femur and the acetabulum to die.

E. Although this type of fracture takes a long time to heal, the patient should not experience any long-term disability as a result of the injury.

CHECKYOURANSWERHERECHECKYOURANSWERHERECHECKYOURANSWERHERE
CHECKYOURANSWERHERECHECKYOURANSWERHERECHECKYOURANSWERHERE
CHECKYOURANSWERHERECHECKYOURANSWERHERECHECKYOURANSWERHERE
CHECKYOURANSWERHERECHECKYOURANSWERHERECHECKYOURANSWERHERE

51. True or false?
    A. Fractures into the knee joint may result in loss of mobility.
       ( ) True   ( ) False
    B. Arthritis often results from a fractured knee joint.   ( ) True   ( ) False
    C. The patella is rarely injured because it is well protected by surrounding muscles.   ( ) True   ( ) False
    D. A fracture to the patella often causes instability and loss of mobility of the knee joint.   ( ) True   ( ) False
    E. One of the most common knee injuries is a tear in the meniscus, which is a ligament surrounding the patella.   ( ) True   ( ) False
    F. Injuries to the meniscus are most common in young athletes, although they also occur to older adults.   ( ) True   ( ) False
    G. Injuries to the meniscus usually have to be treated surgically, either through arthroscopy or more conventional surgical measures.
       ( ) True   ( ) False

CHECKYOURANSWERHERECHECKYOURANSWERHERECHECKYOURANSWERHERE
CHECKYOURANSWERHERECHECKYOURANSWERHERECHECKYOURANSWERHERE
CHECKYOURANSWERHERECHECKYOURANSWERHERECHECKYOURANSWERHERE
CHECKYOURANSWERHERECHECKYOURANSWERHERECHECKYOURANSWERHERE

52. Answer the following multiple choice questions on injuries to the lower leg and feet.
    A. If a patient suffers a fracture to the distal third of the tibia,
       1. poor blood circulation in the area will probably make the fracture difficult to heal.
       2. the fracture will heal quickly since there is good blood circulation in the area.
       3. the patient may develop bursitis as a result of the injury.
    B. Which one of the following is the correct definition of a Pott's fracture?
       1. Avulsion fracture to the calcaneous
       2. Tibia is broken near the lateral malleolus
       3. Both the tibia and fibula are broken in the area of the malleoli; foot is dislocated outward and backward

C. Avulsion fractures occur most frequently to which one of the following bones?

1. Talus
2. Calcaneus
3. Metatarsals

CHECKYOURANSWERHERECHECKYOURANSWERHERECHECKYOURANSWERHERE
CHECKYOURANSWERHERECHECKYOURANSWERHERECHECKYOURANSWERHERE
CHECKYOURANSWERHERECHECKYOURANSWERHERECHECKYOURANSWERHERE
CHECKYOURANSWERHERECHECKYOURANSWERHERECHECKYOURANSWERHERE

53. Write in the correct definition for each healing complication.

A. Arthritis _____
_____

B. Gangrene _____
_____

C. Osteomyelitis _____
_____

D. Bursitis _____
_____

E. Diabetes mellitus _____
_____

CHECKYOURANSWERHERECHECKYOURANSWERHERECHECKYOURANSWERHERE
CHECKYOURANSWERHERECHECKYOURANSWERHERECHECKYOURANSWERHERE
CHECKYOURANSWERHERECHECKYOURANSWERHERECHECKYOURANSWERHERE
CHECKYOURANSWERHERECHECKYOURANSWERHERECHECKYOURANSWERHERE
CHECKYOURANSWERHERECHECKYOURANSWERHERECHECKYOURANSWERHERE
CHECKYOURANSWERHERECHECKYOURANSWERHERECHECKYOURANSWERHERE

7

The Abdominal Organs

INTRODUCTION

1. In this unit, you will study some of the organs in the abdominal area of the body that are susceptible to traumatic injury. An **organ** is any body part that has a specific function. Organs have specialized cells which exist only to serve the specific functions of that organ, and also have their own blood and nerve supplies.

    The four organs you will learn about in this unit are the **liver, spleen, kidneys**, and **urinary bladder**. You'll learn about the location and function of each of these organs, as well as the effects of trauma on them.

    An organ

    A. is a body part that has a specific function.
    B. has specialized cells which serve only the functions of that organ.
    C. has its own blood and nerve supplies.
    D. all of the above are correct.

LOCATION AND FUNCTION OF ABDOMINAL ORGANS

Liver

2. The largest organ in the human body, and the one that performs the most functions, is the **liver**. It is one of the organs that humans cannot survive without.

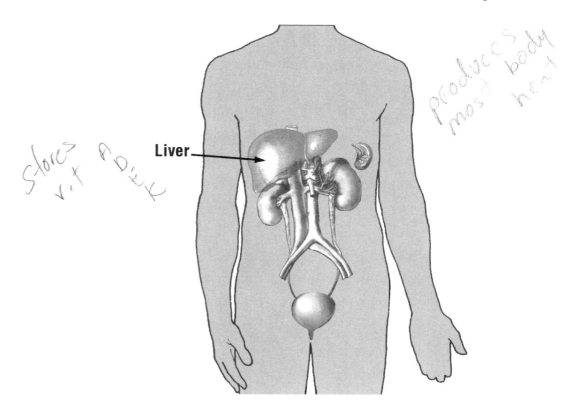

The liver has two sources of blood: the **portal vein** and the **hepatic artery**. It is part of the **gastrointestinal system**. Some of the liver's functions are:

- Regulating the blood's sugar level

- Forming bile, which is a substance used to digest food, and sending it to the gallbladder

- Converting amino acids into proteins

- Detoxifying certain harmful substances, such as alcohol, that are absorbed into the blood

- Storing certain vitamins

- Providing a source of body heat

The liver is also one of the few organs in the body that can *regenerate itself* when it is damaged. However, certain diseases such as cirrhosis of the liver (a disease which causes progressive damage to the liver) can interfere with blood supply and cause the liver to die.

Which of the following statements concerning the liver are correct?

A. It is the smallest organ in the body.

B. Its only function is to regulate the blood's sugar level.

C. It has two sources of blood: the hepatic artery and the portal vein.

D. It is one of the organs that the human body cannot survive without.

E. It can usually regenerate itself when it is damaged.

CHECKYOURANSWERHERECHECKYOURANSWERHERECHECKYOURANSWERHERE
CHECKYOURANSWERHERECHECKYOURANSWERHERECHECKYOURANSWERHERE
CHECKYOURANSWERHERECHECKYOURANSWERHERECHECKYOURANSWERHERE
CHECKYOURANSWERHERECHECKYOURANSWERHERECHECKYOURANSWERHERE

Spleen

3. The **spleen** is part of the **lymphatic system.** It filters bacteria within the blood and produces and distributes certain types of blood cells.

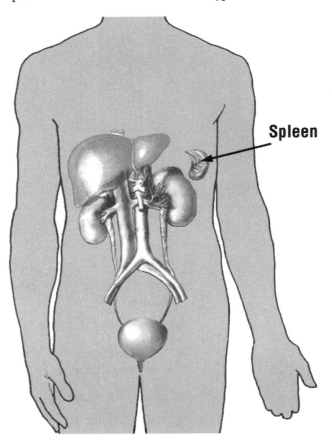

The spleen forms all types of blood cells during fetal development. By the time an individual reaches adulthood, the bone marrow has taken over most of this function, with the spleen manufacturing only a couple of types of blood cells. However, the spleen is capable of taking over full blood cell production if the bone marrow is damaged.

Which of the following are functions of the spleen?

A. Providing a source of body heat

B. Producing all blood cells during fetal development

C. Producing certain types of blood cells in adults

D. Taking over full blood cell production in an adult if the bone marrow is damaged

E. Forming bile used to digest food

F. Distributing blood cells

4. Another function of the spleen is to help the body ward off infections by:

- Producing specific antibodies to toxins within the body

- Filtering bacteria and other microorganisms from the blood

While an individual can survive without a spleen, surgically removing the spleen before the age of two results in the loss of both of the infection fighting functions listed above. Since a child younger than two will not have had a chance to produce many antibodies, he or she may always be susceptible to infections because no other antibodies will be produced by the spleen. This lack of antibodies also means that infections may be very serious, even life-threatening, for the individual, especially since the bacteria-filtering function of the spleen is also lost.

Which one of the following claimants would suffer the most adverse effects if his or her spleen were removed?

A. Louella Garwood, age 60

B. Steve Martin, age 40

C. Hector Mendoza, age 1

Explain your answer. _____
_____
_____
_____

Kidneys

5. The two **kidneys** are part of the **urinary system**. They produce urine and regulate certain elements, such as water and acids, in the blood. The kidneys are located in the back of the abdominal area on either side of the spine. In the illustration on the right, the kidneys have been moved forward slightly for clarity.

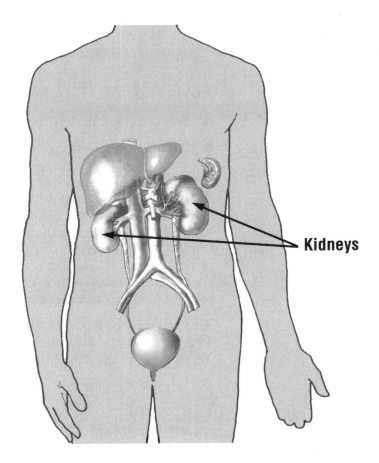

Kidneys

Of all of the organs we will discuss in this unit, the kidneys are the best protected against trauma because they are surrounded by large amounts of **adipose** (fatty) **tissue**.

A. Where are the kidneys located?_____

_____

B. Why are the kidneys better protected against trauma than some of the other abdominal organs?_____

_____

CHECKYOURANSWERHERECHECKYOURANSWERHERECHECKYOURANSWERHERE
CHECKYOURANSWERHERECHECKYOURANSWERHERECHECKYOURANSWERHERE
CHECKYOURANSWERHERECHECKYOURANSWERHERECHECKYOURANSWERHERE
CHECKYOURANSWERHERECHECKYOURANSWERHERECHECKYOURANSWERHERE

Urinary Bladder

6. The **urinary bladder** is also a part of the **urinary system**. Although the body has other types of bladders, such as the gallbladder, we will use the term **bladder** to refer to the urinary bladder.

bladder
infectio

Vinegar
water
sugar

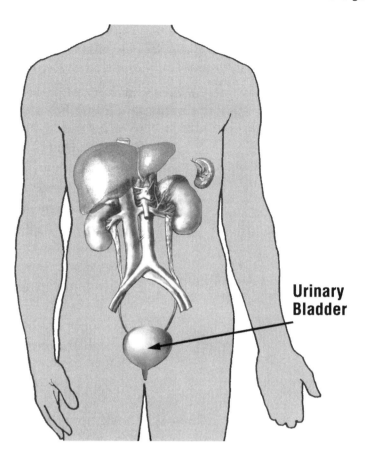

**Urinary
Bladder**

The bladder is a hollow, muscular organ which can be stretched or inflated. This allows the bladder to fulfill its primary purpose, which is to act as a holding tank for urine as it passes from the kidneys out of the body.

The bladder is technically located in the pelvis, not the abdomen, but we are including it here because it is often involved in traumatic injuries. In addition, when the bladder is full, it reaches up into the abdominal cavity.

The bladder is located in the anterior portion of the pelvic cavity, posterior to the pubic bones. In females, it is in front of the uterus and vagina; in males, it is in front of the rectum.

A. What is the primary purpose of the urinary bladder? _____
    _____

B. What features of the bladder allow it to perform the function you
    referred to in your answer to the previous question?_____
    _____

CHECKYOURANSWERHERECHECKYOURANSWERHERECHECKYOURANSWERHERE
CHECKYOURANSWERHERECHECKYOURANSWERHERECHECKYOURANSWERHERE
CHECKYOURANSWERHERECHECKYOURANSWERHERECHECKYOURANSWERHERE
CHECKYOURANSWERHERECHECKYOURANSWERHERECHECKYOURANSWERHERE
CHECKYOURANSWERHERECHECKYOURANSWERHERECHECKYOURANSWERHERE

7. This concludes our discussion of the location and functions of the liver, spleen, kidneys, and urinary bladder. Complete the following review exercise before going on to the next part of this unit.

For each statement below, write in an **L** if it pertains to the liver, an **S** if it describes the spleen, a **K** if it refers to the kidneys, or a **U** if it pertains to the urinary bladder. *Some statements may have more than one correct answer.*

_____ A. Part of the lymphatic system

_____ B. Part of the urinary system

_____ C. Part of the gastrointestinal system

_____ D. Capable of regenerating itself when damaged

_____ E. Helps body fight off infections by producing antibodies and filtering bacteria from the blood

_____ F. Protected against trauma by surrounding adipose tissue

_____ G. Located in the anterior portion of the pelvic cavity, posterior to the pubic bones

_____ H. Largest organ in the body

_____ I. Although this organ is part of the pelvis, it extends into the abdominal area when it is full

_____ J. Located in the back of the abdominal area on either side of the spine

_____ K. Should not be removed before an individual reaches the age of two

_____ L. Performs more functions than any other organ in the human body

CHECKYOURANSWERHERECHECKYOURANSWERHERECHECKYOURANSWERHERE
CHECKYOURANSWERHERECHECKYOURANSWERHERECHECKYOURANSWERHERE
CHECKYOURANSWERHERECHECKYOURANSWERHERECHECKYOURANSWERHERE
CHECKYOURANSWERHERECHECKYOURANSWERHERECHECKYOURANSWERHERE

INJURIES TO THE ABDOMINAL ORGANS

Injuries to the Liver

8. The liver is located underneath the ribs, as you can see in the illustration on the right.

   This means that the liver is susceptible to injury when an individual suffers a traumatic injury to the chest. For example, the liver may be punctured by a fractured rib, or a blunt, crushing force to the chest may damage the liver without actually penetrating it. Either type of injury to the liver may result in either a **lesion** or an **abscess**. *Lesion* is a broad term used to describe an area of damaged tissue. An *abscess* is a collection of pus resulting from damage to tissue.

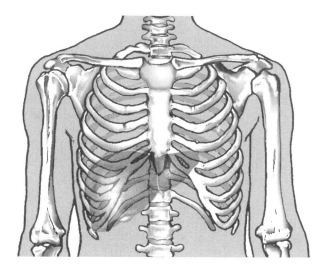

A. The liver's proximity to which body part makes it more susceptible to traumatic injury?

   1. Scapulas

   2. Ribs

   3. Pelvis

B. Name two common results of an injury to the liver.

   1. _____

   2. _____

CHECKYOURANSWERHERECHECKYOURANSWERHERECHECKYOURANSWERHERE
CHECKYOURANSWERHERECHECKYOURANSWERHERECHECKYOURANSWERHERE
CHECKYOURANSWERHERECHECKYOURANSWERHERECHECKYOURANSWERHERE
CHECKYOURANSWERHERECHECKYOURANSWERHERECHECKYOURANSWERHERE

9. A lesion in the hepatic artery is a common result of traumatic injury to the liver. In this case, the lesion is usually an **aneurysm**, or an abnormal dilation of the wall of the artery caused by weakness of the artery. Without treatment, an aneurysm in the hepatic artery can cause the artery itself to rupture, which can cause death.

   An abscess is caused by bacteria. Bacteria can be introduced directly into the liver by a penetrating injury, or it can be introduced indirectly when a crushing injury causes a hematoma. If the hematoma should somehow become infected by bacteria, then an abscess may result.

   A. Which one of the following statements are true about an aneurysm in the hepatic artery?

   1. It can cause the artery to rupture.

   2. It is a minor condition that rarely has to be treated.

   3. It is rarely caused by trauma.

B. Which of the following statements are true about an abscess in the liver?

1. It may result from bacteria introduced directly into the liver.

2. It may arise out of a crushing injury if the injury causes a hematoma, and the hematoma becomes infected.

3. It is never caused by bacterial infection.

CHECKYOURANSWERHERECHECKYOURANSWERHERECHECKYOURANSWERHERE
CHECKYOURANSWERHERECHECKYOURANSWERHERECHECKYOURANSWERHERE
CHECKYOURANSWERHERECHECKYOURANSWERHERECHECKYOURANSWERHERE
CHECKYOURANSWERHERECHECKYOURANSWERHERECHECKYOURANSWERHERE

10. Symptoms of a hepatic abscess may develop slowly over a period of weeks. Fever is the primary, and sometimes the only, symptom, although most patients will have other symptoms such as anorexia (loss of appetite), weight loss, nausea, and general body weakness. Some individuals may experience pain and tenderness in the upper right portion of the trunk.

   Most liver abscesses can be treated by draining the pus and administering medication. Surgery is usually not required unless there are other complications.

A. Gina was injured when she fell off a ladder. Two weeks later, she begins to run a high temperature and complains of anorexia and weakness. Her physician diagnoses a liver abscess. Since two weeks elapsed between Gina's injury and the discovery of the liver abscess,

1. there is no relationship between her injury and the liver abscess.

2. it is possible that her liver abscess is related to her injury.

B. Assuming there are no other complications involved, Gina's liver abscess will probably be treated

1. surgically.

2. by draining the pus and administering medication.

3. by allowing it to heal on its own.

CHECKYOURANSWERHERECHECKYOURANSWERHERECHECKYOURANSWERHERE
CHECKYOURANSWERHERECHECKYOURANSWERHERECHECKYOURANSWERHERE
CHECKYOURANSWERHERECHECKYOURANSWERHERECHECKYOURANSWERHERE
CHECKYOURANSWERHERECHECKYOURANSWERHERECHECKYOURANSWERHERE

Injuries to the Spleen

11. Like the liver, the spleen is susceptible to abscesses as a result of either a penetrating or blunt traumatic injury. Symptoms of an abscess in the spleen are fever and pain on the left side of the body, including the upper abdomen and lower chest. This pain may also extend up into the left shoulder.

   Treatment for a spleen abscess depends on its severity. Milder cases can be treated with antibiotics; for more serious abscesses, a splenectomy may have to be performed. As you'll recall from our earlier discussion of the function of the spleen, a splenectomy should not be performed on a child under the age of two unless it is absolutely necessary, because the vital functions of antibody production and filtering bacteria from the blood will be lost.

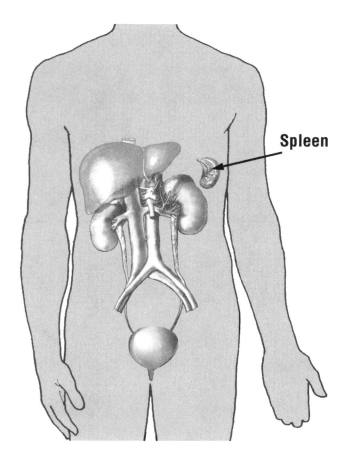

Severe traumatic injuries, such as those caused by auto accidents, may cause the spleen to rupture. An emergency **splenectomy** must be performed to remove a ruptured spleen.

A. Name two symptoms of an abscess in the spleen.

1. _____

2. _____

B. Name two treatment methods used for spleen abscesses.

1. _____

2. _____

CHECKYOURANSWERHERECHECKYOURANSWERHERECHECKYOURANSWERHERE
CHECKYOURANSWERHERECHECKYOURANSWERHERECHECKYOURANSWERHERE
CHECKYOURANSWERHERECHECKYOURANSWERHERECHECKYOURANSWERHERE
CHECKYOURANSWERHERECHECKYOURANSWERHERECHECKYOURANSWERHERE

Injuries to the Kidneys

12. Traumatic injuries to the kidneys are often caused by a forceful blow of some kind in the area of the kidneys, such as being struck in the back by a heavy or fast-moving object. Other types of traumatic injuries that may occur to the kidneys are knife or gunshot wounds.

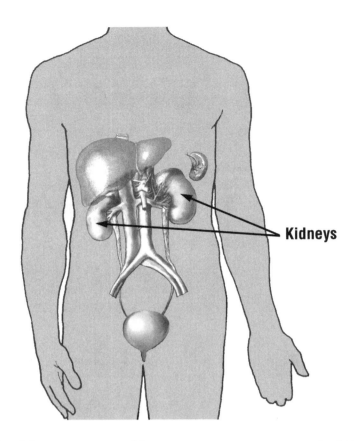

Which of these injuries could cause a traumatic injury to the kidneys?

A. A pedestrian is struck from behind by a hit-and-run driver.

B. A bank robber is shot in the back as he flees from the scene of the crime.

C. An editor slips on a wet bathroom floor and lands on her left hip.

D. A motorist runs off the road and crashes head-on into a tree.

13. The effects of injuries to the kidneys vary.

    A contusion might cause severe hematuria, even though the kidney itself is not badly damaged. While hematuria is not necessarily a serious condition, neither should it be taken lightly because it may be a sign of a more serious problem, such as laceration of a vein or artery in the kidney.

    Another potentially serious condition is laceration of the kidney itself, with bleeding and the escape of urine directly into the tissues surrounding the kidney.

    Either of these conditions can cause the patient to go into **shock** (sudden collapse of the circulatory system) and die quickly. Replacing the blood to control shock, monitoring blood pressure, and ensuring the normal flow of urine are immediate steps that should be taken. Surgery may be required for more severe injuries where bleeding cannot be stopped or large amounts of urine are escaping.

A. You know that a kidney injury may cause hematuria. Name two potentially serious conditions that may be indicated by hematuria in this case.

1. _____

2. _____

B. If the conditions you named in the preceding question are not treated promptly, the patient is at risk for

1. shock.

2. sudden death.

3. both of the above.

CHECKYOURANSWERHERECHECKYOURANSWERHERECHECKYOURANSWERHERE
CHECKYOURANSWERHERECHECKYOURANSWERHERECHECKYOURANSWERHERE
CHECKYOURANSWERHERECHECKYOURANSWERHERECHECKYOURANSWERHERE
CHECKYOURANSWERHERECHECKYOURANSWERHERECHECKYOURANSWERHERE

Injuries to the Urinary Bladder

14. Earlier, you learned that the primary purpose of the urinary bladder is to store urine as it passes from the kidneys out of the body. If the bladder happens to be full when a traumatic injury occurs, it is likely to rupture. Auto accidents are a common cause of ruptured bladders, usually as a result of a crushing injury to a full bladder. In addition, men are more likely than women to suffer ruptured bladders.

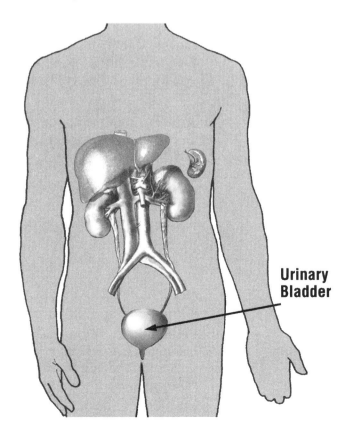

Urinary Bladder

A patient who has a ruptured bladder will either:

- Have blood in the urine

- Produce a lesser amount of urine

- Produce no urine at all

Severe bladder injuries may need to be treated surgically, while patients with less serious injuries may be treated by inserting a catheter into the bladder to drain urine.

Which of the following statements concerning traumatic injuries to the bladder are correct?

A. They are more common in women than in men.
B. If the bladder is empty at the time of the injury, it will probably rupture.
C. Signs of a ruptured bladder may include blood in the urine or a lessening or loss of urine production.
D. All bladder injuries require surgical treatment.
E. Auto accidents are often the cause of ruptured bladders.

15. Let's review what you've learned about injuries to the abdominal organs. Following is a list of conditions that may arise out of a traumatic injury to an abdominal organ. For each condition, write in an **L** if it is likely to be caused by an injury to the liver, a **K** if it may arise from a kidney injury, an **S** if the condition is seen with spleen injuries, or a **U** if it may arise from a urinary bladder injury. **There may be more than one correct answer.**

_____ A. Abscess
_____ B. Hematuria
_____ C. Aneurysm in hepatic artery
_____ D. Lessening or loss of urine production

PERITONITIS

16. **Peritonitis** is a serious infection that may arise after an injury to an abdominal organ. It is an inflammation of the **peritoneum**, a membrane that surrounds the abdominal organs and lines the abdominal cavity. There are two basic types of peritonitis:

■ **Primary peritonitis**, which results from bacteria transmitted through the blood

■ **Secondary peritonitis**, which results when an infection from another area, such as the site of a traumatic injury or an abscess, spreads to the peritoneum

Two other types of peritonitis that you may see described in medical reports are **traumatic peritonitis** and **aseptic peritonitis**. *Traumatic peritonitis* refers specifically to infection of an injury or wound. *Aseptic peritonitis* describes peritonitis which develops *without* a bacterial infection. Aseptic peritonitis can also result from trauma.

Match the type of peritonitis listed in the left-hand column with the correct description of its cause in the right-hand column.

1. Secondary peritonitis
2. Aseptic peritonitis
3. Primary peritonitis
4. Traumatic peritonitis

_____ A. Bacteria transmitted through the blood
_____ B. Infection of an injury or wound
_____ C. Infection from another area spreads to the peritoneum
_____ D. Develops without bacterial infection

CHECKYOURANSWERHERECHECKYOURANSWERHERECHECKYOURANSWERHERE
CHECKYOURANSWERHERECHECKYOURANSWERHERECHECKYOURANSWERHERE
CHECKYOURANSWERHERECHECKYOURANSWERHERECHECKYOURANSWERHERE
CHECKYOURANSWERHERECHECKYOURANSWERHERECHECKYOURANSWERHERE

17. Peritonitis may also be described as:

■ **Diffuse** or **generalized**, meaning it is widely spread throughout the peritoneum

■ **Localized** or **circumscribed**, meaning it is confined to a small area of the peritoneum

A. When peritonitis is described in a medical report as diffuse or generalized, this means that the infection is
   1. confined to a small area of the peritoneum.
   2. widely spread throughout the peritoneum.

B. When peritonitis is described in a medical report as localized or circumscribed, this means that the infection is
   1. confined to a small area of the peritoneum.
   2. widely spread throughout the peritoneum.

C. Based on what you have just read, peritonitis is more serious if it is
   1. localized or circumscribed.
   2. diffuse or generalized.

CHECKYOURANSWERHERECHECKYOURANSWERHERECHECKYOURANSWERHERE
CHECKYOURANSWERHERECHECKYOURANSWERHERECHECKYOURANSWERHERE
CHECKYOURANSWERHERECHECKYOURANSWERHERECHECKYOURANSWERHERE
CHECKYOURANSWERHERECHECKYOURANSWERHERECHECKYOURANSWERHERE

18. The symptoms of peritonitis vary depending on how long the infection has been present and how much of the peritoneum is involved.

Early symptoms of peritonitis include severe abdominal pain, which may be either diffuse or localized, nausea, vomiting, and a distended abdomen. Later symptoms, which indicate the infection has progressed severely, include fever, chills, rapid breathing, and tachycardia, which is an abnormally fast heartbeat. Complications such as shock, kidney failure, liver failure, and the inability to breathe properly may make the patient's condition even worse.

Peritonitis is treated by first eliminating the *cause* of the infection. For example, if the peritonitis was caused by an infection of an abdominal injury, this infection must be treated first. Then, the infection of the peritoneum can be treated. If peritonitis is left untreated, the patient may die.

A. A medical report indicates that a claimant was diagnosed with peritonitis based on her symptoms of severe abdominal pain, vomiting, and a distended abdomen. These symptoms indicate that the claimant is in the (early/late) _____ stage of peritonitis.

B. You receive a claim for a patient whose peritonitis was caused by an infection of an abdominal injury. How will this patient's condition probably be treated?_____

_____

_____

19. Answer the following true/false questions to review what you've learned about peritonitis before going on to the next section.

A. Peritonitis is always caused by a bacterial infection.
( ) True   ( ) False

B. Traumatic peritonitis is a type of peritonitis which results when an infection from another area spreads to the peritoneum.
( ) True   ( ) False

C. In general, peritonitis is more serious when it is diffuse or generalized.
( ) True   ( ) False

D. When peritonitis is described as localized or circumscribed, it means that the infection is confined to a small area of the peritoneum.
( ) True   ( ) False

E. Early symptoms of peritonitis include tachycardia, fever, and chills.
( ) True   ( ) False

F. The late stage of peritonitis can be complicated by kidney failure, liver failure, shock, and the inability to breathe properly.
( ) True   ( ) False

G. Late symptoms of peritonitis include severe abdominal pain, nausea, and vomiting.   ( ) True   ( ) False

H. Peritonitis is treated by first treating the underlying cause of the infection.   ( ) True   ( ) False

ABDOMINAL HERNIAS

20. A **hernia** is the protrusion of all or part of an organ through the wall of the cavity that normally contains it. This can happen with any organ, such as a cerebral hernia, where the brain protrudes through the wall of the cranium. However, we'll focus on the most common type of hernia seen in claim work, which is a protrusion of some portion of the **intestine** outside of its normal boundaries. The intestines are shown in the following illustration:

The Intestines

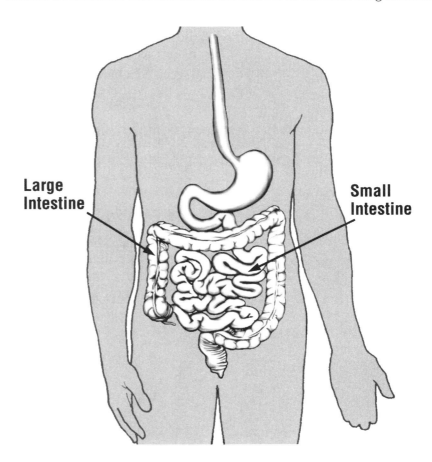

A. What is a hernia?_____
_____

B. The most common type of hernia seen in claim work involves the
_____.

21. Although a traumatic injury is often claimed to be the cause of a hernia, in most cases a hernia results from a natural defect in body development which fails to close normal openings present in early life, or from the progressive weakening of body tissues due to aging. Hernias may also be caused by increased pressure within the abdomen from heavy lifting or coughing. In order for a hernia to be caused by an injury, the injury must be a *direct blow to the abdomen* with enough force to rupture surrounding tissues and create an opening through which the organ can protrude.

    Assume all of the following individuals have filed a claim alleging that a traumatic injury caused them to develop a hernia. Based on what you just read, which one of them probably has a valid claim?

    A. Elvis tripped down the basement stairs and landed on his hands and knees.

    B. Lucille fractured two ribs when she was thrown against the dashboard in an auto accident.

    C. Tom received a hard kick in the abdomen during a karate class.

    D. Wendy was struck by a falling tree limb and landed on her left side.

Inguinal and Femoral Hernias

22. An **inguinal hernia** is the most common type of intestinal hernia, accounting for about 80% of all hernia cases. An inguinal hernia refers to a protrusion of part of the intestine into the inguinal area, or groin. It usually causes a lump to appear in the groin, as shown in the illustration below.

Inguinal Hernia

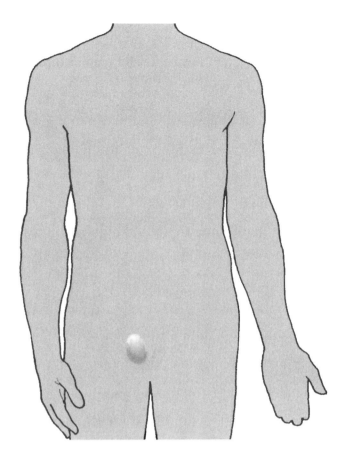

Inguinal hernias are classified as either **direct** or **indirect,** based on how the hernia progresses in the inguinal area. A *direct* inguinal hernia passes directly through the abdominal wall. An *indirect* inguinal hernia passes into the inguinal canal, and is the most common type of inguinal hernia.

A. You're reviewing a medical report for a patient who was diagnosed with a direct inguinal hernia. You know that this patient's hernia passes

  1. directly through the abdominal wall.
  2. into the inguinal canal.

B. You receive a claim for a patient with an indirect inguinal hernia. This claimant's hernia passes

  1. directly through the abdominal wall.
  2. into the inguinal canal.

C. Which type of inguinal hernia is most common?

  1. Direct
  2. Indirect

CHECKYOURANSWERHERECHECKYOURANSWERHERECHECKYOURANSWERHERE
CHECKYOURANSWERHERECHECKYOURANSWERHERECHECKYOURANSWERHERE
CHECKYOURANSWERHERECHECKYOURANSWERHERECHECKYOURANSWERHERE
CHECKYOURANSWERHERECHECKYOURANSWERHERECHECKYOURANSWERHERE

23. A **femoral hernia** occurs in a canal between the abdomen and thigh where the femoral artery, vein, and nerve join the abdomen and thigh. A femoral hernia usually causes a lump on the inner side of the thigh, as shown in the illustration on the right.

Femoral Hernia

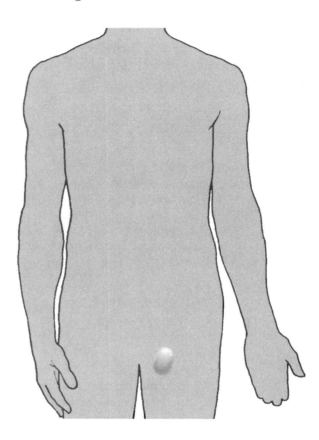

In some cases, a femoral hernia occurs closer to the groin, making it difficult to distinguish from an inguinal hernia.

Both inguinal and femoral hernias are usually repaired surgically, although mechanical devices, such as trusses, may be worn to provide support.

A. A lump on the inner side of the thigh is characteristic of (femoral/inguinal/both femoral and inguinal) _____ _____ hernias.

B. Surgery is the usual treatment method for (femoral/inguinal/both femoral and inguinal) _____ hernias.

CHECKYOURANSWERHERECHECKYOURANSWERHERECHECKYOURANSWERHERE
CHECKYOURANSWERHERECHECKYOURANSWERHERECHECKYOURANSWERHERE
CHECKYOURANSWERHERECHECKYOURANSWERHERECHECKYOURANSWERHERE
CHECKYOURANSWERHERECHECKYOURANSWERHERECHECKYOURANSWERHERE

24. We mentioned earlier that in order for an injury to cause a hernia, the injury must involve a direct blow to the abdomen of sufficient force to rupture the tissues. This statement makes your job sound easy; the claimant either did or did not receive such a blow, so the claim is or is not valid.

Unfortunately, it's not all that simple. As we said in an earlier unit, a claim for *aggravation of an existing condition* may be compensable. Therefore, even if it can be proven that the hernia was a preexisting condition, a claim may be made that the injury increased the size of the hernia or made it more serious. This is determined by the physician, but in order for this type of claim to be valid, certain symptoms should have appeared at the time of the injury. If any of the following symptoms are reported to have occurred, then the injury is probably responsible for the hernia or aggravation of an existing hernia:

■ Swelling

■ Bruising as evidence of hemorrhage

■ Tenderness in the area within 48 hours after the incident

■ Definite pain at the time of the injury

Which, if either, of the following claims would probably be valid?

A. Claim for a hernia caused by a direct blow to the abdomen of sufficient force to rupture surrounding tissues.

B. Claim for aggravation of a preexisting hernia by a traumatic injury.

C. Both A and B are probably valid claims.

D. Neither A nor B are valid claims.

CHECKYOURANSWERHERECHECKYOURANSWERHERECHECKYOURANSWERHERE
CHECKYOURANSWERHERECHECKYOURANSWERHERECHECKYOURANSWERHERE
CHECKYOURANSWERHERECHECKYOURANSWERHERECHECKYOURANSWERHERE
CHECKYOURANSWERHERECHECKYOURANSWERHERECHECKYOURANSWERHERE

25. Review what you've learned about hernias by matching the term in the left-hand column with its correct description in the right-hand column.

1. Hernia
2. Inguinal hernia
3. Indirect inguinal hernia
4. Direct inguinal hernia
5. Femoral hernia

_____ A. Type of inguinal hernia that passes directly through the abdominal wall.

_____ B. Protrusion of all or part of an organ through the cavity that normally contains it.

_____ C. Protrusion of part of the intestine into the groin.

_____ D. Type of inguinal hernia that passes into the inguinal canal.

_____ E. Protrusion of part of the intestine into the area where the femoral artery, vein, and nerve join the abdomen and thigh.

CHECKYOURANSWERHERECHECKYOURANSWERHERECHECKYOURANSWERHERE
CHECKYOURANSWERHERECHECKYOURANSWERHERECHECKYOURANSWERHERE
CHECKYOURANSWERHERECHECKYOURANSWERHERECHECKYOURANSWERHERE
CHECKYOURANSWERHERECHECKYOURANSWERHERECHECKYOURANSWERHERE

REVIEW

26. This concludes our discussion of the abdominal organs and the effect of traumatic injury and other conditions on these organs. Complete the following review exercises before going on to the next unit.

    True or false?

    A. The liver serves as a holding tank for urine as it passes from the kidneys out of the body.   ( ) True   ( ) False

    B. The kidneys are protected against trauma because they are surrounded by large amounts of adipose tissue.   ( ) True   ( ) False

    C. The spleen helps the body fight infection by producing antibodies to certain toxins and filtering bacteria from the blood.   ( ) True ( ) False

    D. Providing a source of body heat is just one of the many functions of the liver.   ( ) True   ( ) False

    E. The spleen is part of the gastrointestinal system.   ( ) True   ( ) False

    F. The kidneys regulate water and acids in the blood.   ( ) True   ( ) False

    G. The liver should not be removed in children under the age of two because this will make the child more susceptible to infections.   ( ) True   ( ) False

    H. The urinary bladder is the only organ in the body that can regenerate itself if it is damaged.   ( ) True   ( ) False

    I. The liver is the largest organ in the human body, and it performs more functions than any other organs.   ( ) True   ( ) False

    J. Regulating the blood's sugar level is one of the functions of the spleen.   ( ) True   ( ) False

27. Check all of the following statements that are correct concerning traumatic injuries to the abdominal organs.

    A. The liver is rarely damaged when an individual suffers a chest injury because it is protected by the ribs.

    B. The spleen is susceptible to abscesses as a result of penetrating or blunt injuries.

    C. Injuries to the kidneys are often caused by a forceful blow to the abdomen.

    D. The urinary bladder may rupture if it is full at the time of the injury.

    E. Injuries to the kidneys may result in laceration of a vein or artery within the kidney, or laceration of the kidney itself.

F. Two common results of an injury to the liver are abscesses and aneurysms in the hepatic artery.

G. An abscess in the spleen can only be treated by surgically removing the spleen.

H. Signs of a ruptured bladder are blood in the urine or a lessening or loss of urine production.

I. Symptoms of hepatic abscesses always appear within 24 hours of the injury to the liver.

J. Injuries to the kidneys often result in hematuria, which is a mild condition that can be allowed to heal on its own.

CHECKYOURANSWERHERECHECKYOURANSWERHERECHECKYOURANSWERHERE
CHECKYOURANSWERHERECHECKYOURANSWERHERECHECKYOURANSWERHERE
CHECKYOURANSWERHERECHECKYOURANSWERHERECHECKYOURANSWERHERE
CHECKYOURANSWERHERECHECKYOURANSWERHERECHECKYOURANSWERHERE

28. Following is a list of the common symptoms of peritonitis. Label each symptom with an **E** if it is most likely to be present in the early stages of peritonitis or an **L** if it is most likely to be present in the late stages.

_____ A. Tachycardia

_____ B. Severe abdominal pain

_____ C. Rapid breathing

_____ D. Fever and chills

_____ E. Distended abdomen

_____ F. Nausea and vomiting

CHECKYOURANSWERHERECHECKYOURANSWERHERECHECKYOURANSWERHERE
CHECKYOURANSWERHERECHECKYOURANSWERHERECHECKYOURANSWERHERE
CHECKYOURANSWERHERECHECKYOURANSWERHERECHECKYOURANSWERHERE
CHECKYOURANSWERHERECHECKYOURANSWERHERECHECKYOURANSWERHERE

29. Answer the following questions about hernias.

A. The most common type of hernia seen in claim work involves the (intestine/brain/liver) _____.

B. Describe an inguinal hernia. _____
_____

C. An inguinal hernia that passes into the inguinal canal is classified as a/an (direct/indirect) _____ inguinal hernia.

D. A an (femoral/inguinal) _____ hernia usually causes a lump on the inner side of the thigh.

E. A claim that a traumatic injury aggravated an already existing hernia is (always/sometimes/never) _____ compensable.

CHECKYOURANSWERHERECHECKYOURANSWERHERECHECKYOURANSWERHERE
CHECKYOURANSWERHERECHECKYOURANSWERHERECHECKYOURANSWERHERE
CHECKYOURANSWERHERECHECKYOURANSWERHERECHECKYOURANSWERHERE
CHECKYOURANSWERHERECHECKYOURANSWERHERECHECKYOURANSWERHERE

UNIT

8

The Cardiovascular System

INTRODUCTION

1. In this unit, we'll talk about the cardiovascular system—the heart and blood vessels that provide blood circulation to the entire body. Heart disease continues to be a major health problem, and one which increasingly affects the insurance industry, especially in the area of workers compensation. We'll also talk about strokes, which involve the brain, in this section because of their relationship to the vascular system.

   You should understand that heart attacks and strokes frequently have no direct relationship to traumatic injuries or physical or psychological job stress. In most cases, heart attacks and strokes result from a preexisting condition or disease. Nevertheless, claimants have sometimes been able to make a valid insurance claim for aggravation of the problem.

   For these reasons, we hope to give you a basic understanding of heart anatomy and discuss what happens when a heart attack or stroke occurs. Our discussion of the heart's anatomy will be broad rather than detailed, focusing on the functions you need to know to understand what occurs in diseased hearts and how that relates to claims.

   For the most part, when you see a claim involving a heart attack or stroke, you know that the claimant's condition was most likely caused by

   A. a traumatic injury.

   B. job stress.

   C. a preexisting condition or disease.

HEART ANATOMY AND FUNCTION

2. The heart acts as a pump to circulate blood throughout the body. It has two sides, each with a distinct function.

   Let's first examine how the **right side** of the heart functions. As you study the following illustrations, keep in mind that the *right* side of the heart is on *your left* as you look at the illustrations.

How the Right Side of the Heart
Functions

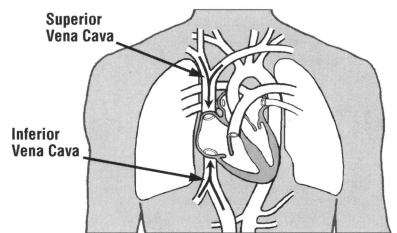

**Superior
Vena Cava**

**Inferior
Vena Cava**

The right side of the heart
receives blood returning
from other parts of the body
through the large veins
called *vena cavae.*

Each vena cava empties the
blood into the *right atrium,*
which is a kind of holding tank.

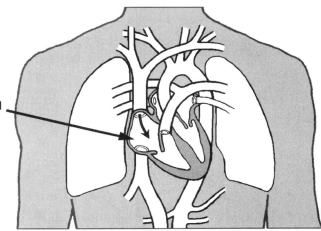

**Right
Atrium**

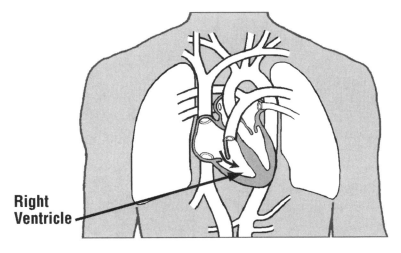

At the next heartbeat, blood
from the right atrium is
released into the *right
ventricle,* which is the
actual pumping mechanism.

**Right
Ventricle**

Match the description of the heart function in the left-hand column with the part of the heart that performs this function in the right-hand column.

1. Bring blood returning from other parts of the body into the right side of the heart

2. Holding receptacle for blood returning from the body

3. Pumping mechanism for the right side of the heart

_____ A. Right ventricle

_____ B. Superior and inferior vena cavae

_____ C. Right atrium

CHECKYOURANSWERHERECHECKYOURANSWERHERECHECKYOURANSWERHERE
CHECKYOURANSWERHERECHECKYOURANSWERHERECHECKYOURANSWERHERE
CHECKYOURANSWERHERECHECKYOURANSWERHERECHECKYOURANSWERHERE
CHECKYOURANSWERHERECHECKYOURANSWERHERECHECKYOURANSWERHERE

3. The blood received by the right atrium is "used" because it has expended all of its oxygen in other parts of the body. It must receive more oxygen before it is recirculated into the body. The blood is circulated to the lungs and back to the heart through the **pulmonary arteries** and the **pulmonary veins**, as shown in the following illustrations:

The Pulmonary Arteries and Pulmonary Veins

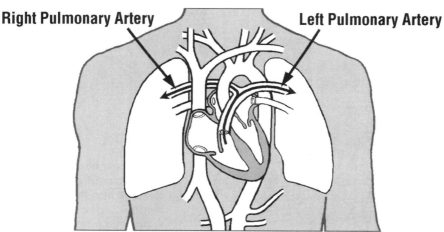

Right Pulmonary Artery   **Left Pulmonary Artery**

The right ventricle pumps the blood into the right and left *pulmonary arteries*, which carry the blood to the lungs.

Having picked up oxygen in the lungs, the blood is returned to the *left atrium* by the *pulmonary veins*. As in the right atrium, the left atrium holds the blood until a heartbeat sends it into the *left ventricle*.

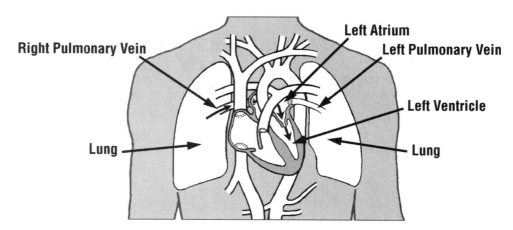

Right Pulmonary Vein   **Left Atrium**
Left Pulmonary Vein
Left Ventricle
Lung   **Lung**

True or false?

A. Blood is carried from the right ventricle to the lungs by the pulmonary arteries.   ( ) True   ( ) False

B. Blood returns to the heart from the lungs through the pulmonary veins.   ( ) True   ( ) False

C. Blood is circulated to the lungs so that oxygen can be added to the blood.   ( ) True   ( ) False

D. The right side of the heart receives the oxygenated blood returning from the lungs.   ( ) True   ( ) False

E. Blood returning from the lungs is held in the left ventricle until a heartbeat sends it to the left atrium.   ( ) True   ( ) False

CHECKYOURANSWERHERECHECKYOURANSWERHERECHECKYOURANSWERHERE
CHECKYOURANSWERHERECHECKYOURANSWERHERECHECKYOURANSWERHERE
CHECKYOURANSWERHERECHECKYOURANSWERHERECHECKYOURANSWERHERE
CHECKYOURANSWERHERECHECKYOURANSWERHERECHECKYOURANSWERHERE

4. After the left ventricle has received the oxygenated blood, the blood is circulated throughout the body through the aorta, arteries, and capillaries, as shown in the following illustrations:

Aorta, Arteries, and Capillaries

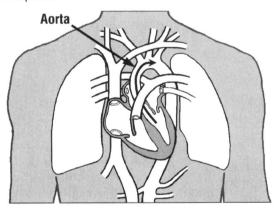

When the left ventricle receives the oxygenated blood, it then pumps it through the *aorta*, which is the large main trunk of the circulatory system.

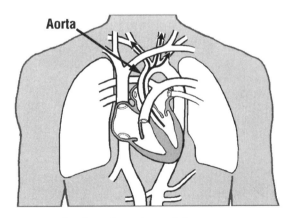

The three branches of the aorta carry the blood to all parts of the body through the *arteries*.

The arteries branch to smaller and smaller arteries, and finally, to microscopic *capillaries*, where the functions of the blood (such as carrying nutrients and oxygen to tissues) are performed,

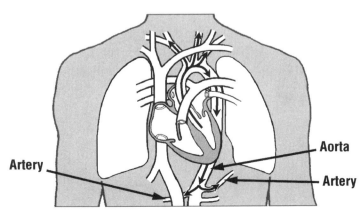

Having performed its functions, the blood flows on into veins of ever-increasing size as the blood is returned, finally, through the large vena cavae into the right atrium. The blood has now come full circle and is once again ready to be pumped to the lungs.

Following are the four steps involved as the left ventricle pumps oxygenated blood into the aorta and throughout the body. Put these steps in the order that they occur by labeling them 1, 2, 3, or 4.

_____ A. Blood is carried through arteries and into the capillaries, where the functions of the blood are performed.

_____ B. After having circulated throughout the body, the blood is returned through the large vena cavae into the right atrium, ready to be pumped into the lungs.

_____ C. The three branches of the aorta carry the blood to the arteries.

_____ D. The left ventricle pumps oxygenated blood through the aorta.

CHECKYOURANSWERHERECHECKYOURANSWERHERECHECKYOURANSWERHERE
CHECKYOURANSWERHERECHECKYOURANSWERHERECHECKYOURANSWERHERE
CHECKYOURANSWERHERECHECKYOURANSWERHERECHECKYOURANSWERHERE
CHECKYOURANSWERHERECHECKYOURANSWERHERECHECKYOURANSWERHERE

5. The heart itself receives its blood supply from the **coronary arteries**, which are the first branches of the aorta. The coronary arteries function as the other arteries do, carrying blood to the capillaries, then on to veins which return to the right atrium. As you will see, it is the coronary arteries that are most often affected by heart disease, resulting in conditions which may arise in claims.

Coronary Arteries

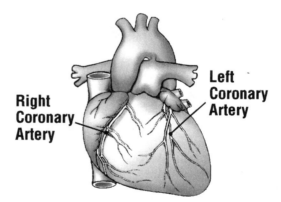

Right Coronary Artery

Left Coronary Artery

Which of the following statements concerning the coronary arteries are true?

A. They supply blood to the heart.

B. They are never affected by heart disease.

C. They are the first branches of the aorta.

CHECKYOURANSWERHERECHECKYOURANSWERHERECHECKYOURANSWERHERE
CHECKYOURANSWERHERECHECKYOURANSWERHERECHECKYOURANSWERHERE
CHECKYOURANSWERHERECHECKYOURANSWERHERECHECKYOURANSWERHERE
CHECKYOURANSWERHERECHECKYOURANSWERHERECHECKYOURANSWERHERE

6. Take a moment to review what you've just learned about the heart and blood circulation. Check all of the following statements that are correct.

   A. Blood that has circulated throughout the body is returned to the right side of the heart through large veins called pulmonary arteries.

   B. The holding receptacle of each side of the heart is called the atrium.

   C. The heartbeat releases blood from the holding receptacles on each side of the heart into the ventricles.

   D. Blood is pumped from the right ventricle to the lungs through the pulmonary veins.

   E. Blood is pumped to the lungs to receive oxygen.

   F. The vessels that return the blood to the left atrium from the lungs are called pulmonary veins.

   G. Blood is pumped from the left ventricle into the arteries through the capillaries.

   H. The microscopic vessels where the blood performs its functions for the rest of the body are called capillaries.

   I. The veins lead to the vessels that return the blood to the heart, which are called capillaries.

   J. The first branches of the aorta to the arteries which supply blood to the heart itself are called coronary arteries.

CHECKYOURANSWERHERECHECKYOURANSWERHERECHECKYOURANSWERHERE
CHECKYOURANSWERHERECHECKYOURANSWERHERECHECKYOURANSWERHERE
CHECKYOURANSWERHERECHECKYOURANSWERHERECHECKYOURANSWERHERE
CHECKYOURANSWERHERECHECKYOURANSWERHERECHECKYOURANSWERHERE

MYOCARDIAL INFARCTION

7. Having studied the heart's circulatory function in an elementary way, we can begin to sense the importance of its continuing to operate normally. Unfortunately, a large percentage of the United States population suffers from some type of **heart disease** which eventually leads to an event called a **heart attack**.

   The term *heart attack* actually describes the symptoms preceding and accompanying a condition called **myocardial infarction**. *Myocardial* refers to the muscular part of the heart. *Infarction* is the cell death of an area of tissue which occurs when its blood supply is cut off.

   What, then, is myocardial infarction?

   A. The condition of the heart muscle that precedes a heart attack

   B. A lack of blood supply to the heart

   C. The death of some areas of tissue in the heart muscle

   D. The death of any muscle in the human body

CHECKYOURANSWERHERECHECKYOURANSWERHERECHECKYOURANSWERHERE
CHECKYOURANSWERHERECHECKYOURANSWERHERECHECKYOURANSWERHERE
CHECKYOURANSWERHERECHECKYOURANSWERHERECHECKYOURANSWERHERE
CHECKYOURANSWERHERECHECKYOURANSWERHERECHECKYOURANSWERHERE

8. Myocardial infarction usually occurs because blood is no longer flowing to a portion of the heart. This disruption in blood flow causes a squeezing type of pain in the middle of the chest that sometimes radiates down the arm or into the jaw or back.

   But what causes the blood to stop flowing? There are a number of possibilities, including **atherosclerosis of the coronary arteries** and **coronary thrombosis**. There are also other, more remote reasons for myocardial infarctions, but they will not be discussed here.

   A. What is the usual cause of myocardial infarction? _____
   _____

   B. Name two conditions that may cause the situation you named in the previous question.

   1. _____

   2. _____

CHECKYOURANSWERHERECHECKYOURANSWERHERECHECKYOURANSWERHERE
CHECKYOURANSWERHERECHECKYOURANSWERHERECHECKYOURANSWERHERE
CHECKYOURANSWERHERECHECKYOURANSWERHERECHECKYOURANSWERHERE
CHECKYOURANSWERHERECHECKYOURANSWERHERECHECKYOURANSWERHERE

Atherosclerosis

9. **Atherosclerosis** is the most prevalent form of **arteriosclerosis** (hardening of the arteries). Atherosclerosis is a buildup of plaque in an artery which provides blood to the heart itself caused by accumulated **lipids,** or fatty substances. The following illustrations depict the difference between a healthy artery and one with atherosclerosis:

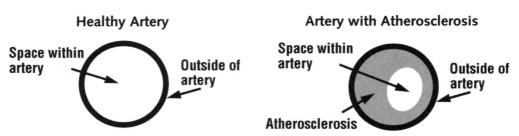

   Some factors which may increase the incidence of atherosclerosis include:

   ■ Hypertension

   ■ Abnormalities in blood lipids, such as high cholesterol levels

   ■ Genetic factors

   ■ Diabetes mellitus

   ■ Smoking

   ■ Obesity

Other factors which may have a relationship to atherosclerosis include emotional stress and a lack of physical activity.

Which of the following individuals may be at risk for atherosclerosis?

A. Mai Chang has a history of low blood pressure.

B. Margaret Hope is obese and confined to a wheelchair.

C. Brian Sellers smokes three packs of cigarettes per day.

D. Bess Williams is extremely underweight.

E. George Adams has a high blood cholesterol level.

CHECKYOURANSWERHERECHECKYOURANSWERHERECHECKYOURANSWERHERE
CHECKYOURANSWERHERECHECKYOURANSWERHERECHECKYOURANSWERHERE
CHECKYOURANSWERHERECHECKYOURANSWERHERECHECKYOURANSWERHERE
CHECKYOURANSWERHERECHECKYOURANSWERHERECHECKYOURANSWERHERE

10. Atherosclerosis is a progressive heart disease, which means the condition gradually worsens, and it usually does not have any symptoms until some other closely related condition occurs, and the combined effect brings about myocardial infarction. The subsequent hospitalization then frequently reveals atherosclerosis for the first time.

    There are other conditions that arise from atherosclerosis in addition to myocardial infarction, but at this point, we're only interested in how it affects myocardial infarction.

    Review what you know about atherosclerosis and its effect on myocardial infarction by answering the following true/false questions.

    A. Myocardial infarction in a patient with a history of smoking, high blood pressure, obesity, diabetes, or high blood cholesterol levels may have been caused by atherosclerosis.   ( ) True   ( ) False

    B. Atherosclerosis always results in myocardial infarction.   ( ) True   ( ) False

    C. The arteries involved in atherosclerosis causing myocardial infarction are those which pump blood to the heart for its own use.   ( ) True   ( ) False

    D. The occurrence of myocardial infarction frequently coincides with the first diagnosis of atherosclerosis.   ( ) True   ( ) False

CHECKYOURANSWERHERECHECKYOURANSWERHERECHECKYOURANSWERHERE
CHECKYOURANSWERHERECHECKYOURANSWERHERECHECKYOURANSWERHERE
CHECKYOURANSWERHERECHECKYOURANSWERHERECHECKYOURANSWERHERE
CHECKYOURANSWERHERECHECKYOURANSWERHERECHECKYOURANSWERHERE

Coronary Thrombosis

11. A **coronary thrombosis** may also cause the lack of blood flow to the heart that results in myocardial infarction. A **thrombosis** is the presence of a blood clot which can close off the passageway through an artery.

    A closed passageway is known as an **occlusion,** and the terms **coronary thrombosis** and **coronary occlusion** are often used interchangeably, even though an occlusion can be caused by something other than a blood clot.

Which of the following statements concerning a coronary thrombosis are true?

A. It may be the cause of myocardial infarction.

B. It refers to a blood clot in a coronary artery.

C. It is caused by a coronary occlusion.

D. It may prevent the flow of blood through a coronary artery.

E. It is the only type of occlusion that occurs in a coronary artery.

Physical Activity and Emotional Stress

12. We've seen that atherosclerosis and coronary thrombosis may be the primary factors in myocardial infarction. But what exactly causes myocardial infarction to occur at a given time is still not completely understood.

    In some cases, physical activity or emotional stress is believed to be the immediate cause; but there are many cases where nothing different in the person's life occurred prior to the myocardial infarction, and in fact, many times it happens while the patient is asleep.

    In a heart diseased with atherosclerosis, it's generally agreed that an increase in physical activity or emotional stress—either of which can cause the heart to work harder—may aggravate the condition and cause myocardial infarction.

    The fact that the heart is not healthy is primary; a normal heart is rarely damaged by physical activity or emotional stress. It is important to remember, however, that there is not complete agreement regarding the effects of physical activity or emotional stress on the heart generally, and its relationship to myocardial infarction specifically.

    Which one of the following statements concerning the relationship between an increase in physical activity or emotional stress and myocardial infarction is true?

    A. Myocardial infarction is always caused by an increase in physical activity or emotional stress, even in patients with healthy hearts.

    B. Myocardial infarction is never caused by an increase in physical activity or emotional stress, even in patients with atherosclerosis.

    C. The relationship between increases in physical activity or emotional stress and myocardial infarction is unclear.

13. The effects of physical effort or emotional stress on the formation of a coronary thrombus leading to myocardial infarction are even less clearly defined, since it's often difficult to determine what produces the clot. To

further complicate matters, advanced atherosclerosis may cause changes in the artery, which in turn eventually cause a thrombus. In this case, the thrombus is believed to have been caused by stress or effort.

However, it's important to note that if stress or effort is a factor in forming the blood clot, hours or even days may pass before the symptoms of myocardial infarction appear. This is because a thrombus can form and move through the blood vessels without causing symptoms until it reaches a vessel that is too small for it to pass through. At that point, occlusion of the vessel occurs, and is soon followed by symptoms as the blood stops flowing normally. If this happens in a coronary artery, myocardial infarction occurs.

On the other hand, parts of the thrombus may break off, and if the pieces are small enough, they can pass through the arteries without causing occlusion. However, even small parts of a thrombus can cause occlusion in some of the very small blood vessels.

The important thing to remember about the time lapse between the formation of a thrombus and the appearance of symptoms is that if the thrombus forms near the heart, it has less time to break up before entering the coronary arteries. Therefore, if the thrombus occurs some distance from the heart, myocardial infarction symptoms are more likely to begin later.

Why is there sometimes a time lapse of hours or even days between the formation of a thrombus and the appearance of the symptoms of myocardial infarction? _____

_____

_____

CHECKYOURANSWERHERECHECKYOURANSWERHERECHECKYOURANSWERHERE
CHECKYOURANSWERHERECHECKYOURANSWERHERECHECKYOURANSWERHERE
CHECKYOURANSWERHERECHECKYOURANSWERHERECHECKYOURANSWERHERE
CHECKYOURANSWERHERECHECKYOURANSWERHERECHECKYOURANSWERHERE

14. It's apparent that there are many uncertainties about the relationship of physical activity and emotional stress to myocardial infarction, and it is beyond the scope of this course to look at all of the possibilities. This is an area which requires experience and continued learning on the part of the claim examiner. The information you've received here should give you the foundation for that continuing growth in understanding the many nuances of cardiovascular claims.

Answer the following questions to review your knowledge of myocardial infarction before proceeding to the next section.

A. Name the two most common causes of myocardial infarction.

1. _____

2. _____

B. What is atherosclerosis? _____

_____

C. What is a coronary thrombosis? _____

_____

D. Select the best answer. What causes myocardial infarction?

1. An increase in physical activity or emotional stress, which causes the heart to work harder.

2. A decrease in physical activity or emotional stress, which causes the heart to stop beating.

3. Exactly what causes myocardial infarction to occur at a given time is not completely understood.

CEREBROVASCULAR ACCIDENTS

15. A **cerebrovascular accident (CVA)** is a **stroke**. The terms CVA and *stroke* are actually more descriptive than technical. They generally refer to the signs and symptoms of either **ischemia** or **hemorrhage**.

   The term *ischemia* means a temporary disruption of blood flow to a part of the body, so an *ischemic stroke* is one where the blood flow to the brain is temporarily interrupted. *Hemorrhage* is uncontrolled bleeding anywhere in the body; a *hemorrhagic stroke* involves heavy bleeding within the brain.

   A. An ischemic stroke involves

   1. a temporary disruption of blood flow to the brain.

   2. bleeding within the brain.

   B. A hemorrhagic stroke involves

   1. bleeding within the brain.

   2. a temporary disruption of blood flow to the brain.

16. A stroke usually comes on abruptly, and the symptoms may last anywhere from 24 to 48 hours. Some of the more common symptoms of a stroke are:

   ■ Paralysis or numbness that affects only one side of the body **(hemiplegia, hemianesthesia)**

   ■ Loss of half of the field of vision in one or both eyes **(hemianopia)**

   ■ Loss or impairment of the ability to communicate orally or in writing **(aphasia)**

■ Loss or impairment of the ability to move the body when there is no underlying muscular paralysis **(apraxia)**

Headaches, coma, a sudden rise in blood pressure, mental confusion, and seizures are common symptoms of a hemorrhagic stroke.

A stroke almost always has permanent effects on the patient, the most common of which are speech problems and paralysis.

Which of the followings statements concerning strokes and stroke symptoms are correct?

A. A stroke never has any type of permanent effect on the patient.

B. Headaches, mental confusion, and seizures are usually present with ischemic strokes.

C. Hemiplegia is paralysis that affects only one side of the body.

D. Aphasia is the loss or impairment of the ability to communicate, either orally or in writing.

E. A stroke usually comes on abruptly, and the symptoms usually last anywhere from 24–48 hours.

F. Apraxia is a loss of sensation that affects both sides of the body.

Ischemic Stroke

17. An **ischemic stroke** is one that occurs when an obstruction prevents the flow of blood through an artery to a portion of the brain. In the brain, if ischemia lasts for more than a few minutes, infarction results.

From our discussion of myocardial infarction, you know this means that a portion of the brain tissue

A. occludes.

B. becomes filled with blood.

C. becomes atherosclerotic.

D. dies.

18. An ischemic stroke may result from a number of causes, including the presence of a thrombus, a term you've already learned, or the presence of an **embolus.**

An embolus is **any kind of obstruction in an artery**. It might be a blood clot or another substance, such as air, fat, or a tumor. With an ischemic stroke, however, an embolus is frequently a blood clot which became detached from another thrombus within the body and moved to a cranial artery, stopping the blood flow there.

Let's clarify the difference between a thrombus and an embolus before we go on.

A. A/an (thrombus/embolus) _____ is always made up of blood; it is never formed by any other substance, such as air or fat.

B. A/an (thrombus/embolus) _____ can be made up of blood or of other substances, such as air or fat.

CHECKYOURANSWERHERECHECKYOURANSWERHERECHECKYOURANSWERHERE
CHECKYOURANSWERHERECHECKYOURANSWERHERECHECKYOURANSWERHERE
CHECKYOURANSWERHERECHECKYOURANSWERHERECHECKYOURANSWERHERE
CHECKYOURANSWERHERECHECKYOURANSWERHERECHECKYOURANSWERHERE

19. It would be impossible for us to discuss all of the causes which might result in a thrombus or embolus developing, leading to an ischemic stroke. Some of the more common causes are:

■ Atherosclerosis

■ Arteritis (inflammation of an artery)

■ Rheumatic heart disease

■ Hypertension

■ Hypotension

■ Acute blood loss

■ Myocardial infarction

Because ischemia follows many of the same patterns as myocardial infarction, a claim involving this type of stroke requires many of the same considerations—previous medical history, disease, and any stress or physical exertion that may have preceded or precipitated the stroke. However, it should also be noted that ischemic stroke more often occurs when the individual is asleep or resting, when the blood is flowing more slowly and is more likely to clot.

A. Which of the following conditions can cause a thrombus or embolus to form, thus leading to an ischemic stroke?
   1. Atherosclerosis
   2. Arteritis
   3. Rheumatic heart disease
   4. Hypertension or hypotension
   5. Acute blood loss
   6. Myocardial infarction
   7. All of these conditions can cause a thrombus or embolus to form and cause an ischemic stroke

B. An ischemic stroke is more likely to occur when the individual is asleep or resting because _____
_____.

Transient Ischemic Attack

20. **Transient ischemic attacks (TIAs)** produce the same symptoms as ischemic strokes, except the symptoms are of a shorter duration (anywhere from a few minutes to an hour or two) and there are no permanent effects. A TIA may be a warning signal of an impending ischemic stroke, although some patients may suffer a series of TIAs without ever having an ischemic stroke. Hypertension and atherosclerosis may be contributing causes of TIAs.

    Hubert Parker has suffered a TIA. Which of the following statements concerning his condition are true?

    A. He will definitely suffer an ischemic stroke in the future.

    B. He may suffer a series of TIAs without ever having an ischemic stroke.

    C. He will not have any permanent effects from the TIA.

Hemorrhagic Stroke

21. **Hemorrhagic stroke** occurs when there is bleeding into brain tissue (such as an **intracerebral hemorrhage**) or into the spaces between the meninges (such as a **subarachnoid hemorrhage**). We discussed some of this type of bleeding in an earlier unit as it applied to traumatic injuries to the head. With a stroke, however, the hemorrhage usually does not result from trauma, but from the rupture of a blood vessel diseased from hypertension or, occasionally, other diseases.

    A hemorrhagic stroke, unlike an ischemic stroke, often occurs during overexertion or excitement, which increases the blood pressure. This increased pressure then causes the diseased and weakened vessel to rupture.

    Why do hemorrhagic strokes occur more often during overexertion or excitement? _____

    _____

22. For each statement below, write in an **I** if it applies to an ischemic stroke, an **H** if it applies to a hemorrhagic stroke, or a **T** if it applies to a transient ischemic attack.

_____ A. Lasts a short time and has no permanent effects

_____ B. Temporary disruption of blood flow to the brain

_____ C. Bleeding into the brain or the spaces between the meninges

_____ D. Headaches, coma, seizures, mental confusion, and a sudden rise in blood pressure are all common symptoms of this type of stroke

_____ E. Usually caused by a thrombus or an embolus

_____ F. Usually caused by a sudden rupture of a diseased blood vessel

_____ G. Produces the same symptoms as an ischemic stroke

CHECKYOURANSWERHERECHECKYOURANSWERHERECHECKYOURANSWERHERE
CHECKYOURANSWERHERECHECKYOURANSWERHERECHECKYOURANSWERHERE
CHECKYOURANSWERHERECHECKYOURANSWERHERECHECKYOURANSWERHERE
CHECKYOURANSWERHERECHECKYOURANSWERHERECHECKYOURANSWERHERE

REVIEW

23. Both heart attacks and strokes present special problems and challenges to a claim professional. The general understanding you've gained in this unit should serve you well as your education continues.

   You'll discover a similar challenge when you study the respiratory system in the next unit. But before you proceed, complete the following review exercises.

Match the description of the heart or circulatory system function in the left-hand column with the part of the heart or circulatory system listed in the right-hand column that performs this function.

1. Main trunk of the circulatory system

2. Bring unoxygenated blood returning from the body into the right side of the heart

3. Pumps oxygenated blood through the aorta

4. Holding receptacle for blood returning from the body

5. Carry unoxygenated blood to the lungs

6. Carry oxygenated blood to the left atrium

7. Holds oxygenated blood until a heartbeat sends it into the left ventricle

8. Supply blood to the heart itself

9. Receive blood from the aorta and circulate it into the capillaries

10. Pumping mechanism for the right side of the heart

_____ A. Left ventricle

_____ B. Right atrium

_____ C. Coronary arteries

_____ D. Vena cavae

_____ E. Arteries

_____ F. Aorta

_____ G. Right ventricle

_____ H. Left atrium

_____ I. Pulmonary veins

_____ J. Pulmonary arteries

CHECKYOURANSWERHERECHECKYOURANSWERHERECHECKYOURANSWERHERE
CHECKYOURANSWERHERECHECKYOURANSWERHERECHECKYOURANSWERHERE
CHECKYOURANSWERHERECHECKYOURANSWERHERECHECKYOURANSWERHERE
CHECKYOURANSWERHERECHECKYOURANSWERHERECHECKYOURANSWERHERE

24. Answer the following true/false questions about myocardial infarction.

A. It is a condition where tissue in the heart muscle dies because the blood supply to the heart has been cut off for some reason.   ( ) True   ( ) False

B. Two of the most common causes of myocardial infarction as stated in the text are atherosclerosis of the coronary arteries and physical or emotional stress.   ( ) True   ( ) False

C. A thrombosis is a blood clot that can close off the passageway through an artery.   ( ) True   ( ) False

D. The terms *coronary thrombosis* and *coronary occlusion* are often used interchangeably because both terms describe a blood clot that has blocked an artery.   ( ) True   ( ) False

E. It is generally agreed that an increase in physical activity or emotional stress can cause myocardial infarction in a person with atherosclerosis.   ( ) True   ( ) False

25. Complete the following *fill in the blank* exercises about cardiovascular accidents.

   A. The terms CVA and stroke actually refer to the signs and symptoms of either a temporary disruption of blood flow to the brain, which is called _____ stroke; or bleeding into the brain tissues or between the meninges, which is called _____ stroke.

   B. Which type of stroke is usually caused by a thrombus or embolus?
   _____

   C. How does an embolus differ from a thrombus? _____
   _____
   _____

   D. If ischemia in the brain lasts for more than a few minutes, what results? _____

   E. Describe the difference between ischemic and hemorrhagic stroke regarding when they are likely to occur. _____
   _____

   F. How does an increase in blood pressure often cause a hemorrhagic stroke? _____

   G. Name two key differences between an ischemic stroke and a transient ischemic attack. _____
   _____

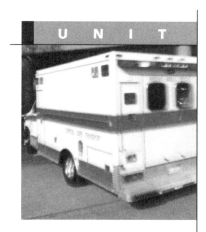

UNIT

9

The Respiratory System

INTRODUCTION

1. In this unit, we'll study the respiratory system in much the same way that we did the cardiovascular system. We'll start with a simple explanation of the anatomy and functions of the lung, then move on to brief discussions of lung injuries that may be involved in chest injuries and common occupational lung diseases.

    As in the previous unit, we will cover basic introductory information only. While the complete respiratory, or pulmonary, system includes all of the structures that lead to the lungs, such as the nasal passages, we will only discuss the anatomy of the lungs themselves.

    After you have completed this unit, you should

    A. understand the anatomy and functions of the complete respiratory system.
    B. have a basic understanding of the anatomy and functions of the lungs.
    C. know more about common injuries and occupational diseases involving the lungs.

CHECKYOURANSWERHERECHECKYOURANSWERHERECHECKYOURANSWERHERE
CHECKYOURANSWERHERECHECKYOURANSWERHERECHECKYOURANSWERHERE
CHECKYOURANSWERHERECHECKYOURANSWERHERECHECKYOURANSWERHERE
CHECKYOURANSWERHERECHECKYOURANSWERHERECHECKYOURANSWERHERE

LUNG ANATOMY AND FUNCTION

2. The lungs lie on either side of the heart, within and protected by the rib cage. They are divided into **lobes**, with one lung having two lobes and the other three. Study the following illustration, then go on to the questions that follow.

Right and Left Lungs

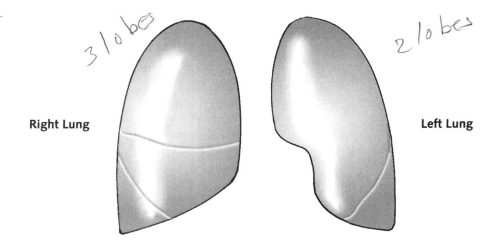

Right Lung   **Left Lung**

A. Which lung has three lobes?
   1. Right lung
   2. Left lung

B. How many lobes does the left lung have?
   1. 3
   2. 2
   3. 1
   4. 4

CHECKYOURANSWERHERECHECKYOURANSWERHERECHECKYOURANSWERHERE
CHECKYOURANSWERHERECHECKYOURANSWERHERECHECKYOURANSWERHERE
CHECKYOURANSWERHERECHECKYOURANSWERHERECHECKYOURANSWERHERE
CHECKYOURANSWERHERECHECKYOURANSWERHERECHECKYOURANSWERHERE

3.   The following illustrations show how the lungs work:

Trachea and Primary Bronchi

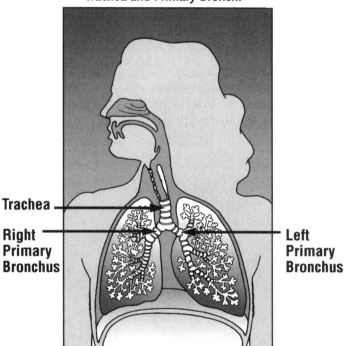

Secondary Bronchi

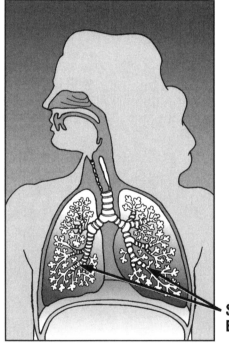

Air is brought into the lobes of the lungs through the *trachea*, or *windpipe*, which divides into two primary branches, one going into each lung. Each branch is called a *bronchus* (plural is *bronchi*).

The primary bronchi divide into smaller *secondary bronchi*. A secondary bronchus reaches into each of the lobes in both the right and left lungs.

Bronchioles and Alveoli

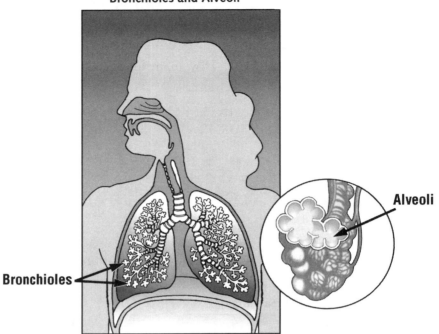

In each lobe, the bronchi continue to subdivide into smaller and smaller branches called *bronchioles,* such as the *respiratory bronchioles* and the *terminal bronchioles,* until finally they end in *alveoli* (singular is *alveolus*), or *air sacs.*

A. The air-carrying structures that extend from the windpipe into each lung are called the _____.

B. What is the technical name for the windpipe? _____

C. How many primary bronchi are there? _____

D. Where do the secondary bronchi lead? _____

E. The termination point of the bronchi and bronchioles are the _____.

CHECKYOURANSWERHERECHECKYOURANSWERHERECHECKYOURANSWERHERE
CHECKYOURANSWERHERECHECKYOURANSWERHERECHECKYOURANSWERHERE
CHECKYOURANSWERHERECHECKYOURANSWERHERECHECKYOURANSWERHERE
CHECKYOURANSWERHERECHECKYOURANSWERHERECHECKYOURANSWERHERE

4. You'll recall from our discussion of the cardiovascular system that the blood picks up oxygen in the lungs. This occurs at each alveolus. At the alveolus, only a thin membrane separates the blood from the inhaled air, allowing the blood to be oxygenated.

Where in the lungs does the blood pick up oxygen?

A. Trachea

B. Primary bronchi

C. Secondary bronchi

D. Alveoli

CHECKYOURANSWERHERECHECKYOURANSWERHERECHECKYOURANSWERHERE
CHECKYOURANSWERHERECHECKYOURANSWERHERECHECKYOURANSWERHERE
CHECKYOURANSWERHERECHECKYOURANSWERHERECHECKYOURANSWERHERE
CHECKYOURANSWERHERECHECKYOURANSWERHERECHECKYOURANSWERHERE

5. The lungs are designed to:

■ Move air in and out of the alveoli

■ Distribute air in the alveoli

■ Diffuse gases, such as oxygen and carbon dioxide, into the blood

These functions can be impaired by various forms of injury or disease to the lungs, as you will see as you progress through this unit.

Before you go on to the next section, review what you've learned about basic lung anatomy and functions by matching the part of the lung listed in the left-hand column with its correct description in the right-hand column.

1. Right lung
2. Trachea
3. Primary bronchi
4. Secondary bronchi
5. Bronchioles
6. Alveoli
7. Left lung

_____ A. Smaller branches of the secondary bronchi that end in alveoli
_____ B. Has three lobes
_____ C. Divides into smaller secondary branches
_____ D. Reaches into each of the lobes in both the right and left lungs
_____ E. Add oxygen to blood
_____ F. Has two lobes
_____ G. Divides into two primary branches

LUNG INJURIES

6. Traumatic chest injuries often cause injury to the lungs. The most common type of lung injuries involve the **pleural space**, or **chest cavity**.

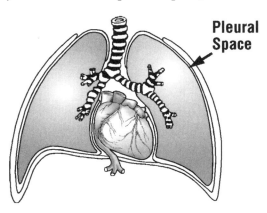

Pleural Space

Pleural refers to a membrane called the **pleura** that surrounds the lungs. It releases a secretion that reduces friction during the lungs' breathing motions.

The **pleural space** is the potential space between two layers of the pleura, including a layer that enters into the lungs' lobes. If it is damaged, the lungs can malfunction.

A. What is the function of the pleura?_____

_____

B. What is the pleural space?_____

_____

C. What can happen if the pleural space is damaged?_____

_____

7. Three common conditions that may occur if a chest injury damages the pleural space are:

   ■ Hemothorax

   ■ Pneumothorax

   ■ Hemopneumothorax

   In each of these conditions, **thorax** means **in the pleural space**. **Hemothorax** is **blood** in the pleural space; **pneumothorax** is **air** in the pleural space. **Hemopneumothorax**, then, is **both** blood and air in the pleural space. We'll discuss each of these conditions in more detail in the next few frames.

   A. A claimant who has a hemothorax has (blood/air/both blood and air) _____ in the pleural space.

   B. A claimant who has air in the pleural space has a (hemothorax/ pneumothorax) _____.

   C. A claimant with a hemopneumothorax has (blood/air/both blood and air) _____ in the pleural space.

Hemothorax

8. **Hemothorax** is caused by laceration of the blood vessels in the lungs, or of the lungs themselves. When blood is present in the pleural space, pressure builds up, and the lungs can collapse, as shown in the illustration on the right:

Hemothorax

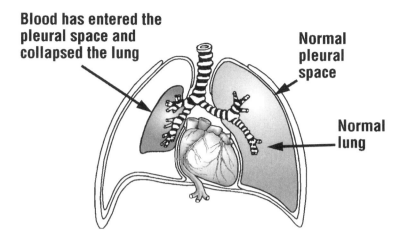

Blood has entered the pleural space and collapsed the lung

Normal pleural space

Normal lung

A hemothorax interferes with the normal functioning of the respiratory system, so the patient will have trouble breathing. If it is not treated promptly, the patient may go into shock.

A. Which of the following can cause a hemothorax?

   1. Laceration of blood vessels in the lungs

   2. Laceration of the lungs

   3. Both of the above

B. A fracture to which one of these bones might cause a hemothorax?

   1. Humerus

   2. Rib

   3. Hip

C. Name two possible complications of a hemothorax.

   1. _____

   2. _____

CHECKYOURANSWERHERECHECKYOURANSWERHERECHECKYOURANSWERHERE
CHECKYOURANSWERHERECHECKYOURANSWERHERECHECKYOURANSWERHERE
CHECKYOURANSWERHERECHECKYOURANSWERHERECHECKYOURANSWERHERE
CHECKYOURANSWERHERECHECKYOURANSWERHERECHECKYOURANSWERHERE

Treatment of Hemothorax

9. A hemothorax can be diagnosed and, occasionally, treated through a procedure called **thoracentesis:**

Thoracentesis

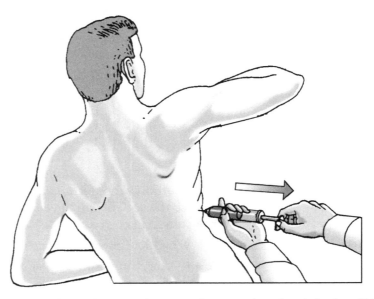

A needle is inserted into the space between the seventh and eighth ribs. If blood can be drawn out, a hemathorax is confirmed. In minor cases, if the bleeding has stopped, drawing out the blood by needle may solve the problem. A thoracentesis may also be performed in emergency situations before regular medical care is available.

A more common procedure is **closed chest drainage,** where catheter tubes are surgically inserted into the pleural space to drain the blood:

Closed Chest Drainage

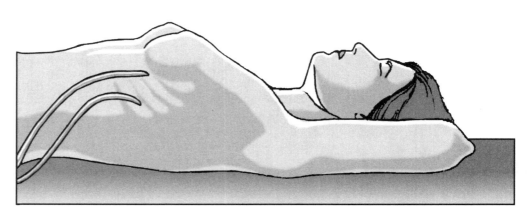

This procedure helps the collapsed lung expand again because the pressure that has built up is returned to normal.

If the bleeding continues for an extended period of time or is unusually heavy, a **thoracotomy,** or surgical incision into the chest wall, may be performed. In this situation, treatment of the hemothorax depends on what the surgeon finds after the incision is made.

For each of the following statements, write in a **TH** if it describes thoracentesis, a **C** if it describes closed chest drainage, or a **TC** if it describes a thoracotomy.

____ A. Catheter tubes are surgically inserted into the pleural space to drain blood.

____ B. Surgical incision is made into the chest wall.

____ C. It may be used to treat a hemothorax if the bleeding has stopped.

____ D. It is sometimes used in emergency situations before regular medical care is available.

____ E. It is generally used only if the bleeding has continued for an extended period of time or is unusually heavy.

Pneumothorax

10. A **pneumothorax**, or air in the pleural space, can occur in one of three ways:

■ A traumatic injury to the chest creates a hole in the chest wall which allows air to flow in and out of the pleural space. This is called an **open pneumothorax**.

■ Chronic lung disorders, such as emphysema, cause a part of the respiratory system to rupture and leak air into the pleural space. This is called a **spontaneous pneumothorax**. In some cases, a spontaneous pneumothorax will develop in a previously healthy individual for no apparent reason.

■ A puncture wound to the chest allows air to enter the pleural space which then becomes trapped, rather than being expelled through the respiratory processes. This is called a **tension pneumothorax**. Some treatment methods may also cause a tension pneumothorax, such as a mechanical ventilator causing a part of the respiratory system to burst, or a faulty closed chest drainage procedure.

Air in the pleural space causes most of the same problems as blood in this space: a buildup of pressure within the pleural space, the possibility of the lung collapsing, and difficulty in breathing. The same treatment methods used for a hemothorax—thoracentesis, closed chest drainage, thoracotomy—are also used to treat a pneumothorax.

For each of the following statements, write in an **O** if it describes an open pneumothorax, an **S** if it describes a spontaneous pneumothorax, or a **T** if it refers to a tension pneumothorax.

_____ A. It may develop in previously healthy individuals for no apparent reason.

_____ B. A hole in the chest wall caused by traumatic injury allows air to flow in and out of the pleural space.

_____ C. It may be a complication of the use of a mechanical ventilator or a faulty closed chest drainage procedure.

_____ D. Occurs when air enters the pleural space and becomes trapped.

_____ E. It may develop when a chronic lung disease causes part of the respiratory system to collapse and leak air into the pleural space.

CHECKYOURANSWERHERECHECKYOURANSWERHERECHECKYOURANSWERHERE
CHECKYOURANSWERHERECHECKYOURANSWERHERECHECKYOURANSWERHERE
CHECKYOURANSWERHERECHECKYOURANSWERHERECHECKYOURANSWERHERE
CHECKYOURANSWERHERECHECKYOURANSWERHERECHECKYOURANSWERHERE

11. A tension pneumothorax is the most serious type of pneumothorax. If left untreated, it can cause a life-threatening condition called **mediastinal shift**. The **mediastinum** is a cavity that contains the heart, trachea, esophagus, and some of the large blood vessels. A **mediastinal shift** occurs when pressure from the trapped air causes all of these organs to shift to the unaffected side.

Normal Lung

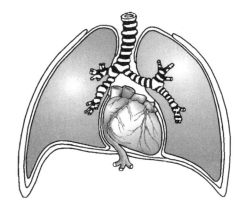

Mediastinal Shift

Air has entered through rupture in pleural space

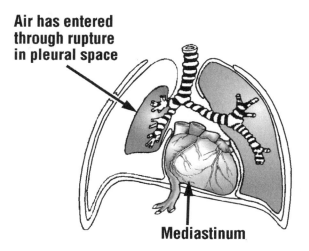

Mediastinum

A mediastinal shift may twist the large blood vessels and impede the flow of blood back to the heart.

A. The cavity that contains the heart, trachea, esophagus, and some of the large blood vessels is the

1. pleural cavity.
2. mediastinum.
3. chest cavity.

B. One of the greatest dangers of a mediastinal shift is that
   1. additional air will flow into the pleural space.
   2. the lungs will rupture.
   3. the flow of blood returning to the heart will be impeded.

CHECKYOURANSWERHERECHECKYOURANSWERHERECHECKYOURANSWERHERE
CHECKYOURANSWERHERECHECKYOURANSWERHERECHECKYOURANSWERHERE
CHECKYOURANSWERHERECHECKYOURANSWERHERECHECKYOURANSWERHERE
CHECKYOURANSWERHERECHECKYOURANSWERHERECHECKYOURANSWERHERE

Hemopneumothorax

12. The final type of problem we mentioned that occurs in the pleural space is **hemopneumothorax**, which involves both blood and air in the pleural space. The problems and treatments we've discussed for hemothorax and pneumothorax also apply to this condition.

    Let's end this section by summarizing with a short review.

    A. Laceration of the blood vessels in the lungs or of the lungs themselves are often the cause of
       1. hemopneumothorax.
       2. hemothorax.
       3. pneumothorax.

    B. All of the following methods may be used to treat a hemothorax, pneumothorax, or hemopneumothorax EXCEPT
       1. closed chest drainage.
       2. thoracentesis.
       3. medication.
       4. thoracotomy.

    C. All of the conditions involving the pleural space discussed in this section can cause the lungs to
       1. collapse.
       2. rupture.
       3. degenerate.

    D. Mediastinal shift is the biggest danger involved with which type of pneumothorax?
       1. Open
       2. Tension
       3. Spontaneous

CHECKYOURANSWERHERECHECKYOURANSWERHERECHECKYOURANSWERHERE
CHECKYOURANSWERHERECHECKYOURANSWERHERECHECKYOURANSWERHERE
CHECKYOURANSWERHERECHECKYOURANSWERHERECHECKYOURANSWERHERE
CHECKYOURANSWERHERECHECKYOURANSWERHERECHECKYOURANSWERHERE

LUNG DISEASES

13. In this section, we'll concentrate on a group of employment-related lung diseases, collectively known as **pneumoconioses**, which can interfere with the proper functioning of the lungs. Pneumoconioses are diseases involving inhalation of various kinds of dusts, such as those from asbestos, rocks, or coal. A patient may be exposed to these various kinds of dusts for a long period of time—anywhere from 10–30 years—before a pneumoconiosis develops.

    Not all types of pneumoconioses result in lung impairment. Some types of dusts—such as those from barium, iron, tin, and most carbons—can be inhaled and retained in the lungs without adverse effects. These are called **benign** pneumoconioses.

    A. Pneumoconioses are a group of lung diseases involving inhalation of various kinds of

       1. toxic chemicals.

       2. dusts.

       3. bacteria.

    B. What type of pneumoconioses do not have an adverse effect on the lungs?

       1. Benign

       2. Toxic

       3. Bacterial

CHECKYOURANSWERHERECHECKYOURANSWERHERECHECKYOURANSWERHERE
CHECKYOURANSWERHERECHECKYOURANSWERHERECHECKYOURANSWERHERE
CHECKYOURANSWERHERECHECKYOURANSWERHERECHECKYOURANSWERHERE
CHECKYOURANSWERHERECHECKYOURANSWERHERECHECKYOURANSWERHERE

14. **Fibrogenic pneumoconioses** are the most common type of pneumoconioses seen in claim work. Fibrogenic pneumoconioses produce abnormal fibrous tissue with nodules scattered throughout the lungs. This impairs the flow and distribution of air and gases within the lungs.

    When a fibrogenic pneumoconiosis is diagnosed, the relationship to the patient's employment environment is often apparent, as you'll see when we look at some specific types of fibrogenic pneumoconioses in the next few frames.

    Fibrogenic pneumoconioses

    A. are the least common type of pneumoconioses seen in claim work.

    B. produce abnormal fibrous tissue with nodules in the lungs.

    C. cause the lungs to collapse.

    D. are usually directly related to the patient's employment.

CHECKYOURANSWERHERECHECKYOURANSWERHERECHECKYOURANSWERHERE
CHECKYOURANSWERHERECHECKYOURANSWERHERECHECKYOURANSWERHERE
CHECKYOURANSWERHERECHECKYOURANSWERHERECHECKYOURANSWERHERE
CHECKYOURANSWERHERECHECKYOURANSWERHERECHECKYOURANSWERHERE

Silicosis

15. **Silicosis** is a fibrogenic pneumoconiosis which results from inhaling **free silica** (quartz) over long periods of time. Free silica is most often found in these industries:

   ■ Mining (lead, copper, hard coal, silver and gold)

   ■ Foundries

   ■ Stonecutting

   ■ Pottery

   Once silicosis is present, it may continue to produce fibroids in the lungs even after the patient is no longer exposed to free silica.

   True or false?

   A. Silicosis always develops within 24 hours of exposure to free silica.
   ( ) True   ( ) False

   B. Silicosis can be cured by simply limiting the patient's exposure to free silica.   ( ) True   ( ) False

   C. People employed in gold mining, stonecutting, and foundries are usually exposed to large amounts of free silica and are therefore at risk of developing silicosis.   ( ) True   ( ) False

16. Two other diseases that often accompany and complicate silicosis are **emphysema** and **tuberculosis**. While we won't discuss either of these diseases in detail, we'll take a brief look at how they interact with silicosis.

   Emphysema causes the air spaces near the **terminal bronchioles** to increase in size, damaging the walls of the alveoli and making it more difficult for the patient to breathe. The patient must breathe harder than normal to force air from the lungs, which in turn may cause the airways to collapse and lead to even more difficulty in breathing. When combined with silicosis, emphysema usually receives the major focus of treatment efforts, since silicosis follows whatever course the emphysema takes. However, one symptom of silicosis which distinguishes it from emphysema is that the lungs' volume eventually becomes greatly reduced.

   Patients who have both silicosis and emphysema are also at risk for spontaneous pneumothorax.

   When emphysema is present with silicosis, it's important to look at the patient's history to see if smoking, pneumonia, or bronchitis may have aggravated either of the conditions.

Which of the following are correct?

A. When emphysema accompanies silicosis, the emphysema usually receives the major focus of treatment efforts.

B. A distinguishing feature of emphysema is the reduction of air volume in the lungs.

C. Emphysema causes an increase in the size of the air spaces near the terminal bronchioles.

D. Smoking, pneumonia, and bronchitis have no effect on silicosis or accompanying emphysema.

CHECKYOURANSWERHERECHECKYOURANSWERHERECHECKYOURANSWERHERE
CHECKYOURANSWERHERECHECKYOURANSWERHERECHECKYOURANSWERHERE
CHECKYOURANSWERHERECHECKYOURANSWERHERECHECKYOURANSWERHERE
CHECKYOURANSWERHERECHECKYOURANSWERHERECHECKYOURANSWERHERE

17. **Tuberculosis** is a bacterial infection that causes inflammation of the lungs. It occurs slightly more often in persons who have silicosis than in the general population, probably because silicosis makes the patient more susceptible to the tuberculosis bacteria. Some symptoms that may point to the presence of tuberculosis in a patient with silicosis are:

■ Fever

■ Disturbed sleep

■ Chest pains

■ Hoarseness

■ Loss of appetite

These symptoms usually appear in the advanced stages of silicosis.

A. What is tuberculosis?_____

_____

B. Tuberculosis is (more/less) _____ likely to occur in a patient who has silicosis than in a patient without silicosis.

C. Which one of the following is NOT a symptom of tuberculosis?

1. Chest pains

2. Hoarseness

3. Loss of appetite

4. Very low fever

CHECKYOURANSWERHERECHECKYOURANSWERHERECHECKYOURANSWERHERE
CHECKYOURANSWERHERECHECKYOURANSWERHERECHECKYOURANSWERHERE
CHECKYOURANSWERHERECHECKYOURANSWERHERECHECKYOURANSWERHERE
CHECKYOURANSWERHERECHECKYOURANSWERHERECHECKYOURANSWERHERE

Coal Workers' Pneumoconiosis

18. **Coal workers' pneumoconiosis (CWP)** is another common type of fibrogenic pneumoconiosis seen in claim work. It is also known as **black lung disease** and **anthracosis**. As the name implies, CWP is caused by the inhalation of coal dust.

    CWP may cause only minimal impairment for the patient. However, in some cases—especially for individuals involved in the mining of hard coal—great impairment can occur, similar to advanced silicosis. When this happens, CWP is called **progressive massive fibrosis**, or PMF, which is descriptive of the course of the disease.

    A. CWP is caused by inhaling _____ dust.

    B. Inhalation and retention of coal dust in the lungs (always/sometimes/never) _____ causes functional impairment of the lungs.

    C. When CWP causes great lung impairment, it is called _____
    _____.

CHECKYOURANSWERHERECHECKYOURANSWERHERECHECKYOURANSWERHERE
CHECKYOURANSWERHERECHECKYOURANSWERHERECHECKYOURANSWERHERE
CHECKYOURANSWERHERECHECKYOURANSWERHERECHECKYOURANSWERHERE
CHECKYOURANSWERHERECHECKYOURANSWERHERECHECKYOURANSWERHERE

Asbestosis

19. The final pneumoconiosis we'll discuss here is **asbestosis**, which is caused by the inhalation of asbestos dust. Asbestosis is a risk with any type of employment that involves asbestos products, such as mining, milling, and manufacturing. Those who install insulation are also at risk. Preventive measures currently in use have somewhat reduced the incidence of asbestosis, but those who have been exposed to asbestos for long periods of time in the past may still be diagnosed with the disease.

    Complicating asbestosis is the fact that there is a higher incidence of lung cancer in those exposed, primarily among smokers. This means that asbestos workers can reduce their own risk of lung cancer by not smoking.

    Which of the following statements concerning asbestosis are correct?

    A. It can result from a number of different jobs involving asbestos products.

    B. The incidence of asbestosis has increased in recent years.

    C. The risk of lung cancer increases with asbestosis, especially if the patient is a smoker.

CHECKYOURANSWERHERECHECKYOURANSWERHERECHECKYOURANSWERHERE
CHECKYOURANSWERHERECHECKYOURANSWERHERECHECKYOURANSWERHERE
CHECKYOURANSWERHERECHECKYOURANSWERHERECHECKYOURANSWERHERE
CHECKYOURANSWERHERECHECKYOURANSWERHERECHECKYOURANSWERHERE

20. In any type of pneumoconiosis, the patient's history of other lung diseases and other factors which may damage the lungs, such as smoking, should be considered. In most cases, a direct relationship to inhalation of certain dusts in an employment situation can be seen. However, it's important to determine whether any preexisting conditions have aggravated the pneumoconiosis, or if the reverse is true.

Now you're ready to review what you just learned about employment-related lung conditions. For each of the following statements, write in an **S** if it describes silicosis, a **C** if it refers to coal workers' pneumoconiosis, or an **A** if it describes asbestosis.

_____ A. Results from inhaling free silica over long periods of time

_____ B. Also known as black lung disease and anthracosis

_____ C. Often complicated by tuberculosis or emphysema

_____ D. Pneumoconiosis caused by the inhalation of asbestos dust

_____ E. May continue to produce fibroids in the lungs even after the patient is no longer exposed to the agent that causes this pneumoconiosis

_____ F. Advanced stage is called progressive massive fibrosis.

CHECKYOURANSWERHERECHECKYOURANSWERHERECHECKYOURANSWERHERE
CHECKYOURANSWERHERECHECKYOURANSWERHERECHECKYOURANSWERHERE
CHECKYOURANSWERHERECHECKYOURANSWERHERECHECKYOURANSWERHERE
CHECKYOURANSWERHERECHECKYOURANSWERHERECHECKYOURANSWERHERE

REVIEW

21. Complete the following review exercises before going on to the next unit.

Answer the following true/false questions about the anatomy and functions of the lungs.

A. The left lung has three lobes.   ( ) True   ( ) False

B. Air is brought into the lobes of the lungs through the trachea.
( ) True   ( ) False

C. The smaller branches of the secondary bronchi that end in alveoli are called the bronchi.   ( ) True   ( ) False

D. The purpose of the alveoli is to add oxygen to the blood.   ( ) True
( ) False

E. A secondary bronchus reaches into each of the lobes in both the right and left lungs.   ( ) True   ( ) False

CHECKYOURANSWERHERECHECKYOURANSWERHERECHECKYOURANSWERHERE
CHECKYOURANSWERHERECHECKYOURANSWERHERECHECKYOURANSWERHERE
CHECKYOURANSWERHERECHECKYOURANSWERHERECHECKYOURANSWERHERE
CHECKYOURANSWERHERECHECKYOURANSWERHERECHECKYOURANSWERHERE

22. Which of these statements concerning lung injuries are correct?

    A. The most common type of lung injuries involve the pleural space.

    B. Hemothorax is the presence of blood in the lungs.

    C. Mediastinal shift is an inherent danger in hemothorax, pneumothorax, and hemopneumothorax.

    D. A tension pneumothorax may develop in previously healthy individuals for no apparent reason.

    E. An open pneumothorax occurs when air enters the pleural space and becomes trapped.

    F. Hemothorax, pneumothorax, and hemopneumothorax may all be treated by thoracentesis, closed chest drainage, or thoracotomy.

    G. A hemopneumothorax is the presence of both blood and air in the pleural space.

CHECKYOURANSWERHERECHECKYOURANSWERHERECHECKYOURANSWERHERE
CHECKYOURANSWERHERECHECKYOURANSWERHERECHECKYOURANSWERHERE
CHECKYOURANSWERHERECHECKYOURANSWERHERECHECKYOURANSWERHERE
CHECKYOURANSWERHERECHECKYOURANSWERHERECHECKYOURANSWERHERE

23. Answer the following questions about employment-related pneumoconioses.

    A. People who work in copper mining, stonecutting, and foundries are at risk of developing

        1. silicosis.

        2. CWP.

        3. asbestosis.

    B. Emphysema and tuberculosis often accompany and complicate

        1. silicosis.

        2. CWP.

        3. asbestosis.

    C. Spontaneous pneumothorax is a possible complication for individuals who suffer from

        1. silicosis and emphysema.

        2. asbestosis and tuberculosis.

        3. CWP and emphysema.

    D. Which pneumoconiosis increases an individual's risk of developing lung cancer, especially for those who are smokers?

        1. Silicosis

        2. CWP

        3. Asbestosis

    E. Anthracosis and black lung disease are other names for

        1. silicosis.

        2. CWP.

        3. asbestosis.

CHECKYOURANSWERHERECHECKYOURANSWERHERECHECKYOURANSWERHERE
CHECKYOURANSWERHERECHECKYOURANSWERHERECHECKYOURANSWERHERE
CHECKYOURANSWERHERECHECKYOURANSWERHERECHECKYOURANSWERHERE
CHECKYOURANSWERHERECHECKYOURANSWERHERECHECKYOURANSWERHERE

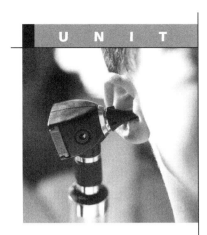

10

The Ears and Eyes

BASIC ANATOMY AND FUNCTIONS OF THE EARS

1. There are three basic divisions of the internal apparatus of the ear: the external ear, the middle ear, and the inner ear. In general terms, here is how they function:

Anatomy and Function of the Ears

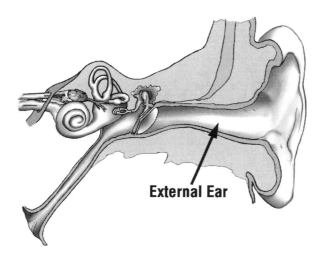

The *external ear* is a canal leading from the opening visible outside the head.

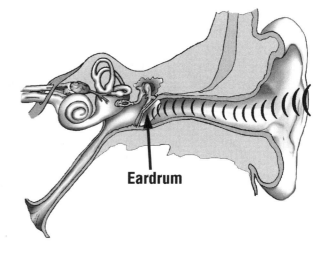

Sound waves pass through the external ear canal and strike the *eardrum* which is a kind of wall between the external ear and the *middle ear*.

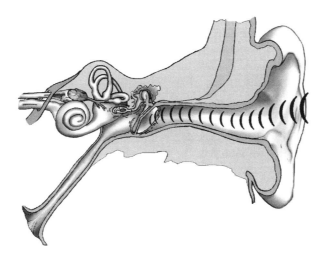

When the eardrum receives the sound waves, it vibrates, activating *three tiny bones in the middle ear*. These bones transmit the sound waves to the nerve endings in the inner ear.

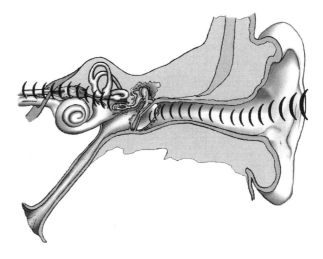

The *hearing nerve* transmits the sound waves on to the brain, where they are interpreted.

Complete the following sentences to review the anatomy and functions of the ear.

A. The canal leading from the opening in the ear visible outside the head is called the
   1. external ear.
   2. eardrum.
   3. middle ear.

B. Sound waves pass through the external ear canal and strike the
   1. inner ear.
   2. hearing nerve.
   3. eardrum.

C. The eardrum is a kind of wall between the external ear and the
   1. hearing nerve.
   2. middle ear.
   3. inner ear.

D. When the eardrum receives the sound waves, it vibrates, activating the
   1. three tiny bones in the middle ear.
   2. hearing nerve.
   3. exterior ear.

E. These bones transmit the sound waves to the nerve endings in the
   1. eardrum.
   2. external ear canal.
   3. inner ear.

F. Sound waves are transmitted to the brain by the
   1. eardrum.
   2. middle ear.
   3. hearing nerve.

CHECKYOURANSWERHERECHECKYOURANSWERHERECHECKYOURANSWERHERE
CHECKYOURANSWERHERECHECKYOURANSWERHERECHECKYOURANSWERHERE
CHECKYOURANSWERHERECHECKYOURANSWERHERECHECKYOURANSWERHERE
CHECKYOURANSWERHERECHECKYOURANSWERHERECHECKYOURANSWERHERE

Hearing Impairments

2. If a hearing impairment occurs in the external or middle ear, it is called a **conductive hearing impairment**. If it occurs in the inner ear, it is called a **neural hearing impairment**. Neural hearing impairments may also be described as **sensory hearing impairments** or **sensorineural hearing impairments**. We will use the term *neural* in the text.

   A. A hearing impairment occurring in the external or middle ear is called a _____ hearing impairment.

B. A hearing impairment occurring in the inner ear is most commonly referred to as a _____ hearing impairment.

C. Other terms used to describe a hearing impairment occurring in the inner ear are _____ and

_____.

Conductive Hearing Impairments

3. A conductive hearing impairment is usually caused by wax or foreign bodies in the external ear or an infection in either the external or middle ear.

   In most cases, the impairment is treated by curing the cause of the impairment (such as removing the wax or clearing up the infection). In some situations, a hearing aid is required to restore functional hearing; surgical treatment is rarely required. A conductive hearing impairment rarely results in deafness.

   Claims for employment-related conductive hearing impairments should be examined carefully. A buildup of wax in the ear would not be job-related; however, a sliver of steel found in the ear could easily be the result of an industrial accident.

   You receive a claim from a person with a conductive hearing impairment. Which of the following statements are true about that person's condition?

   A. Conductive hearing impairments always cause deafness.

   B. Conductive hearing impairments must be treated surgically.

   C. The most common causes of conductive hearing impairments are wax or foreign bodies in the external ear or an infection in the middle ear.

   D. In most cases, a conductive hearing impairment is treated by curing the cause of the impairment.

Neural Hearing Impairments

4. A neural hearing impairment is more serious than a conductive hearing impairment. This type of impairment results from some disturbance to the hearing nerve that transmits sounds to the brain. With a neural hearing impairment, sounds may *reach* the hearing nerve, but the impairment does not allow the sounds to continue on to the brain for interpretation, so, to the patient, they are just incomprehensible noise.

   Common causes for a neural hearing impairment include:

   ■ Extreme noise

- Disease

- Infection

- Tumor

- Hemorrhage

- Trauma

- Reaction to drugs

- Deterioration due to old age

Unlike a conductive hearing impairment, a neural hearing impairment is likely to result in deafness and may not respond to either a hearing aid or surgery.

Work-related claims for neural hearing impairments may be compensable, depending on the cause of the impairment. Assume the following excerpts are claims for work-related neural hearing impairments. Based on what you just read, which of these are probably compensable?

A. Bill, a 70-year-old accountant, has experienced a gradual loss of hearing over the last ten years.

B. Tom is a machinist. His employer has never installed noise pollution controls in the shop or supplied its workers with ear plugs.

C. Freida is a factory line worker. She was injured when a small part flew off a malfunctioning machine and lodged in her inner ear.

CHECKYOURANSWERHERECHECKYOURANSWERHERECHECKYOURANSWERHERE
CHECKYOURANSWERHERECHECKYOURANSWERHERECHECKYOURANSWERHERE
CHECKYOURANSWERHERECHECKYOURANSWERHERECHECKYOURANSWERHERE
CHECKYOURANSWERHERECHECKYOURANSWERHERECHECKYOURANSWERHERE

5. Following are basic descriptions of the five steps involved in the hearing process. Put these steps in the proper order by writing a 1, 2, 3, 4, or 5 in the space next to the description.

_____ A.   Sound waves pass through the external ear canal and strike the eardrum.

_____ B.   Sound waves enter the external ear canal.

_____ C.   Sound waves are transmitted up the hearing nerve in the inner ear to the brain.

_____ D.   The three tiny bones in the middle ear transmit the sound waves to the nerve endings in the internal ear.

_____ E.   When the eardrum receives the sound waves, it vibrates, activating the three tiny bones in the middle ear.

CHECKYOURANSWERHERECHECKYOURANSWERHERECHECKYOURANSWERHERE
CHECKYOURANSWERHERECHECKYOURANSWERHERECHECKYOURANSWERHERE
CHECKYOURANSWERHERECHECKYOURANSWERHERECHECKYOURANSWERHERE
CHECKYOURANSWERHERECHECKYOURANSWERHERECHECKYOURANSWERHERE

COMMON EYE CONDITIONS AND INJURIES

6. The anatomy of the eye is very complicated, and it would be beyond the scope of this course to discuss all of the various structures and functions of the eye and all of the injuries, diseases, and conditions which can affect it. Instead, in this section we'll concentrate on some of the more common conditions and injuries of the eye which you're likely to encounter in medical claims.

    Since most eye conditions can be caused either by a disease or by an injury, any work-related claim involving an eye condition should be examined carefully to determine if it is compensable. So, if you receive a claim for a work-related eye condition, you should

    A. settle the claim promptly without further investigation.

    B. deny the claim immediately without further investigation.

    C. determine the cause of the eye condition before deciding how to handle the claim.

CHECKYOURANSWERHERECHECKYOURANSWERHERECHECKYOURANSWERHERE
CHECKYOURANSWERHERECHECKYOURANSWERHERECHECKYOURANSWERHERE
CHECKYOURANSWERHERECHECKYOURANSWERHERECHECKYOURANSWERHERE
CHECKYOURANSWERHERECHECKYOURANSWERHERECHECKYOURANSWERHERE

Cataracts

7. A **cataract** is a condition where the lens of the eye, which is normally transparent, becomes opaque. Most patients who suffer from cataracts experience a progressive, painless loss of vision; the vision becomes blurred, like a foggy camera lens.

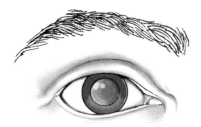

Normal Eye   **Eye with Cataract**

    Cataracts may develop progressively as one grows older, or they may be caused by other factors, such as disease or an injury to the lens of the eye. Common injuries to the lens are contusions or penetrations by small flying objects, such as steel or metal.

    Cataracts may be removed surgically, but there must be some substitute made for the missing lens, such as eyeglasses, contact lenses, or an artificial lens implanted into the eye.

    Which of the following statements are true?

    A. When the lens of the eye becomes opaque, it is called a cataract.

    B. Persons who suffer from cataracts experience a sudden, total loss of vision.

C. A cataract may develop progressively as one grows older, or it may be caused by an injury to the lens.

D. Since removal of a cataract results in blindness, there is no need to provide a substitute lens.

CHECKYOURANSWERHERECHECKYOURANSWERHERECHECKYOURANSWERHERE
CHECKYOURANSWERHERECHECKYOURANSWERHERECHECKYOURANSWERHERE
CHECKYOURANSWERHERECHECKYOURANSWERHERECHECKYOURANSWERHERE
CHECKYOURANSWERHERECHECKYOURANSWERHERECHECKYOURANSWERHERE

Conjunctivitis

8. **Conjunctivitis** is a highly contagious disease that causes inflammation of the **conjunctiva**, which is a membrane covering the eye. The most common causes of conjunctivitis are viruses, bacteria, and allergies. Smoke, chemicals, dust, and other types of air pollution may also irritate the conjunctiva. The treatment for conjunctivitis depends on what caused the disorder. In most cases, conjunctivitis can be treated successfully with no lasting effects, although some patients may have chronic recurrences.

   A. What is conjunctivitis? _____

   _____

   _____

   B. Name the three most common causes of conjunctivitis.

   1. _____

   2. _____

   3. _____

CHECKYOURANSWERHERECHECKYOURANSWERHERECHECKYOURANSWERHERE
CHECKYOURANSWERHERECHECKYOURANSWERHERECHECKYOURANSWERHERE
CHECKYOURANSWERHERECHECKYOURANSWERHERECHECKYOURANSWERHERE
CHECKYOURANSWERHERECHECKYOURANSWERHERECHECKYOURANSWERHERE

Diplopia

9. **Diplopia** is another name for double vision, which occurs when both eyeballs do not function together. Diplopia results in the patient looking at one object and seeing two. This condition is a result of injury or disease to the eye muscles or the nerves that control the muscles. Diplopia can also result from a skull fracture with accompanying damage to the brain or meninges. Depending on the severity of the case, diplopia may be treated with eyeglasses or surgery.

   Which of the following statements are true?

   A. Either disease or injury may be a cause of diplopia.

   B. Skull fractures cannot cause diplopia.

   C. Diplopia is another name for double vision.

   D. A person with diplopia looks at one object and sees two.

Enucleation of the Eye

10. **Enucleation of the eye** is the act of removing the eye completely from its socket. Obviously, the eye must be seriously damaged for this type of radical treatment, which leaves the patient blind on one side. If enucleation is necessary, it is usually the result of a violent injury or trauma to the eye.

    Enucleation of the eye is usually the result of

    A. an inflammation of the conjunctiva.

    B. a violent injury or trauma to the eye.

    C. looking at one object and seeing two.

Glaucoma

11. **Glaucoma** is an increase in pressure within the eyeball. This causes pressure on the **optic nerve**, which is the nerve that transmits visual messages to the brain, and leads to impaired vision. If the pressure becomes extreme, the nerve dies, and blindness results.

    There are several causes of glaucoma. It may be caused by another eye disease or, occasionally, by an injury to the eye. Sometimes, the cause is unknown. If discovered and treated early, glaucoma may respond to medication, and blindness may be prevented. If medication fails, surgery is advised, although this might not prevent blindness if the condition reappears.

    Glaucoma

    A. means the removal of the eye from its socket.

    B. is an increase in pressure within the eyeball.

    C. never causes blindness.

    D. cannot be treated with medication; surgery is the only treatment option.

    E. may be caused by an injury to the eye or by another eye disease.

Retinal Detachment

12. Before we learn about **retinal detachment**, let's discuss the anatomy of the eyeball. The eyeball is made up of three layers of tissue:

Anatomy of the Eyeball

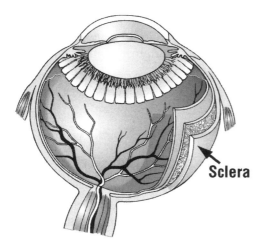

The outermost layer of the eyeball is called the *sclera*. The nontechnical term for the sclera is the *white of the eye*.

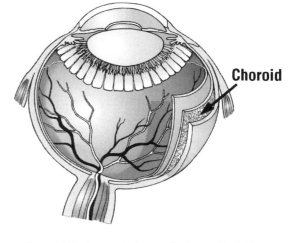

The middle layer of the eyeball is called the *choroid*. The choroid is attached to the sclera.

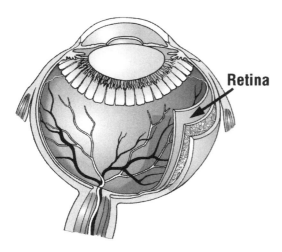

The innermost layer of the eyeball is called the *retina*. The retina is attached to the choroid.

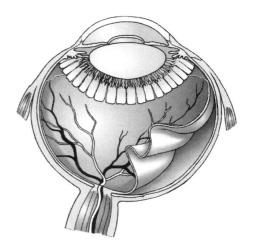

Retinal detachment occurs when the retina becomes completely or partially separated from the choroid. It can be caused by trauma, hemorrhaging, or tumors. Vision in the affected area will be lost until the retina can be reattached surgically.

A claimant is suffering from a detached retina. Which of the following statements are true about this condition?

A. A detached retina can be caused by trauma.

B. It always results in permanent blindness, even after the retina is reattached.

C. It affects vision in the affected area until the retina is reattached surgically.

D. It is never caused by hemorrhaging or tumors.

13. To review what you've just learned, match the eye condition listed in the left-hand column with its correct description in the right-hand column.

1. Cataracts	____ A.	Removal of the eye from its socket
2. Conjunctivitis	____ B.	Double vision
3. Diplopia	____ C.	Lens of the eye becomes opaque
4. Enucleation of the eye		
5. Glaucoma	____ D.	Increase in pressure within the eye puts pressure on the optic nerve
6. Retinal detachment		
	____ E.	Innermost layer of the eyeball detaches from the second layer of the eyeball
	____ F.	Inflammation of the membrane covering the eye

REVIEW

14. Briefly review what you've learned about the ears and eyes by answering the following questions.

    Which of the following are some common causes of **neural** hearing disorders?

    A. Foreign objects in the external or middle ear

    B. Buildup of ear wax in the external ear canal

    C. Disease

    D. Excessive noise

    E. Trauma

    F. Tumor

15. A (conductive/neural) _____ hearing disorder affects the external or middle ear.

CHECKYOURANSWERHERECHECKYOURANSWERHERECHECKYOURANSWERHERE
CHECKYOURANSWERHERECHECKYOURANSWERHERECHECKYOURANSWERHERE
CHECKYOURANSWERHERECHECKYOURANSWERHERECHECKYOURANSWERHERE
CHECKYOURANSWERHERECHECKYOURANSWERHERECHECKYOURANSWERHERE

16. In addition to viruses, bacteria, and allergies, which of the following can irritate the conjunctiva and lead to conjunctivitis?
    A. Smoke
    B. Chemicals
    C. Air pollution
    D. Hemorrhage
    E. Tumor

CHECKYOURANSWERHERECHECKYOURANSWERHERECHECKYOURANSWERHERE
CHECKYOURANSWERHERECHECKYOURANSWERHERECHECKYOURANSWERHERE
CHECKYOURANSWERHERECHECKYOURANSWERHERECHECKYOURANSWERHERE
CHECKYOURANSWERHERECHECKYOURANSWERHERECHECKYOURANSWERHERE

17. A claim for a work-related hearing impairment or eye condition should be
    A. paid immediately without further investigation.
    B. investigated thoroughly to determine the cause of the impairment or condition.
    C. denied without further investigation.

CHECKYOURANSWERHERECHECKYOURANSWERHERECHECKYOURANSWERHERE
CHECKYOURANSWERHERECHECKYOURANSWERHERECHECKYOURANSWERHERE
CHECKYOURANSWERHERECHECKYOURANSWERHERECHECKYOURANSWERHERE
CHECKYOURANSWERHERECHECKYOURANSWERHERECHECKYOURANSWERHERE

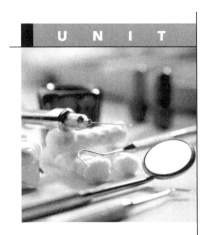

11

The Teeth

DECIDUOUS AND PERMANENT TEETH

1. Each person has two sets of teeth during his or her lifetime. The first set, the **deciduous**, or **baby**, teeth, start falling out at around age six to be replaced by the second set, the **permanent teeth**. The permanent teeth are usually completely in by around age 16, with the exception of the wisdom teeth.
   A. The (deciduous/permanent) ______________________________ teeth start falling out at around age 6.
   B. The (deciduous/permanent) teeth ______________________________ are usually completely in by around age 16, with the exception of the wisdom teeth.

CHECKYOURANSWERHERECHECKYOURANSWERHERECHECKYOURANSWERHERE
CHECKYOURANSWERHERECHECKYOURANSWERHERECHECKYOURANSWERHERE
CHECKYOURANSWERHERECHECKYOURANSWERHERECHECKYOURANSWERHERE
CHECKYOURANSWERHERECHECKYOURANSWERHERECHECKYOURANSWERHERE

Answer: A. deciduous B. permanent

Deciduous Teeth

2. There are 20 deciduous teeth. The deciduous teeth usually begin to erupt at the age of about six months, and all 20 teeth are usually in by age two.

   Let's learn the names of the deciduous teeth. As you're reviewing the names, note that the corresponding teeth in the upper and lower jaws share the same names, even though they look different.

right to left
upper

left to ri
lower

The Deciduous Teeth

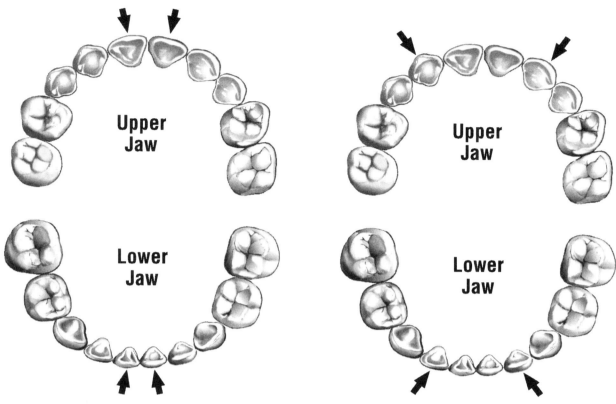

The two center teeth in the upper and lower jaw are the *central incisors*.

The *lateral incisors* are located to the side of the central incisors.

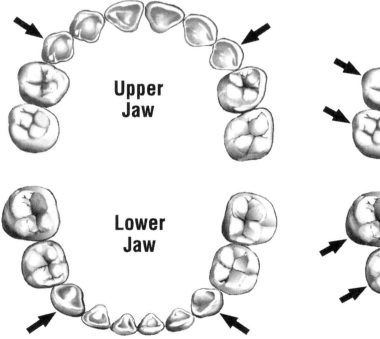

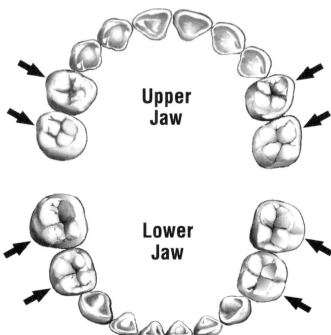

Next to each lateral incisor is a *cuspid*. Cuspids are also called *eye teeth* or *canine teeth*.

The last two teeth on each side of the upper and lower jaw are the *first molar* and the *second molar*.

True or false?

A. The central incisors are the two center teeth in the upper and lower jaw.   ( ) True   ( ) False

B. The lateral incisors are located next to the molars.   ( ) True   ( ) False

C. The last two teeth on each side of the upper and lower jaw are the molars.   ( ) True   ( ) False

D. The cuspids are located between the central and lateral incisors.   ( ) True   ( ) False

CHECKYOURANSWERHERECHECKYOURANSWERHERECHECKYOURANSWERHERE
CHECKYOURANSWERHERECHECKYOURANSWERHERECHECKYOURANSWERHERE
CHECKYOURANSWERHERECHECKYOURANSWERHERECHECKYOURANSWERHERE
CHECKYOURANSWERHERECHECKYOURANSWERHERECHECKYOURANSWERHERE
CHECKYOURANSWERHERECHECKYOURANSWERHERECHECKYOURANSWERHERE
CHECKYOURANSWERHERECHECKYOURANSWERHERECHECKYOURANSWERHERE

Universal Lettering System for Deciduous Teeth

3. In addition to the names you have just learned, the deciduous teeth are also referred to in medical reports and claims by specific **letters**. The following illustration shows the **Universal Lettering System** for deciduous teeth.

Universal Lettering System— Deciduous Teeth

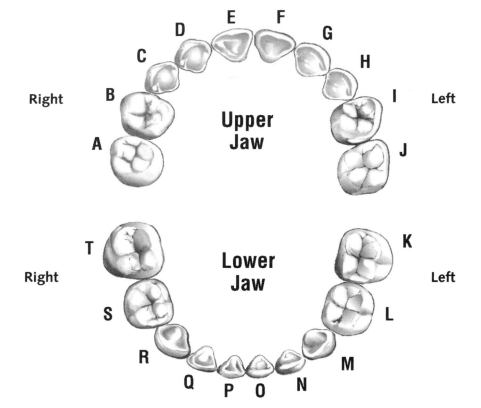

Use the Universal Lettering System to identify the following teeth.

A. Tooth "T" refers to a

    1. cuspid.

    2. central incisor.

    3. molar.

B. Tooth "E" describes a

    1. central incisor.

    2. cuspid.

    3. lateral incisor.

C. Tooth "M" is a

    1. cuspid.

    2. molar.

    3. central incisor.

CHECKYOURANSWERHERECHECKYOURANSWERHERECHECKYOURANSWERHERE
CHECKYOURANSWERHERECHECKYOURANSWERHERECHECKYOURANSWERHERE
CHECKYOURANSWERHERECHECKYOURANSWERHERECHECKYOURANSWERHERE
CHECKYOURANSWERHERECHECKYOURANSWERHERECHECKYOURANSWERHERE

4. Answer the following questions to review what you've learned about the deciduous teeth.

A. What is the total number of deciduous teeth? _____

B. How many central incisors are there, and where are they located?

    _____

    _____

    _____

C. How many lateral incisors are there? _____

D. What other names are used to describe the cuspids? _____

    _____

    _____

E. Write in the correct letter of the deciduous tooth on the line extending from each tooth in the following illustration.

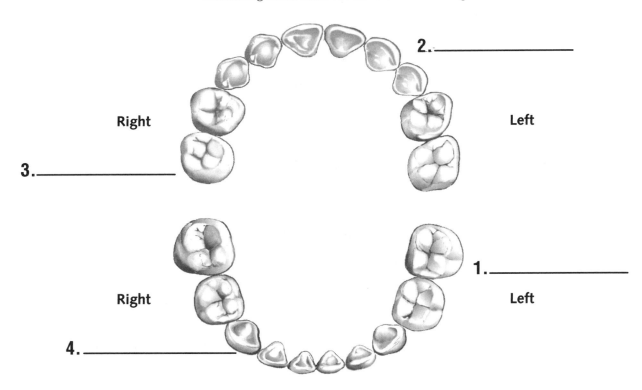

2._____

Right

Left

3._____

Right

1._____

Left

4._____

Permanent Teeth ~ numbered

5. Most adults have 32 permanent teeth: 16 in the upper jaw and 16 in the lower jaw. The permanent teeth have the same names as the deciduous teeth, although some teeth found in the permanent set are not included in the deciduous teeth. The permanent teeth include:

The Permanent Teeth

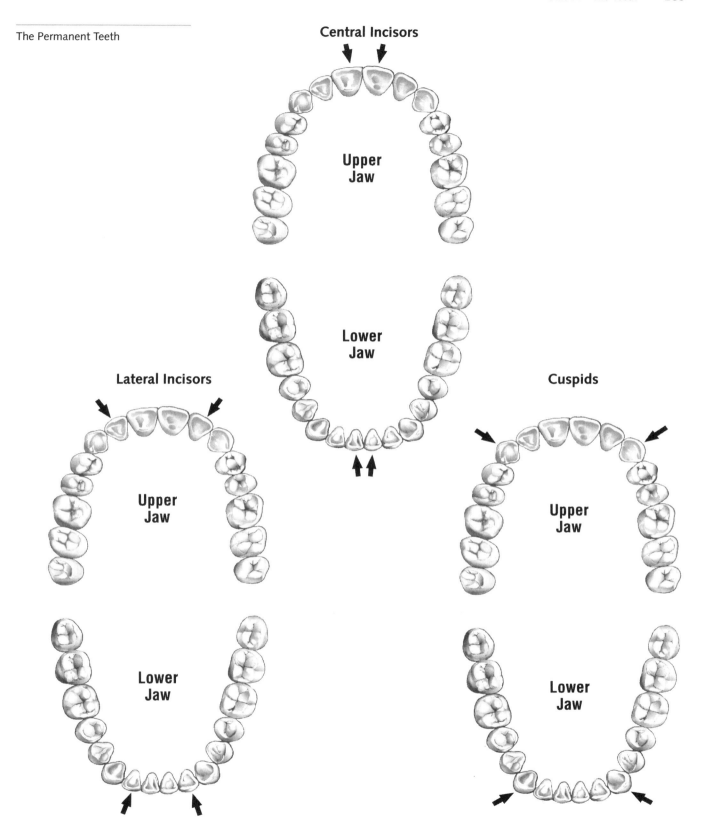

Central Incisors

Upper Jaw

Lower Jaw

Lateral Incisors

Upper Jaw

Lower Jaw

Cuspids

Upper Jaw

Lower Jaw

Also included in the permanent teeth are:

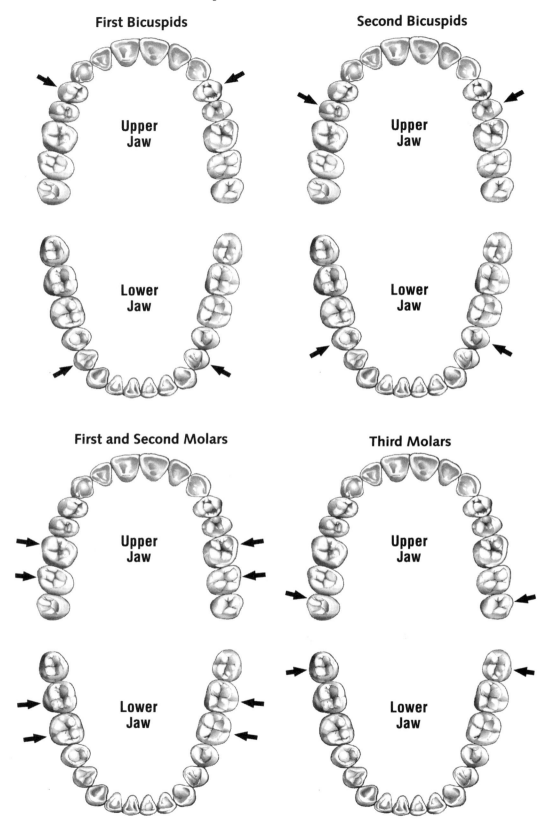

The **third molars** are also called the **wisdom teeth**. The wisdom teeth usually come in between the ages of 16–25. In many adults, the third molars never develop, so these people will have *fewer* than 32 permanent teeth.

A. Which of the following are part of the permanent teeth but are not included in the deciduous teeth?

　　1.　Third molars

　　2.　Central incisors

　　3.　First bicuspids

　　4.　Second bicuspids

　　5.　Cuspids

B. The third molars are also called the

　　1.　wisdom teeth.

　　2.　canine teeth.

　　3.　eyeteeth.

CHECKYOURANSWERHERECHECKYOURANSWERHERECHECKYOURANSWERHERE
CHECKYOURANSWERHERECHECKYOURANSWERHERECHECKYOURANSWERHERE
CHECKYOURANSWERHERECHECKYOURANSWERHERECHECKYOURANSWERHERE
CHECKYOURANSWERHERECHECKYOURANSWERHERECHECKYOURANSWERHERE

Universal Numbering System for Permanent Teeth

6. While deciduous teeth are described by specific letters in medical reports and claims, permanent teeth are identified by specific **numbers**. The following illustration shows the **Universal Numbering System** for permanent teeth.

Universal Numbering System—
Permanent Teeth

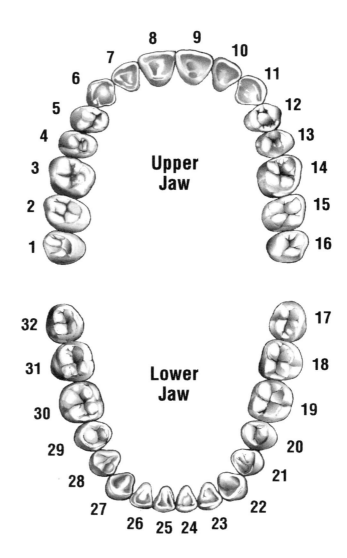

Match the number of the permanent tooth in the left-hand column with its correct description in the right-hand column.

1. 8   _____ A. Second bicuspid
2. 20   _____ B. Central incisor
3. 7   _____ C. Third molar
4. 32   _____ D. Lateral incisor

7. Answer the following questions to review what you've learned about the permanent teeth.

   A. How many permanent teeth do most adults have? _____32_____

   B. Name the three types of teeth that are part of the permanent teeth but are not included in the deciduous teeth.

      1. _____

      2. _____

      3. _____

   C. Write in the correct number of the permanent tooth on the line extending from each tooth in the following illustration.

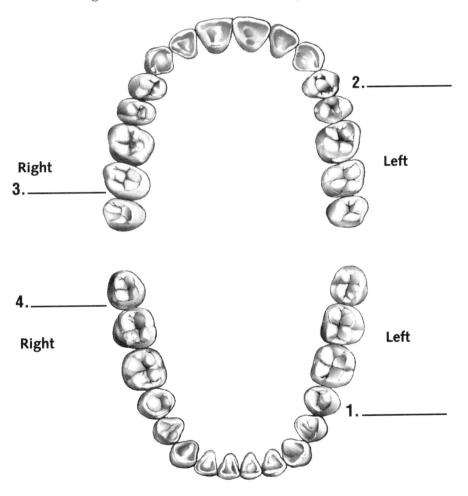

IMPLICATIONS OF TOOTH LOSS

Permanent Teeth

8. From the point of view of a claim examiner, the main problem with teeth is that they are sometimes knocked out. For adults, the loss of teeth is inconvenient, but easily corrected with dental prostheses, or false teeth. This type of claim can be settled with relative ease by simply paying for the adult patient's dental work.

    However, when a child loses permanent teeth, the claim is usually more complicated than merely making a payment for dental services. Since a child is still growing, any dental prosthesis will probably have to be replaced often to keep up with the child's growth.

    John, age 12, lost four permanent teeth in an auto accident. Why is John's loss more complicated than a similar loss by an adult?

    A. Since children are more careless than adults, John will probably have to have his dental prosthesis replaced frequently.

    B. Because John is still growing, any dental prosthesis will probably have to be replaced often to keep up with his growth.

    C. It is more difficult to fit a dental prosthesis to a child's mouth than an adult's.

CHECKYOURANSWERHERECHECKYOURANSWERHERECHECKYOURANSWERHERE
CHECKYOURANSWERHERECHECKYOURANSWERHERECHECKYOURANSWERHERE
CHECKYOURANSWERHERECHECKYOURANSWERHERECHECKYOURANSWERHERE
CHECKYOURANSWERHERECHECKYOURANSWERHERECHECKYOURANSWERHERE

Deciduous Teeth

9. The loss of deciduous teeth before they fall out naturally can cause even more problems for a child than the loss of permanent teeth.

    Many people mistakenly believe that caring for the deciduous teeth is not important, since they are eventually replaced by permanent teeth. On the contrary, the deciduous teeth prepare the way for the permanent teeth to grow in straight and strong. If these teeth are removed before the normal time when they would fall out naturally, the other teeth around that area try to fill in the gap left by the missing tooth. The permanent tooth underneath the gap must then struggle to grow into its rightful place, and often ends up crooked or only partially visible. If this happens, the child will probably have to wear orthodontic braces for several years to correct the situation.

    Check all correct statements.

    A. The only purpose served by deciduous teeth is to aid the child in eating until the permanent teeth come in.

    B. When a deciduous tooth is lost before it naturally falls out, the surrounding teeth tend to try to fill the gap left by the lost tooth.

    C. The deciduous teeth have no effect on the growth of the permanent teeth.

D. The end result of premature loss of a deciduous tooth may be wearing orthodontic braces to correct permanent teeth that didn't come in properly.

CHECKYOURANSWERHERECHECKYOURANSWERHERECHECKYOURANSWERHERE
CHECKYOURANSWERHERECHECKYOURANSWERHERECHECKYOURANSWERHERE
CHECKYOURANSWERHERECHECKYOURANSWERHERECHECKYOURANSWERHERE
CHECKYOURANSWERHERECHECKYOURANSWERHERECHECKYOURANSWERHERE

10. While more problems usually arise when teeth are lost by children than by adults, in some cases adults can also suffer greatly from such a loss. For example, adults who work in occupations where appearance or speaking abilities are important, such as fashion models or teachers, would probably be more affected by the loss of teeth than other adults.

Following are four examples of claims involving adults and children who have lost teeth. Match each example in the left-hand column with the description in the right-hand column that best describes the action that will probably be taken on the claim and/or any problems that may arise.

1. A 22-year-old professional singer lost both upper central incisors and the left upper lateral incisor.

2. A 4-year-old child lost a deciduous lower left cuspid.

3. A 41-year-old accountant lost the lower left second bicuspid and the lower left first and second molars.

4. A 12-year-old lost his permanent right lateral incisor and first bicuspid.

____ A. The claimant may have to get orthodontic braces if the permanent cuspid has difficulty in developing, which is likely in this case.

____ B. Although the claimant can probably be properly fitted with a dental prosthesis, it is difficult to determine if the prosthesis will affect the claimant's singing abilities.

____ C. Since the claimant is still growing, it is likely that the dental prosthesis will probably have to be replaced several times before the claimant reaches adulthood.

____ D. This claimant can probably be successfully fitted with a dental prosthesis that will be adequate for some time.

CHECKYOURANSWERHERECHECKYOURANSWERHERECHECKYOURANSWERHERE
CHECKYOURANSWERHERECHECKYOURANSWERHERECHECKYOURANSWERHERE
CHECKYOURANSWERHERECHECKYOURANSWERHERECHECKYOURANSWERHERE
CHECKYOURANSWERHERECHECKYOURANSWERHERECHECKYOURANSWERHERE

▌REVIEW

11. Review what you've learned about the teeth by completing the following exercises.

Match the name of the permanent tooth in the left-hand column with its correct description in the right-hand column.

1. Molars
2. Bicuspids
3. Cuspids
4. Central incisors
5. Lateral incisors

____ A. Two center teeth in the upper and lower jaw

____ B. Last three teeth in the upper and lower jaws

____ C. Located to the side of the central incisors

____ D. Also called eye teeth or canine teeth

____ E. Located between the molars and the cuspids

CHECKYOURANSWERHERECHECKYOURANSWERHERECHECKYOURANSWERHERE
CHECKYOURANSWERHERECHECKYOURANSWERHERECHECKYOURANSWERHERE
CHECKYOURANSWERHERECHECKYOURANSWERHERECHECKYOURANSWERHERE
CHECKYOURANSWERHERECHECKYOURANSWERHERECHECKYOURANSWERHERE

12. Which of the following statements concerning the deciduous teeth are true?

A. There are 32 deciduous teeth.

B. The deciduous teeth include central incisors, lateral incisors, cuspids, and first and second molars.

C. The deciduous teeth begin to erupt at around age six months.

D. The deciduous teeth begin to fall out at around age two.

CHECKYOURANSWERHERECHECKYOURANSWERHERECHECKYOURANSWERHERE
CHECKYOURANSWERHERECHECKYOURANSWERHERECHECKYOURANSWERHERE
CHECKYOURANSWERHERECHECKYOURANSWERHERECHECKYOURANSWERHERE
CHECKYOURANSWERHERECHECKYOURANSWERHERECHECKYOURANSWERHERE

13. Use the Universal Lettering System to describe the following deciduous teeth.

A. Tooth A: _____

B. Tooth F: _____

C. Tooth C: _____

D. Tooth N: _____

E. Tooth L: _____

CHECKYOURANSWERHERECHECKYOURANSWERHERECHECKYOURANSWERHERE
CHECKYOURANSWERHERECHECKYOURANSWERHERECHECKYOURANSWERHERE
CHECKYOURANSWERHERECHECKYOURANSWERHERECHECKYOURANSWERHERE
CHECKYOURANSWERHERECHECKYOURANSWERHERECHECKYOURANSWERHERE

14. Use the Universal Numbering System to describe the following permanent teeth.

   A. Tooth 3: _____

   B. Tooth 29: _____

   C. Tooth 23: _____

   D. Tooth 28: _____

   E. Tooth 11: _____

15. True or false?

   A. The loss of permanent teeth causes more problems for children than the loss of deciduous teeth before they fall out naturally.
   ( ) True   ( ) False

   B. Most adults who lose permanent teeth can be successfully fitted with dental prostheses.   ( ) True   ( ) False

   C. A child who loses permanent teeth will probably outgrow several dental prostheses before adulthood.   ( ) True   ( ) False

   D. The loss of deciduous teeth before they fall out naturally has no effect on how the permanent teeth come in.   ( ) True   ( ) False

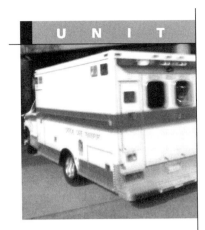

12

Burns

CLASSIFYING BURNS BY DEGREE

First-Degree Burns

1. In an earlier unit, we discussed various injuries to the skin, such as bruises, abrasions and lacerations. Another type of skin injury commonly seen in claim work is a **burn**. A burn is damage or injury to the skin or underlying tissues caused by fire, heat, electricity, or chemicals. There are three broad classifications of burns, each referring to the depth to which the burn extends into the body.

   First-degree burns are superficial, with damage limited to the **outer layer**, or **epidermis**, of the skin. The skin is red, tender, and painful, but not blistered. Swelling is often present with first-degree burns. First-degree burns usually heal within 1–10 days with no lasting effects. Exposure to the sun and brief contact with a hot object are common causes of first-degree burns.

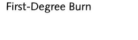

First-Degree Burn

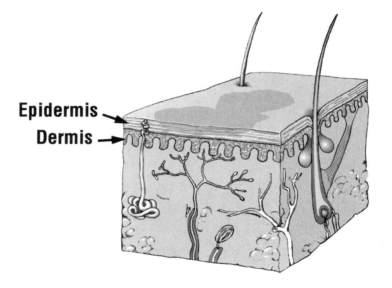

Epidermis
Dermis

Which one of the following examples describes a first-degree burn?

A. The patient suffered burns on the epidermis of the left forearm. The area was red and swollen, but no blisters were present.

B. The patient was extensively burned over the lateral aspect of the right thigh. Burns extended through all layers of skin, damaging much of the soft tissue in the thigh.

C. The patient was burned on the face. Blisters were present.

CHECKYOURANSWERHERECHECKYOURANSWERHERECHECKYOURANSWERHERE
CHECKYOURANSWERHERECHECKYOURANSWERHERECHECKYOURANSWERHERE
CHECKYOURANSWERHERECHECKYOURANSWERHERECHECKYOURANSWERHERE
CHECKYOURANSWERHERECHECKYOURANSWERHERECHECKYOURANSWERHERE

Second-Degree Burns

most painful

2. **Second-degree burns** extend through the epidermis into the **dermis,** the lower layer of skin. The skin blisters and swells. A second-degree burn can cause severe damage but usually not of sufficient extent to prevent the skin from healing. Second-degree burns usually heal completely within 14 days, unless infection is involved. Intense exposure to the sun, prolonged contact with a hot object, scalding liquids, and gasoline are common causes of second-degree burns.

Second-Degree Burn

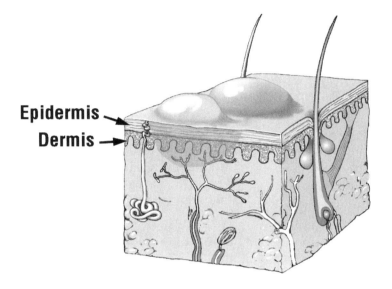

Second-degree burns

A. extend into the lower layer of skin.

B. cause the skin to blister and swell.

C. damage only the outer layer of skin.

D. prevent the skin from healing.

CHECKYOURANSWERHERECHECKYOURANSWERHERECHECKYOURANSWERHERE
CHECKYOURANSWERHERECHECKYOURANSWERHERECHECKYOURANSWERHERE
CHECKYOURANSWERHERECHECKYOURANSWERHERECHECKYOURANSWERHERE
CHECKYOURANSWERHERECHECKYOURANSWERHERECHECKYOURANSWERHERE

Answer: A and B are correct.

Third-Degree Burns

- nerves are damaged - no pain

3. In **third-degree burns**, both the epidermis and dermis are destroyed, and underlying tissues are either damaged or destroyed. The skin may be charred or white. Blisters may be present, but in very severe third-degree burns, they are often absent. Usually, little swelling is involved. Because the nerve endings are destroyed, there is little or no pain.

Third-Degree Burn

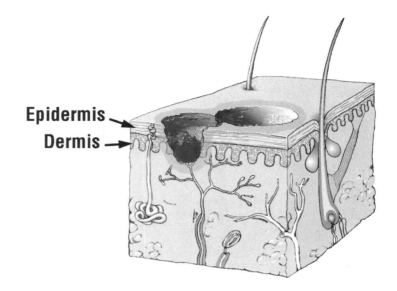

Epidermis
Dermis

Healing, if possible, requires more than 21 days, and scarring usually results even when skin grafting is performed. Patients with third-degree burns are at high risk of infection. The patient may also experience severe fluid loss through the burned tissue. Third-degree burns are usually caused by fire, electrical shock, or contact with corrosive chemicals.

Describe a third-degree burn. _____

_____

_____

_____

CHECKYOURANSWERHERECHECKYOURANSWERHERECHECKYOURANSWERHERE
CHECKYOURANSWERHERECHECKYOURANSWERHERECHECKYOURANSWERHERE
CHECKYOURANSWERHERECHECKYOURANSWERHERECHECKYOURANSWERHERE
CHECKYOURANSWERHERECHECKYOURANSWERHERECHECKYOURANSWERHERE

4. Each of the following excerpts from medical reports represents a classification of a burn. Label each description with a **1** if it describes a first-degree burn, a **2** if it describes a second-degree burn, or a **3** if it represents a third-degree burn.

_____ A. There is complete destruction of dermis and epidermis on the lateral side of the right forearm. Tissue damage is extensive.

_____ B. All burns are confined to the epidermis of the patient's left hand. The burned areas are painful, but no blisters are present.

_____ C. The patient's burns have caused massive blistering on the left arm. However, it is apparent that the dermis and epidermis have already begun healing.

_____ D. The patient's right thigh is severely burned, with charring of an area of thigh tissue about three inches in diameter. All of the overlying skin is completely destroyed in an area about four inches in diameter.

APPRAISING BURNS

Percentage of Body Burned

5. When appraising the seriousness of a burn, the most important consideration is the **percentage of the surface of the body that has been burned in any degree**. A first- or second-degree burn to a large percentage of the body may be considerably more damaging than a very small third-degree burn, unless the third-degree burn destroys important nerves or blood vessels.

    In order to determine what percentage of the body is burned, physicians use a rather complicated chart dividing the body into percentages based on the patient's age and height. It is not necessary to learn this procedure for interpreting medical reports, since they will contain the doctor's findings in percentages.

    When appraising the seriousness of burns, the most important consideration is the

    A. degree of the burn.

    B. percentage of the surface of the body that has been burned in any degree.

    C. age of the patient.

Other Factors in Appraising Burns

6. In addition to the percentage of the body burned, other factors also play a role in determining the severity of a burn. One of these is the **site of the burn**. Even a small burn in certain parts of the body is extremely deforming. These parts include the face, hands, feet, external genitalia, and the joint areas which perform flexion and extension, such as the back of the knee or the inside of the elbow.

    The following factors also are taken into consideration in determining the severity of a burn:

    ■ Burn is complicated by a fracture or extensive injury to soft tissues

    ■ Burn occurs to the lungs or other parts of the respiratory system

    ■ Burn is caused by exposure to electricity

Burns to the lungs or other parts of the respiratory system occur when flames or very hot gases are inhaled.

A small burn might be considered severe if it is located on the

A. inside of the elbow.

B. abdomen.

C. face.

D. hands.

E. back.

F. lower leg.

CHECKYOURANSWERHERECHECKYOURANSWERHERECHECKYOURANSWERHERE
CHECKYOURANSWERHERECHECKYOURANSWERHERECHECKYOURANSWERHERE
CHECKYOURANSWERHERECHECKYOURANSWERHERECHECKYOURANSWERHERE
CHECKYOURANSWERHERECHECKYOURANSWERHERECHECKYOURANSWERHERE

7. Which of the following factors may increase the severity of a burn?

A. Burn caused by exposure to electricity

B. Fracture in the area of the burn

C. Location of the burn

D. Extensive soft tissue injury

E. Involvement of the respiratory system

F. All of the above factors may increase the severity of a burn

CHECKYOURANSWERHERECHECKYOURANSWERHERECHECKYOURANSWERHERE
CHECKYOURANSWERHERECHECKYOURANSWERHERECHECKYOURANSWERHERE
CHECKYOURANSWERHERECHECKYOURANSWERHERECHECKYOURANSWERHERE
CHECKYOURANSWERHERECHECKYOURANSWERHERECHECKYOURANSWERHERE

CLASSIFICATION OF BURNS

8. Burns are classified as **minor**, **moderate**, or **critical** based on all of the criteria we've discussed in this unit. These groups are outlined in the following chart.

Minor Burns	Moderate Burns	Critical Burns
■ Second-degree burns of less than 15% of the body, or	■ Second-degree burns of 15–30% of the body, or	■ Second-degree burns over 30% or more of the body, or
■ Third-degree burns of less than 2% of the body, unless the burned area is: — Hands or feet — Face — Genitalia — Joints involving flexion and extension	■ Third-degree burns of less than 10% of the body, unless the burned area is: — Hands or feet — Face — Genitalia — Joints involving flexion and extension	■ Third-degree burns of face, hands, feet, genitalia, or joints involving flexion and extension, or ■ Third-degree burns over 10% or more of the body, or ■ Electrical burns, or ■ Burns complicated by: — Fractures — Extensive soft tissue damage — Lung or other respiratory system involvement

Answer the following questions based on the information in the preceding chart. Assume that none of these burns involve the hands, feet, face, genitalia, or joints.

A. According to the chart, a person who has third-degree burns over 15% of the body is said to have (critical/moderate/minor) _____ burns.

B. A person who has third-degree burns over less than 2% of the body has (critical/moderate/minor) _____ burns.

C. An electrical burn accompanied by fractures is (critical/moderate/minor) _____.

D. A second-degree burn of 25% of the body is (critical/moderate/minor) _____.

CHECKYOURANSWERHERECHECKYOURANSWERHERECHECKYOURANSWERHERE
CHECKYOURANSWERHERECHECKYOURANSWERHERECHECKYOURANSWERHERE
CHECKYOURANSWERHERECHECKYOURANSWERHERECHECKYOURANSWERHERE
CHECKYOURANSWERHERECHECKYOURANSWERHERECHECKYOURANSWERHERE

REVIEW

9. Review what you've learned about burns by answering the following questions.

Briefly describe the three degrees of burns.

A. First-degree: _____
    _____
    _____
    _____

B. Second-degree: _____
    _____
    _____

C. Third-degree: _____
    _____
    _____

CHECKYOURANSWERHERECHECKYOURANSWERHERECHECKYOURANSWERHERE
CHECKYOURANSWERHERECHECKYOURANSWERHERECHECKYOURANSWERHERE
CHECKYOURANSWERHERECHECKYOURANSWERHERECHECKYOURANSWERHERE
CHECKYOURANSWERHERECHECKYOURANSWERHERECHECKYOURANSWERHERE
CHECKYOURANSWERHERECHECKYOURANSWERHERECHECKYOURANSWERHERE
CHECKYOURANSWERHERECHECKYOURANSWERHERECHECKYOURANSWERHERE
CHECKYOURANSWERHERECHECKYOURANSWERHERECHECKYOURANSWERHERE

10. All of the following factors are taken into consideration when determining the severity of a burn EXCEPT

A. age of the patient.

B. percentage of the body burned.

C. site of the burn.

D. whether the burn is complicated by a fracture or extensive soft tissue injury.

11. Label each of the following burns **C** for critical, **MOD** for moderate, or **MIN** for minor.

    ____ A. Third-degree burns over 7% of the body, involving the right aspect of the back.

    ____ B. Second-degree burns over 29% of the body; extensive damage to soft tissues in several areas.

    ____ C. Second-degree burns over 10% of the body.

    ____ D. Third-degree burns over 15% of the body, including both legs and feet.

This completes your study of the basic structures and functions of the human body. We hope you'll draw on your new-found knowledge throughout your career as a claim examiner.

When you're ready, take the examination that accompanies this course. Before you do so, you may want to review the Glossary and Job Aids included at the end of the text. Good luck.

Review Test

Important Information Regarding This Review Test

This exam was designed for review purposes and may be used to fulfill your training and firm element requirements. This exam has not been approved for insurance continuing education and cannot be used for this purpose. If you need insurance continuing education credit for this course, a different exam is required; please contact Kaplan Financial at 1-800-423-4723.

1. A claimant who has been diagnosed with arthritis is suffering from
   - A. an earache.
   - B. weakness in a joint.
   - C. extreme pain in the liver.
   - D. an inflammation of a joint.

2. Which one of the following is the correct definition of hematoma?
   - A. Presence of blood
   - B. Abnormal flow of blood
   - C. Blood in the urine
   - D. Blood tumor

3. What does the root word chondri mean?
   - A. Bone marrow
   - B. Joint
   - C. Cartilage
   - D. Muscle

4. An arthrotomy is a/an
   - A. surgical incision into a joint.
   - B. condition of a joint.
   - C. surgical removal of a joint.
   - D. inflammation of a joint.

5. A person who specializes in disorders of the skin is a/an
   - A. cardiologist.
   - B. dermatologist.
   - C. oncologist.
   - D. orthopedist.

6. Which one of the following prefixes means on or upon?
   - A. Inter
   - B. Peri
   - C. Intra
   - D. Epi

7. Translate the following instructions: Patient should take ss dos of medication p.o. q2h e.m.p.
   - A. Patient should take a half dose of medication by mouth every two hours as directed.
   - B. Patient should take a half dose of medication every two hours or as needed.
   - C. Patient should take a half tablet of medication by mouth every two hours without food or water.
   - D. Patient should take a full dose of medication every two days or as needed.

8. Select the correct abbreviation for the following instructions: Patient's vital signs should be checked at bedtime.
   - A. Patient's v.s.s. should be checked q.h.
   - B. Patient's v.s. should be checked h.s.
   - C. Patient's v.s.s. should be checked h.s.
   - D. Patient's v.s. should be checked e.m.p.

9. Marty Schoenstein fractured his leg when he fell off a ladder. Which one of the following specialists would probably treat Marty's injury?
   - A. Otologist
   - B. Radiologist
   - C. Orthopedist
   - D. Otolaryngologist

10. Which one of the following is the correct abbreviation for dosage?
    - A. q.d.
    - B. dos
    - C. ss
    - D. gtt.

11. Dionne Walters suffered a detached retina when she was involved in a serious auto accident. Which one of the following specialists would probably treat her injury?
    - A. Otolaryngologist
    - B. Orthopedist
    - C. Otologist
    - D. Ophthalmologist

12. You're reviewing a medical report on a patient who suffered multiple contusions in the right malar area. This means that the skin in the area was

    A. penetrated by an object, causing a deep, narrow hole.

    B. torn irregularly.

    C. bruised severely, but not enough to break the skin.

    D. scraped.

13. Which one of the following statements does NOT apply to an abrasion?

    A. It scrapes away part of the skin.

    B. It is protected during healing by scab formation.

    C. It is a nonthreatening injury in healthy individuals.

    D. It may cause swelling and pain, but does not break the skin.

14. The type of wound characterized by a clean, straight cut from a sharp-edged object is a/an

    A. perforating wound.

    B. crushing wound.

    C. incised wound.

    D. lacerating wound.

15. A claimant was diagnosed with a sprained hip after she slipped and fell on a wet floor in the company lunchroom. This means that the claimant has

    A. stretched the tendons around her hip beyond their usual limits.

    B. fractured a bone in her hip.

    C. torn the ligaments in her hip.

    D. stretched her hip muscles beyond their usual limits.

16. You're reviewing a medical report on a patient who was diagnosed with a back strain. This means that the claimant has

    A. fractured a bone in his back.

    B. torn the ligaments in his back.

    C. stretched his back muscles or tendons beyond their usual limits.

    D. torn the cartilage in his back.

17. A skull fracture is most dangerous when it is located in what area of the skull?

    A. Basal

    B. Occipital

    C. Frontal

    D. Parietal

18. Which one of the following is NOT a residual symptom of a cerebral concussion?

    A. Light-headedness

    B. Headache

    C. Deafness

    D. Insomnia

19. Which cranial bone is located at the front of the head?

    A. Parietal

    B. Occipital

    C. Temporal

    D. Frontal

20. A medical report lists the following symptoms for a claimant: severe pain in the area of the right temporomandibular joint, difficulty in opening the mouth, grating sounds when opening the mouth, and loose teeth. Based on these symptoms, the claimant will probably be diagnosed as having

    A. thoracic outlet syndrome.

    B. a TMJ disorder.

    C. a depressed skull fracture.

    D. carpal tunnel syndrome.

21. Which one of the following statements is correct concerning computerized tomography (CT)?

    A. It is a color-enhanced video image of a single two-dimensional image made from two plain film x-rays taken from different angles.

    B. It produces a series of radiographs from a revolving x-ray tube that are converted first to digital code, then to a two-dimensional image on a screen.

    C. It takes two or more plain film x-rays and converts them to a one-dimensional 'slice' of tissue or bone on a screen.

    D. It blurs all structures except the part being studied, allowing a single-angle plain film x-ray of the unblurred part to be converted to a one-dimensional image on a screen.

22. A comminuted fracture in which one or more of the bone pieces are driven inward and press on the brain is called a

    A. depressed skull fracture.
    B. closed skull fracture.
    C. simple skull fracture.
    D. basal skull fracture.

23. A brain contusion

    A. bruises the brain but does not tear the brain or the meninges.
    B. is usually caused by a depressed skull fracture.
    C. tears into the substance of the brain.
    D. never results in permanent brain damage.

24. What is an epidural hematoma?

    A. A blood tumor located below the dura mater
    B. Abnormal bleeding on or above the dura mater
    C. Abnormal bleeding in the area below the dura mater
    D. A blood tumor located on or above the dura mater

25. A claimant has suffered a cerebral concussion. Which one of the following statements concerning this claimant's condition are correct?

    A. It never produces any residual symptoms, such as headaches or blurred vision.
    B. It is considered the most serious of all injuries that can occur to the brain.
    C. It always causes severe hemorrhaging within the brain.
    D. It usually causes a short period of unconsciousness.

26. Name the bone that forms the lower back portion of the skull and is located between the parietal and temporal bones.

    A. Occipital
    B. Zygomatic
    C. Frontal
    D. Sphenoid

27. The original use of MRI, and an area for which MRI remains a major testing device, is

    A. neurology.
    B. pathology.
    C. pediatrics.
    D. orthopedics.

28. Which one of the following answer choices correctly lists the two bones that make up the jaw?

    A. Maxilla and mandible
    B. Mandible and temporomandibular bone
    C. Mandible and occipital bone
    D. Maxilla and sphenoid

29. Babinski's reflex is positive when the

    A. patient cannot maintain equilibrium.
    B. big toe flexes backward.
    C. ankle joint flexes forward.
    D. patient experiences pain when the hip joint is flexed.

30. What portion of the vertebra allows joint movement in the spine?

    A. Intervertebral disc
    B. Vertebral body
    C. Neural arch
    D. Articular processes

31. The spinal cord extends from the

    A. first cervical vertebra to the fifth lumbar vertebra.
    B. first cervical vertebra to the coccyx.
    C. medulla oblongata to the sacrum.
    D. medulla oblongata to approximately the second lumbar vertebra.

32. A herniated intervertebral disc

    A. occurs most frequently in the thoracic region of the spine.
    B. can be caused by trauma or deterioration during the aging process.
    C. always causes pain for the patient regardless of whether the disc is pressing on spinal nerve roots.
    D. will repair itself in time as the blood supply to the disc helps regenerate the nerves.

33. Fractures, dislocations and other types of injuries usually occur more frequently in which region of the spine?

    A. Lumbar/sacral
    B. Coccyx
    C. Thoracic
    D. Dorsal

34. What is the most common type of back injury seen in claim work?

    A. Spondylolisthesis
    B. Sprain/strain
    C. Subluxation
    D. Compression fracture

35. Which one of the following spinal fractures would be most likely to result in permanent, total paralysis of the patient's trunk and limbs?

    A. Simple linear fracture to the coccyx
    B. Comminuted fracture to C-4
    C. Complete, undisplaced fracture to T-12
    D. Compression fracture to L-5

36. Which one of the following diagnostic tests or signs is positive when the patient is unable to maintain balance while standing with the feet together and the eyes closed?

    A. Romberg's sign
    B. Straight leg-raising test
    C. Electromyography
    D. Myelography

37. Which one of the following medical report excerpts describes a subjective complaint?

    A. The pain in Mrs. Jay's lower back was determined to be caused by a herniated intervertebral disc between L-4 and L-5.
    B. Although all tests were negative, Mr. Grover continues to complain of pain in the lumbar region upon movement.
    C. Tests revealed that a compression fracture between L-2 and L-3 was the reason Mr. Wilson had difficulty in movement.
    D. Ms. Chang's neck pain is the result of a hyperextension-hyperflexion injury she suffered in an auto accident.

38. What is spondylolisthesis?

    A. Forward displacement of one vertebra over another
    B. Compression of a vertebra into the one beneath it
    C. Partial dislocation of a vertebra
    D. Type of injury where the neck is first extended excessively backward, then thrown forward

39. Another name for the membranes that cover the brain and spinal cord is

    A. medulla oblongata.
    B. articular processes.
    C. cerebrospinal fluid.
    D. meninges.

40. Which one of the following diagnostic tests or signs is used to distinguish between sciatica and hip joint disease?

    A. Electromyography
    B. Babinski's reflex
    C. Straight leg-raising test
    D. Myelography

41. A partial union of a bone fracture occurs when

    A. only tissue holds the bone fragments together.
    B. callus does not adequately bridge the fracture site.
    C. the callus does not harden.
    D. bone fragments do not heal in a functional position.

42. The type of disability present when a person is partially able to perform usual activities, but will never be completely able to perform them as before, is called

    A. temporary total.
    B. permanent partial.
    C. permanent total.
    D. temporary partial.

43. Which one of the following is NOT a possible complication of a sternal fracture?

    A. Fractured spine
    B. Bruising of the heart
    C. Ruptured spleen
    D. Detachment of the ribs from the sternum

44. The purpose of bursae is to

    A. protect the vertebrae from damaging each other during movement.
    B. facilitate joint movement.
    C. prevent friction between bone and muscle.
    D. attach muscles to bone.

45. Why is a fracture to the middle third of the humerus considered more serious than a fracture to the proximal end of the humerus?
    A. The presence of the radial nerve in this area poses the possibility of nerve damage.
    B. A fracture in this area is likely to involve a joint, causing loss of motion.
    C. This part of the bone is responsible for movement of the entire arm.
    D. The middle third of the humerus always requires a longer healing period than the proximal third.

46. The olecranon process is
    A. the part of the pelvis that receives the head of the femur.
    B. often involved in an injury called a silver fork deformity.
    C. located between the femur and the tibia.
    D. a part of the ulna that articulates with the humerus to form the elbow joint.

47. What is the name of the group of bones that forms the hand?
    A. Carpals
    B. Phalanges
    C. Metacarpals
    D. Tarsals

48. Which one of the following injuries is most likely to result in loss of use of the hand?
    A. Simple linear fracture of the distal phalanx of the right little finger
    B. Total amputation of the left index finger
    C. Total amputation of the thumb
    D. Compound fracture of a metacarpal

49. Select the correct definition of temporary total disability.
    A. Individual is only partially able to perform pre-injury activities for a temporary period of time
    B. Individual is totally unable to perform any pre-injury activities for a temporary period of time
    C. Individual cannot perform any pre-injury activities
    D. Individual will never be able to fully perform any pre-injury activities

50. Which one of the following answer choices lists the two bones that make up the forearm?
    A. Ulna and humerus
    B. Radius and tarsal
    C. Radius and ulna
    D. Humerus and olecranon process

51. Which one of the following answer choices lists the two conditions that are often misdiagnosed as carpal tunnel syndrome?
    A. Lumbar disc herniation and thoracic outlet syndromes
    B. Thoracic outlet syndromes and cervical disc herniation
    C. Epiphysis injuries and cervical disc herniation
    D. Compression fractures and thoracic outlet syndromes

52. A Colles fracture is a fracture
    A. of the lower end of the fibula and the medial malleolus of the tibia.
    B. in which the bone is partially bent and partially broken.
    C. of the distal end of the radius.
    D. of any bone that extends into a joint.

53. A fracture of the lower end of the fibula and the medial malleolus of the tibia is a
    A. transverse fracture.
    B. Pott's fracture.
    C. Colles fracture.
    D. greenstick fracture.

54. Which one of the following bones is NOT a part of the pelvic area?
    A. Ilium
    B. Ischium
    C. Sacrum
    D. Tarsal

55. Which one of the following is a possible complication of a fracture to the pubic bone, especially for male patients?
    A. Loss of mobility in the hip joint
    B. Atrophy of thigh muscles
    C. Torn urethra
    D. Ruptured spleen

56. Which one of the following knee injuries is most common in young athletes, usually as a result of over-twisting the knee?

    A. Horizontal meniscus tear
    B. Arthritis
    C. Fractured patella
    D. Longitudinal meniscus tear

57. What surgical technique is often used to diagnose and treat meniscus tears?

    A. Arthroscopy
    B. MRI
    C. Open reduction of the meniscus
    D. Closed reduction of the meniscus

58. You're reviewing a medical report for a patient who has suffered a compound fracture in the middle third of his right tibia. Which one of the following healing complications may arise as a result of this type of fracture?

    A. Bursitis
    B. Arthritis
    C. Diabetes mellitus
    D. Osteomyelitis

59. The lower end of the fibula is known as the

    A. acetabulum.
    B. medial malleolus.
    C. proximal malleolus.
    D. lateral malleolus.

60. All of the following are possible results of a fracture into the knee joint EXCEPT

    A. arthritis.
    B. atrophy of thigh muscles.
    C. loss of motion in the joint.
    D. instability when walking or standing.

61. Bursitis most often arises after an injury to which one of the following joints?

    A. Ankle
    B. Shoulder
    C. Knee
    D. Wrist

62. The two most frequently fractured tarsal bones are the

    A. achilles and talus.
    B. tibia and calcaneus.
    C. talus and calcaneus.
    D. fibula and achilles.

63. Where is the fibula located?

    A. On the inside of the lower leg
    B. On the outside of the lower leg
    C. Between the pelvis and the knee joint
    D. On the lower portion of the tibia

64. A claimant has suffered a fractured acetabulum. All of the following are possible complications of this type of fracture EXCEPT

    A. avascular necrosis.
    B. need for replacement of the hip joint with an artificial joint.
    C. osteoarthritis.
    D. atrophy of the muscles in the lower leg.

65. Which organ is especially susceptible to damage from a traumatic chest injury because it is located underneath the ribs?

    A. Kidney
    B. Bladder
    C. Liver
    D. Spleen

66. Which one of the following situations would be most likely to cause injury to the kidneys?

    A. A warehouse clerk falls off a ladder and lands on his right hip.
    B. A football coach trips over a bench and falls flat on his face.
    C. A mail carrier slips on an icy sidewalk and lands on her hands and knees.
    D. A jogger is struck from behind by a fast-moving car.

67. Which one of the following statements best describes the relationship between trauma and hernias?
    A. Trauma has never been determined to be the cause of a hernia.
    B. A direct inguinal hernia is usually caused by a traumatic injury.
    C. In order to be the cause of a hernia, a traumatic injury must be of sufficient force to rupture the tissues.
    D. A hernia is always the direct result of a severe traumatic injury to the abdominal wall.

68. If the urinary bladder is full when a traumatic injury occurs, it is likely to
    A. develop an aneurysm.
    B. develop an abscess.
    C. bruise.
    D. rupture.

69. A lump on the inner side of the thigh is characteristic of a/an
    A. indirect inguinal hernia.
    B. direct inguinal hernia.
    C. ruptured bladder.
    D. femoral hernia.

70. When peritonitis is described as diffuse, this means it
    A. developed without a bacterial infection.
    B. has spread through the peritoneum.
    C. arose from trauma.
    D. affects only a small area of the peritoneum.

71. A claimant fractured four ribs in an auto accident. Three weeks later, she returned to her physician complaining of high fever, weight loss, anorexia, and nausea. Based on the type of injury, the time frame and her symptoms, the claimant probably has a
    A. ruptured bladder.
    B. hepatic aneurysm.
    C. lacerated kidney.
    D. liver abscess.

72. The heart receives its blood supply from the
    A. left ventricle.
    B. pulmonary arteries.
    C. coronary arteries.
    D. right atrium.

73. The term "stroke" can be used to describe any of the following EXCEPT
    A. ischemia.
    B. cerebral hemorrhage.
    C. myocardial infarction.
    D. cerebrovascular accident.

74. The condition in which lipids accumulate in the arteries is called
    A. thrombosis.
    B. embolus.
    C. occlusion.
    D. atherosclerosis.

75. When you see a claim involving myocardial infarction or a cerebrovascular accident, you know that the claimant's condition was most likely caused by
    A. an allergic reaction to medication.
    B. job stress.
    C. a preexisting condition or disease.
    D. a traumatic injury.

76. The purpose of the pulmonary arteries is to carry
    A. nutrients and oxygen to tissues.
    B. used blood returning from other parts of the body to the heart.
    C. unoxygenated blood to the lungs.
    D. oxygenated blood from the lungs to the heart.

77. What is myocardial infarction?
    A. The death of tissue in the heart muscle
    B. A lack of blood supply to the heart
    C. A blockage in a coronary artery
    D. Excessive hemorrhaging within the heart

78. All of the following are common symptoms of a stroke EXCEPT
    A. hemianopia.
    B. nausea.
    C. apraxia.
    D. aphasia.

79. All of the following terms are related to the inhalation of hard coal dust EXCEPT
    A. progressive massive fibrosis.
    B. asbestosis.
    C. anthracosis.
    D. black lung disease.

80. Long employment in the stonecutting industry is known to have a relationship to the development of a pneumoconiosis called
    A. silicosis.
    B. asbestosis.
    C. fibrosis.
    D. CWP.

81. What is the technical name for the windpipe?
    A. Alveolus
    B. Trachea
    C. Bronchus
    D. Lung

82. What is a hemopneumothorax?
    A. Blood in the pleural space
    B. Air in the pleural space
    C. Blood and air in the pleural space
    D. Blood and air in the lungs

83. Which one of the following answer choices correctly lists the two diseases that often accompany and complicate silicosis?
    A. Tuberculosis and emphysema
    B. Anthracosis and emphysema
    C. Tuberculosis and CWP
    D. Asbestosis and CWP

84. If not treated, a pneumothorax can cause the lungs to
    A. degenerate.
    B. fill with blood.
    C. atrophy.
    D. collapse.

85. What part of the lungs supply oxygen for the blood?
    A. Bronchiole
    B. Alveoli
    C. Trachea
    D. Bronchus

86. When you encounter a claim for a neural hearing impairment, you know that
    A. compensation is probably in order, since a nerve impairment is always the result of either trauma or prolonged exposure to loud noise.
    B. following proper treatment, the nerve will regenerate, but will have to be supplemented by a hearing aid.
    C. the condition is always caused by deterioration due to old age, so the claim is not compensable.
    D. a complete physical examination is necessary since the underlying causes of hearing nerve impairment vary greatly.

87. What is the most common cause of a conductive hearing impairment?
    A. Trauma affecting the hearing nerve in the inner ear
    B. Deterioration due to old age
    C. Prolonged exposure to loud noise
    D. Wax or foreign bodies in the external ear, or an infection in the external or middle ear

88. Which one of the following eye conditions involves the separation of the innermost layer of the eyeball from the middle layer of the eyeball?
    A. Conjunctivitis
    B. Glaucoma
    C. Diplopia
    D. Retinal detachment

89. Which one of the following conditions might require enucleation of the eye?
    A. Cataracts
    B. Violent injury or trauma to the eye
    C. Diplopia
    D. Conjunctivitis

90. Which one of the following answer choices correctly lists the three basic divisions of the internal apparatus of the ear?
    A. External ear, middle ear, inner ear
    B. Eardrum, hearing nerve, middle ear
    C. Middle ear, eardrum, hearing nerve
    D. Inner ear, ear lobe, bones of the middle ear

91. How many teeth are in a full set of permanent teeth?

    A. 28
    B. 32
    C. 30
    D. 20

92. Which one of the following types of teeth are a part of the permanent set of teeth but are not part of the deciduous teeth?

    A. First molars
    B. Central incisors
    C. Lateral incisors
    D. Bicuspids

93. Which one of the following situations involving the loss of teeth would have the most adverse effect on the individual?

    A. Six-year-old Katie lost all four of her deciduous central incisors.
    B. Thirteen-year-old Cassandra lost a permanent lateral incisor.
    C. Larry, a 42-year-old dentist, lost his first and second molars.
    D. Elmer, a 70-year-old retiree, lost his first and second bicuspids.

94. A claimant lost permanent tooth number 8 when she fell down her porch steps and landed face-first on the sidewalk. This claimant has lost a

    A. third molar.
    B. lateral incisor.
    C. bicuspid.
    D. central incisor.

95. A medical report states that a four-year-old child lost deciduous tooth L in an auto accident. This report is describing the loss of a

    A. cuspid.
    B. first molar.
    C. central incisor.
    D. second molar.

96. A third-degree burn that covers more than 10% of the body is classified as a

    A. minor burn.
    B. moderate burn.
    C. critical burn.
    D. superficial burn.

97. Which one of the following factors is NOT taken into consideration when determining the severity of a burn?

    A. Whether the burn is complicated by a fracture or extensive soft tissue injury
    B. Location of the burn
    C. Percentage of body burned
    D. The amount of time that elapsed between the time the patient was burned and the time the patient sought treatment for the burn

98. A third-degree burn over less than 2% of the body that does not occur on the hands, feet, face, genitalia, or joints involved in flexion or extension would be classified as a

    A. moderate burn.
    B. minor burn.
    C. superficial burn.
    D. critical burn.

99. Which one of the following individuals has suffered a second-degree burn?

    A. Lynn was burned on the face. Her skin was blistered.
    B. Jack suffered extensive burns on his back that destroyed all layers of the skin.
    C. Steve suffered burns on the epidermis of the left forearm. His skin was red and swollen, but not blistered.
    D. Leslie burned her left hand. No blistering or swelling was present.

100. Which one of the following conditions is NOT present in a first-degree burn?

    A. Swelling
    B. Redness
    C. Pain and tenderness
    D. Blisters

ANSWERS AND RATIONALES

1. **D.** The word is a combination of the prefix arthr, which means joint, and the suffix itis, which means inflammation.

2. **D.** The word is a combination of the root word hemat, meaning blood, and the suffix oma, meaning tumor.

3. **C.** The root word for muscle is myo. The prefix for a joint is arthr/arthro. The root word for bone marrow is myel/myelo.

4. **A.** The term arthrotomy is a combination of the prefix arthr, meaning joint, and the suffix otomy, meaning surgical incision.

5. **B.** An oncologist specializes in the treatment of cancer. An orthopedist treats disorders of the skeleton and joints. A cardiologist specializes in the heart.

6. **D.** Inter means between. Intra means within. Peri means around.

7. **A.** The abbreviations in these instructions are defined as follows: ss, half; dos, dose; p.o., by mouth; q2h, every two hours; e.m.p., as directed.

8. **B.** The abbreviation for vital signs is v.s. The abbreviation for bedtime is h.s.

9. **C.** An orthopedist treats disorders of the skeleton and joints, including fractures. An otologist treats disorders of the ear. An otolaryngologist treats disorders of the ear, nose and throat. A radiologist specializes in interpreting x-rays.

10. **B.** The abbreviation q.d. stands for every day. Gtt. stands for drops. The abbreviation ss means half.

11. **D.** The root word ophthalmos means eye; an ophthalmologist is a specialist in eye disorders such as detached retinas.

12. **C.** A contusion, or bruise, is a type of injury that causes discoloration but does not break the skin.

13. **D.** Breaking of the skin is characteristic of an abrasion.

14. **C.** A crushing wound is caused by trauma of sufficient force to smash or compress tissues, sometimes without lacerating the skin. A lacerating wound is an irregular tear in the skin, as opposed to a clean cut. A perforating wound is one where an object breaks the skin and then exits at another point.

15. **C.** A sprain is an injury to a joint where the ligaments are partly or completely torn away from the bone.

16. **C.** A strain involves stretching muscles or tendons beyond their usual limits. It is not the same thing as a sprain, which is an injury to a joint where the ligaments are partly or completely torn away from the bone.

17. **A.** While all skull fractures are potentially dangerous, one located in the basal area is particularly serious because cranial nerves, major blood vessels and nerve centers in this area make surgical treatment of the fracture virtually impossible in most cases.

18. **C.** Headache, insomnia and light-headedness were all listed in the text as possible residual symptoms of a cerebral concussion.

19. **D.** The parietal bones form the top and sides of the skull. The occipital bone forms the lower back portion of the skull. The temporal bones are located at the base of the skull and on either side of the head.

20. **B.** These symptoms are characteristic of a TMJ disorder, but do not correspond with those produced by carpal tunnel syndrome, thoracic outlet syndromes or a depressed skull fracture.

21. **B.** The CT produces two-dimensional images from a number of x-rays, not just one.

22. **A.** This type of fracture must be treated surgically; the patient risks both injury to the brain from the fracture itself and the additional possibility of brain damage that occurs when correcting the fracture.

23. **A.** While a brain contusion is less serious than a brain laceration, it still can cause temporary or permanent brain impairment and even death.

24. **D.** A blood tumor located below the dura mater is a subdural hematoma. Abnormal bleeding in the area below the dura mater is a subdural hemorrhage. Abnormal bleeding on or above the dura mater is an epidural hemorrhage.

25. **D.** A cerebral concussion is the least complicated and least damaging injury to the brain, and it does not cause hemorrhaging. Once the patient has recovered, however, the effects of the cerebral concussion can appear in other modes called residual symptoms.

26. **A.** The frontal bone is located at the front of the head. The sphenoid bone is located at the side of the skull between the frontal and temporal bones. The zygomatic bone is one of two bones located below the eyes.

27. **A.** While MRI might be used in any of the specialties listed above, it is used most frequently in neurology because it is very effective for examining soft tissues with high fluid content, such as the brain or spinal cord, or for detecting any condition that increases fluid content.

28. **A.** The upper jaw bone is called the maxilla and the lower jaw bone is called the mandible.

29. **B.** A positive Babinski's reflex indicates damage to the nervous system.

30. **D.** A vertebra's articular processes articulate with the articular processes of the vertebrae above and below. This means that joints are formed between the vertebrae, making movement possible.

31. **D.** The spinal cord does not extend all the way through the spinal column.

32. **B.** A herniated intervertebral disc occurs most often in the lumbar region. An intervertebral disc has no blood supply or nerves, so it cannot regenerate and does not cause pain unless it is pressing on spinal nerves.

33. **A.** The lumbar and sacral areas are subjected to many extremes of motion and bear the strain of most of the lifting and carrying we do.

34. **B.** Strains and sprains can cause the same symptoms and the same amount of pain as a fracture, dislocation or herniated disc, so a diagnostic test may be used to determine the nature of the patient's injury.

35. **B.** The location of a fracture in the spinal column is very significant regarding permanent disability. A fracture in the cervical region that damages the spinal cord is very likely to cause permanent, total paralysis of the patient's trunk and limbs.

36. **A.** A positive Romberg's sign indicates nerve damage.

37. **B.** A subjective complaint is one that has no apparent cause, as opposed to an objective finding, which means the physician has actually found some abnormalities in the patient to back up his or her symptoms. In the other answer choices, objective findings were made.

38. **A.** The other answer choices describe a compression fracture, subluxation and hyperextension-hyperflexion injury.

39. **D.** These three membranes are called the pia mater, arachnoid and dura mater.

40. **C.** Electromyography measures electrical activity in muscles. Myelography involves inspecting the spinal cord by injecting a radiopaque medium and x-raying. Babinski's reflex is used to diagnose nervous system damage.

41. **B.** The other answer choices describe non-union, malunion and fibrous union.

42. **B.** In temporary disabilities, the individual is completely or partially unable to perform usual activities for a temporary period. A permanent total disability means the individual will never be able to perform his or her pre-injury vocation.

43. **C.** The spleen is not located anywhere near the sternum, so there is no chance that it will suffer damage if the sternum is fractured.

44. **C.** The other answer choices describe the functions of intervertebral discs, ligaments and tendons.

45. **A.** The radial nerve winds around the middle third of the humerus. When this area of the humerus is fractured, the radial nerve is susceptible to being lacerated by a bone fragment or pinched as the bone heals.

46. **D.** The olecranon process is a part of the ulna that articulates with the humerus to form the elbow joint.

47. **C.** The phalanges form the fingers and toes. The tarsals make up the ankle. The carpals make up the wrist.

48. **C.** The ability to touch the thumb to the other fingertips is considered 50% of the use of the hand, so the loss of this ability leaves the hand only 50% functional.

49. **B.** In temporary disabilities, the individual is completely or partially unable to perform usual activities for a temporary period. In

permanent disabilities, an individual is completely or partially unable to perform usual activities on a permanent basis.

50. **C.** The humerus is the long bone in the upper arm. The olecranon process is part of the ulna that articulates with the lower end of the humerus to form the elbow. Tarsals are the ankle bones.

51. **B.** Both thoracic outlet syndromes and cervical disc herniation produce symptoms that are similar to carpal tunnel syndrome, such as tingling and pain in the arm.

52. **C.** Other characteristics of a Colles fracture are that it is a transverse fracture and that the lower fragment of the radius is displaced backward and outward, causing the hand to be displaced in the same manner.

53. **B.** In a greenstick fracture, the bone is partially bent and partially broken. A Colles fracture is a type of fracture that involves the radius. In a transverse fracture, the break is at right angles to the bone.

54. **D.** Tarsals form the ankle bones.

55. **C.** While fractures to the pelvic bones are rare, they can be serious and very painful since the pelvic bones provide support for both the abdomen and lower spine.

56. **D.** The patella is usually damaged as a result of a direct blow to the knee. A horizontal meniscus tear is more common in older adults and occurs as a result of aging. Arthritis may develop after an injury, but is rarely the primary result of an injury.

57. **A.** With arthroscopy, the physician observes the interior of the knee with an endoscope.

58. **D.** Bursitis and arthritis involve joints, and the middle third of the tibia is not a joint. Diabetes mellitus is never caused by an injury.

59. **D.** The medial malleolus is the lower end of the tibia. The acetabulum is part of the hip joint. There is no such thing as a proximal malleolus.

60. **B.** This type of injury would not cause the thigh muscles to atrophy.

61. **B.** Bursitis in the shoulder is usually very painful for the patient and results in the greatest loss of joint movement, sometimes resulting in permanent disability.

62. **C.** The talus is directly below the tibia. The calcaneus is below the talus. Both of these bones form part of the ankle.

63. **B.** The other answer choices refer to the medial malleoli, femur and tibia.

64. **D.** This type of injury would not affect the muscles in the lower leg.

65. **C.** None of the organs listed in the other answer choices are located underneath the ribs.

66. **D.** The kidneys may be damaged by a forceful blow to the area of the kidneys, such as being struck in the back by a heavy or fast-moving object.

67. **C.** While hernias can arise from trauma, they usually result from a natural defect in body development that fails to close normal openings present in early life, or from progressive weakening of body tissues due to aging.

68. **D.** Auto accidents are a common cause of ruptured bladders, usually as a result of a crushing injury to a full bladder.

69. **D.** This type of hernia occurs in a canal between the abdomen and thigh where the femoral artery, vein and nerve join the abdomen and thigh.

70. **B.** Aseptic peritonitis develops without a bacterial infection. Localized, or circumscribed, peritonitis affects only a small area of the peritoneum. Traumatic peritonitis is caused by trauma.

71. **D.** These symptoms do not correspond with those produced by a ruptured bladder, lacerated kidney or hepatic aneurysm.

72. **C.** The pulmonary arteries carry blood from the right ventricle of the heart to the lungs. The right atrium receives deoxygenated blood and circulates it to the lungs to pick up oxygen. The left ventricle pumps oxygenated blood to the body.

73. **C.** Myocardial infarction is the death of tissue in the heart muscle. Ischemia is a temporary interruption of blood flow to a part of the body, such as the brain. A cerebral hemorrhage is bleeding in the brain. A cerebrovascular accident refers to both ischemic strokes and cerebral hemorrhages.

74. **D.** Atherosclerosis is a common cause of myocardial infarctions. Some factors that may increase the risk of atherosclerosis include high blood pressure, high cholesterol levels, smoking, and obesity.

75. **C.** Most myocardial infarctions and CVAs have no relationship to traumatic injuries, job stress or allergies.

76. **C.** The pulmonary veins transport oxygenated blood from the lungs to the heart. The vena cavae carry used blood returning from other parts of the body to the heart. The blood itself is responsible for providing nutrients and oxygen to tissues.

77. **A.** The term myocardial means heart muscle; the term infarction means cell death of an area of tissue that occurs when its blood supply is cut off.

78. **B.** Nausea is not a usual symptom of a stroke.

79. **B.** Asbestosis arises from the inhalation of asbestos dust.

80. **A.** Silicosis is caused by breathing free silica. CWP is caused by breathing coal dust. Fibrosis is not a type of pneumoconiosis. Asbestosis is caused by breathing asbestos.

81. **B.** The windpipe, or trachea, brings air into the lungs' lobes.

82. **C.** Hemopneumothorax is a combination of the terms hemo, meaning blood; pneumo, meaning air; and thorax, meaning, in this instance, in the pleural space.

83. **A.** Asbestosis, CWP and anthracosis are all types of fibrogenic pneumoconioses.

84. **D.** A pneumothorax, or air in the pleural space, causes a buildup of pressure within the lungs that can eventually cause the lungs to collapse.

85. **B.** The trachea brings air into the lungs' lobes. A bronchus is a branch of the trachea. A bronchiole is a smaller branch of a bronchus.

86. **D.** Neural hearing impairments may be caused by work-related activities, such as trauma or extreme noise, or they may be caused by disease or aging.

87. **D.** The other answer choices are common causes for neural hearing impairments.

88. **D.** Retinal detachment can be caused by trauma, hemorrhaging or tumors. Vision in the affected area will be lost until the retina is reattached surgically.

89. **B.** Enucleation, or removal of the eye from its socket, is only performed if the eye has been seriously damaged. This procedure would not be used to treat relatively minor eye conditions such as diplopia, cataracts or conjunctivitis.

90. **A.** The eardrum separates the external and middle ear. The hearing nerve is found in the inner ear. The ear lobe is not part of the internal apparatus of the ear. The bones of the middle ear are part of the middle ear.

91. **B.** There are 16 teeth in the upper jaw and 16 in the lower jaw.

92. **D.** Bicuspids and third molars are part of the permanent set of teeth but are not part of the deciduous teeth.

93. **A.** A child who loses deciduous teeth before they fall out naturally usually must wear orthodontic braces to correct permanent teeth that didn't come in properly.

94. **D.** The Universal Numbering System uses the number eight to identify one of the two central incisors in the upper jaw.

95. **B.** The Universal Lettering System uses the letter L to identify one of the two first molars in the lower jaw.

96. **C.** Any third-degree burn that covers more than 10% of the body is considered a critical burn.

97. **D.** Other factors taken into account to determine the severity of the burn are whether the burn was caused by exposure to electricity or whether the burn involves the lungs or other parts of the respiratory system.

98. **B.** A third-degree burn that covers less than 10% of the body is considered a moderate burn unless the burn occurs on the hands, feet, face, genitalia, or joints involved in flexion or extension.

99. **A.** Steve and Leslie have first-degree burns. Jack has a third-degree burn.

100. **D.** Blisters are characteristic of second-degree burns and, in some cases, third-degree burns.

Glossary

A

Abduction Lateral movement of a part of the body away from the median line of the body.

Abrasion Scraping away of a portion of skin as a result of injury.

Abscess Localized accumulation of pus resulting from breakdown or displacement of tissue.

Acetabulum Rounded cavity on the external surface of the hip which receives the head of the femur.

Achilles Tendon Large tendon that attaches muscles to the calcaneus.

Acute Sharp, severe; having a rapid onset, severe symptoms, and a short course; opposite of *chronic*.

Adduction Lateral movement of a part of the body toward the median line of the body.

Adipose Pertaining to fat.

Alignment The placing of portions of a fractured bone into their correct anatomical position.

Alveolus, Pulmonary Terminal sac of an alveolar duct where gases are exchanged in respiration. Plural is *alveoli*.

Aneurysm A dilation of an area in a blood vessel, most commonly an artery.

Annulus A ring-shaped structure.

Anomaly Considerable deviation from normal.

Anterior Before or in front of.

Anteriorposterior (A.P.) Passing from front to back.

Anthracosis See *Coal Workers' Pneumoconiosis*

Aorta Main trunk of the arterial system; originates in the left ventricle of the heart and distributes blood throughout the body.

Aphasia Loss or impairment of the ability to communicate orally or in writing.

Apraxia Loss or impairment of the ability to move the body when there is no underlying muscular paralysis.

Arachnoid One of the three membranes covering the brain and spinal cord; located between the dura mater and pia mater.

Arteriosclerosis Condition in which the arteries thicken, harden, and lose elasticity.

Artery One of the vessels that carries blood from the heart to body tissues.

Artery, Coronary An artery that supplies blood to the heart.

Artery, Pulmonary The artery that carries blood from the right ventricle of the heart to the lungs.

Arthritis Inflammation of a joint.

Arthroplasty Surgical formation or reformation of a joint.

Arthroscopy Direct observation of the interior of a joint using an endoscope.

Articular Pertaining to articulation.

Articular Process Outgrowth of bone or tissue that forms part of a joint.

Articulation The point of juncture of two bones; also called a joint.

Asbestosis A pneumoconiosis resulting from inhalation of asbestos particles over a long period of time.

Atherosclerosis A type of arteriosclerosis characterized by a lesion in an artery caused by accumulated fatty deposits.

Atrium The upper chamber of the left and right sides of the heart. The right atrium receives deoxygenated blood and circulates it to the lungs to pick up oxygen; the left atrium receives the oxygenated blood.

Atrophy Wasting away from lack of nourishment.

Avascular Necrosis A condition where poor blood circulation to an injured area causes tissues in the area to die.

B

Babinski's Reflex Used to diagnose damage to the nervous system; positive if the big toe flexes backward when the lateral side of the foot is stroked; the other toes may also fan out.

Backbone See *Spine*

Black Lung Disease See *Coal Workers' Pneumoconiosis*

Bony Union Reunion of pieces of fractured bones. See also *Fibrous Union*, *Malunion*, *Nonunion*, and *Partial Union*

Brachial Plexus Network of lower cervical and upper thoracic spinal nerves supplying the arm, forearm, and hand.

Bronchiole A smaller subdivision of the bronchi.

Bronchiole, Respiratory Last subdivision of the bronchi which branches off the terminal bronchioles and leads to the alveoli.

Bronchiole, Terminal Subdivision of the bronchi which leads to the respiratory bronchioles.

Bronchus One of the primary branches from the trachea which carries air to the lungs. Plural is *bronchi*.

Bruise Large, irregular-shaped hemorrhage under the skin; first appears as blue-black, then changes to green, brown, or yellow. Also known as *contusion* and *ecchymosis*.

Burn Damage or injury to the skin or underlying tissues caused by fire, heat, electricity, or chemicals.

Burn, First Degree Superficial burn with damage confined to epidermis; skin is red, tender, and painful, but not blistered.

Burn, Second Degree Burn that extends from the epidermis into the dermis; characterized by blistering and swelling.

Burn, Third Degree Burn that destroys both the epidermis and dermis and damages or destroys underlying tissues; blisters may or may not be present.

Bursa Sac or cavity found in connecting tissue, usually near joints.

Bursitis Inflammation of a bursa, especially those between bony prominences and muscle or tendon, such as the shoulder or knee.

C

Calcaneus Heel bone; also called *os calcis*.

Callus Bony material formed between the ends of a fractured bone; also thickening and hypertrophy of a small area of skin.

Capillary Small blood vessel that connects an artery and a vein.

Cardiologist Specialist in diseases and disorders of the heart.

Cardiovascular Pertaining to the heart and blood vessels.

Carpals Bones of the wrist.

Carpal Tunnel Canal in the wrist that contains tendons and the median nerve.

Carpal Tunnel Syndrome Pain, numbness, or weakness of muscles in the hand, fingers, or wrist caused by compression of the median nerve as it travels through the carpal tunnel.

Cartilage Dense connective tissue that has many functions in the human body. It covers the ends of bones where they articulate and helps form body parts such as the ears, nose, and larynx.

Cataract An opacity or clouding of the lens of the eye.

Cerebral Concussion Injury where the brain has been violently shaken about, usually as a result of a blow to the head.

Cerebrospinal Fluid (CSF) A watery liquid that acts as a cushion to protect the brain and spinal cord from impact.

Cerebrovascular Pertaining to the brain and blood vessels.

Cerebrovascular Accident (CVA) General term describing an abnormal interruption of blood flow in the brain. Also see *Stroke*

Cervical Pertaining to the neck or to that part of an organ resembling the neck; also to the upper part of the back.

Chest See *Thorax*

Chiropractor Type of health care professional who focuses on the relationship between the structure of the human body, particularly the spinal column, and how the body functions, primarily the nervous system, in order to preserve health. Chiropractors treat most medical conditions by manipulating and adjusting the body, particularly the spinal column.

Choroid Middle, vascular layer of the eyeball.

Chronic A condition that lasts for a long time or is recurring; opposite of *acute*.

Clavicles Long, slender bones that extend from the sternum to the scapula; also called *collar bones*.

Coal Workers' Pneumoconiosis A pneumoconiosis in which carbon deposits exist in the lungs as a result of inhalation of coal dust. Also called *black lung disease* and *anthracosis*.

Coccyx Lowest portion of the spinal column; in adults, results from the fusion of four smaller vertebrae. Also called the *tailbone*.

Computerized Tomography (CT) A diagnostic technique providing rapid imaging of the brain, spinal cord, and soft tissues. X-ray beams pass through the specified area, and a computer transforms the resulting measurements into high-resolution, two-dimensional images.

Conductive Hearing Impairment Reduction of hearing ability due to an obstruction or infection in the external or middle ear which prevents sound waves from reaching the inner ear.

Condyle Rounded protuberance at the end of a bone which forms an articulation.

Congenital Present at birth.

Conjunctiva Mucous membrane that lines the eyelids and eyeball.

Conjunctivitis Inflammation of the conjunctiva.

Contrast Agent Or Medium In radiology, a radiopaque substance used to set off the tissue or organ being filmed by providing a contrast in density.

Contusion See *Bruise*

Coronary Pertaining to the heart.

Coronary Occlusion Closing off of a coronary artery.

Coronary Thrombosis Blood clot in a coronary artery which can close off the passageway through the artery.

Costal Pits Cup-shaped depressions at the distal ends of the thoracic vertebrae into which the ribs fit.

CSF See *Cerebrospinal Fluid*

CVA See *Cerebrovascular Accident*

CWP See *Coal Workers' Pneumoconiosis*

Cyanosis Condition where the skin turns gray or blue because the blood cannot carry enough oxygen to the skin.

D

Degeneration Deterioration of an organ or body part.

Degenerative Arthritis See *Osteoarthritis*

Dermatologist Specialist in disorders of the skin.

Dermis Lower layer of the skin.

Diabetes Mellitus A metabolic disorder resulting from inadequate production or use of insulin.

Diagnosis Term denoting the name of the disease a person has or is believed to have.

Diaphysis Middle portion of a long bone. Also called *shaft*.

Diplopia Double vision.

Disability, Industrial In some states, refers to an individual's loss of earnings as the basis for total or partial disability.

Disability, Medical In some states, refers to how an individual's physical condition affects functioning as the basis for total or partial disability.

Disability, Permanent Partial A medical condition that has a permanent, partial effect on an individual's earning power or other pre-injury activities.

Disability, Permanent Total A medical condition that has a complete and permanent effect on an individual's earning power or other pre-injury activities.

Disability, Temporary Partial A medical condition that has a temporary, partial effect on an individual's earning power or other pre-injury activities, but from which the individual is expected to recover.

Disability, Temporary Total A medical condition that has a complete but temporary effect on an individual's earning power or other pre-injury activities, and from which the individual is expected to recover.

Dislocation Displacement of any body part, especially temporary displacement of a bone from its normal position in a joint.

Distal Location term meaning farthest from the center, the median line, or the trunk; opposite of *proximal*.

Dorsal Pertaining to the region of the back between the cervical and lumbar areas; also called *thoracic*.

Dura Mater The outermost layer of the meninges covering the brain and spinal cord.

E

Ear Organ of hearing; consists of the external, middle, and inner ear.

Ear Drum Cavity in the middle ear which separates the external ear and middle ear.

Ecchymosis See *Bruise*

Echoencephalography The use of ultrasound as a non-invasive diagnostic method in examining and measuring internal structures of the skull.

Edema Abnormal accumulation of fluid in body tissue.

Electroenchephalography (EEG) The amplification, recording, and analysis of the electrical activity in the brain.

Electromyography (EMG) Electrographic test that involves recording, measuring and analyzing electrical activity in muscles.

Embolus An occlusion in a blood vessel which may be a blood clot or another foreign substance, such as air, fat, or a tumor.

Emphysema Lung disease in which the size of the air spaces is increased.

Endoscope Instrument consisting of a tube and optical system for observing the interior of a hollow organ or cavity. The device may be inserted through a natural body opening or an incision.

Enucleation Removal of an entire body part or mass without rupturing it, especially an eyeball or tumor.

Epicondyle Prominence at the articular end of a bone above a condyle.

Epidermis Outer layer of the skin.

Epidural Occurring over or above the dura mater.

Epiphysis In developing children, the bone growth center at each extremity of long bones, separated from the parent bone by cartilage. As growth proceeds, it becomes a part of the parent bone.

Excise To cut out or remove surgically.

Extension Straightening out of a body part.

Extremity An arm or leg.

F

Facet, Facette Small, smooth area on a bone.

Femur Bone that extends from the hip to the knee; longest and strongest bone in the body. Also called the *thigh bone*.

Fibrous Union Failure of cartilage between fractured bone fragments to harden.

Fibula Smaller of the two lower leg bones; located on the outside of the leg.

Flexion Bending of a body part.

Foramen A hole in a bone for passage of nerves or vessels; plural is *foramina*.

Forearm Part of the arm between the wrist and the elbow.

Fracture A broken bone.

Fracture, Articular Type of fracture that extends into a joint.

Fracture, Avulsion Type of fracture where the bone is torn out of its normal position.

Fracture, Basal Fracture located at the base of the skull.

Fracture, Colles Transverse fracture of the distal end of the radius; the hand is displaced outward and backward. Also called a *silver fork deformity*.

Fracture, Comminuted Fracture in which the bone is broken or splintered into two or more pieces.

Fracture, Complete Fracture in which the bone is broken completely through.

Fracture, Complicated Type of fracture where a bone fragment has injured an internal organ.

Fracture, Compound Fracture in which the bone is broken and an external wound leads to the fracture site, or a piece of bone extends through the skin.

Fracture, Compression Type of fracture where a vertebra is crushed between the ones above and below it.

Fracture, Depressed Fracture in which a piece of the skull is driven into the brain.

Fracture, Displaced Type of fracture where the bone fragments are out of alignment.

Fracture, Greenstick Type of incomplete fracture where the bone is partially bent and partially broken.

Fracture, Impacted Fracture in which one bone fragment is wedged into the interior of another bone fragment.

Fracture, Incomplete Type of fracture where the bone is not broken completely through.

Fracture, Linear A crack in a bone which does not break the bone into pieces.

Fracture, Longitudinal Type of fracture where the fracture line runs lengthwise on the bone.

Fracture, Oblique Fracture in which the fracture line slants across the bone.

Fracture, Potts Fracture of the distal ends of the tibia and fibula in the area of the malleoli; the foot is also displaced backward and outward.

Fracture, Simple Fracture in which there is no external wound leading to the fracture site.

Fracture, Spiral Type of fracture where the fracture line winds around the bone.

Fracture, Transverse Type of fracture where the fracture line is at right angles to the bone.

Fracture, Undisplaced Type of fracture where the bone fragments are not out of alignment.

Frontal Bone Bone that forms the anterior part of the skull. Also called the *forehead bone*.

Fusion The process of fusing or uniting, especially the surgical fusion of two or more vertebrae.

G

Gangrene Decomposition of soft tissue.

Gangrene, Dry Decomposition of soft tissues in the body caused by an interruption of blood supply to the affected area.

Gangrene, Wet Decomposition of soft tissues in the body caused by a bacterial infection in the affected area.

Glaucoma An increase in the pressure within the eye which puts pressure on the optic nerve; this leads to impaired vision and, in some cases, blindness.

Groin Depression between the thigh and the trunk; also called the *inguinal region*.

H

Head The proximal end of a bone.

Heart Organ responsible for circulating blood throughout the body.

Heart Attack See *Myocardial Infarction*

Hematoma A swelling containing blood or a mass of clotted blood caused by a break in a blood vessel; the mass is confined to an organ, tissue, or space.

Hemianesthesia Numbness that affects only one side of the body.

Hemianopia Loss of half of the field of vision in one or both eyes.

Hemiplegia Paralysis that affects only one side of the body.

Hemopneumothorax The presence of both blood and air in the pleural space.

Hemorrhage An abnormal internal or external discharge of blood from the blood vessels.

Hemothorax The presence of blood in the pleural space.

Hernia Protrusion of an organ or a part of an organ through the wall of the cavity that normally contains it.

Hernia, Femoral Type of hernia where a part of the intestine protrudes into the area where the femoral artery, vein, and nerve join the abdomen and thigh.

Hernia, Inguinal Type of hernia where a part of the intestine protrudes into the groin.

Herniated Intervertebral Disc A rupture or herniation of the nucleus within an intervertebral disc, usually between lumbar vertebrae, causing pain and/or numbness on the affected side.

Hip Bone Large, broad bone that forms the largest part of the pelvis; also called the *innominate bone* and the *ilium*.

Humerus Large bone in the upper arm located between the shoulder and the elbow.

Hyperextension Extreme extension.

Hyperflexion Extreme flexion.

Hypertension High blood pressure.

Hyperthermia High fever.

Hypotension Low blood pressure.

I

Ilium See *Hip Bone*

Impairment Medical factor included as part of a disability evaluation.

Incision Cut made with a knife, especially for surgical purposes.

Infarction Cell death of an area of tissue which occurs when blood supply to that area is cut off.

Inferior Beneath; lower

Inguinal Region See *Groin*

Innominate Bone See *Hip Bone*

Internist Specialist who treats diseases by nonsurgical methods.

Intervertebral Disc Fibrocartilaginous tissue between vertebrae.

Ischemia Temporary interruption of blood flow caused by an occlusion.

Ischium Lower portion of the hip bone on which the body rests while sitting.

J

Jaw One of two bones supporting the teeth; the upper bone is the maxilla and the lower bone is the mandible.

Joint See *Articulation*

K

Keloid Overgrowth of scar tissue that results in a thick, raised, irregularly-shaped red scar which is often painful to the touch.

Kidney Pair of organs located in the back of the abdominal area on either side of the spine. Their function is to regulate the composition of blood and urine.

Knee Articulation between the femur and the tibia.

Kneecap See *Patella*

L

Laceration An irregular tear in the flesh.

Lamina A thin, flat layer or membrane; the flattened part of either side of the neural arch of the vertebra.

Laryngologist Specialist in disorders of the throat and larynx.

Larynx Voice organ located at the upper end of the trachea.

Lateral Pertaining to the side.

Lesion An abnormal change in tissue caused by injury or disease; an injury or wound or an infected patch of skin.

Ligament Band of fibrous connective tissue joining articular ends of bones to hold them together and facilitate or limit motion; band of tissue connecting bones, cartilage, and other structures and serving to support or attach muscle.

Lipid A fat or fatty substance.

Lipping Development of bony projection beyond the joint margin.

Liver Large organ located in the upper right quadrant of the abdomen; has a wide variety of functions, including regulating blood sugar level, detoxifying certain harmful substances that are absorbed into the blood, and providing a source of body heat.

Lumbar Pertaining to the loins or to the back between the thorax and pelvis.

Lumen Space within a hollow, tubular structure, such as an artery.

Lungs Two organs of respiration located in the chest cavity.

M

Magnetic Resonance Imaging (MRI, NMRI, NMR) A technique for analyzing the response of certain atomic nuclei to a strong magnetic field by applying a radiofrequency pulse. The results are valuable imaging information of the heart, large blood vessels, brain, and soft tissues.

Malar Bones Two bones located directly below the eyes on either side of the face. Also called *zygomatic bones*.

Malleoli Plural of *malleolus*.

Malleolus, Lateral Lower end of the fibula bone located to the side of the body.

Malleolus, Medial Lower end of the tibia bone located closest to the middle of the body.

Malunion Condition where fractured bone fragments unite in a position that renders the bone useless, or where the fragments unite with another bone.

Mandible Lower jaw bone.

Marrow Soft material that fills the cavities of certain bones.

Maxilla Upper jaw bone.

Medial Pertaining to the middle, or nearer the median plane.

Median Nerve Combined motor and sensory nerve that begins at the brachial plexus and extends down the arm into the hand.

Mediastinum A cavity or septum (dividing wall) between two principal parts of an organ; the mass of organs and tissues separating the lungs.

Medulla Oblongata Enlarged portion of spinal cord in the cranium; the lower portion of the brain stem.

Membrane Thin, soft layer of tissue that covers an organ or structure; separates one part from another; or lines a tube or cavity.

Meninges The three membranes covering the brain and spinal cord. They are called the pia mater, arachnoid, and dura mater.

Meniscus The crescent-shaped fibrous cartilage within a joint, especially the knee.

Metacarpals Bones of the hand.

Metatarsals Bones of the foot.

MI See *Myocardial Infarction*

Midline Cerebral Structures Various cavities in the brain that are typically centered within the skull.

MRI See *Magnetic Resonance Imaging*

Myelography Inspection of the spinal cord by injecting a radiopaque medium and x-raying.

Myocardial Concerning the muscular part of the heart.

Myocardial Infarction (MI) Condition caused by obstruction of one or more coronary arteries producing symptoms of heavy pressure or squeezing pain in the center of the chest. The pain may also radiate down the arm or up into the back or jaw. Also called a *heart attack*.

N

Necrosis Death of areas of tissue or bone surrounded by healthy parts.

Nerve Bundle or group of bundles of nerve fibers outside the central nervous system which connects the brain and spinal cord with other areas of the body.

Nerve Conduction Studies Studies of the nerves' impulses in response to a stimulus in which an oscilloscope records and measures the speed with which the impulse is transmitted. Helps identify the presence of certain nerve injuries and diseases. Used almost exclusively in conjunction with electromyography.

Neural Arch Arch formed by two laminae and two roots located in the posterior portion of a vertebra.

Neural Hearing Impairment Type of hearing impairment that occurs in the inner ear and involves some type of damage to the hearing nerve. Also called *sensory hearing impairment* and *sensorineural hearing impairment*.

Neurologist Specialist in diseases of the nervous system.

NMR, NMRI See *Magnetic Resonance Imaging*

Nonunion Condition where fractured bone fragments fail to unite and are held together only by tissue.

Nucleus Fluid, jelly-like center of an intervertebral disc.

O

Objective Finding Discovery of some type of abnormality in the patient that is causing the patient's symptoms of injury or disease. Opposite of *subjective complaint*.

Oblique Slanting or diagonal.

Occipital Bone Bone in the lower back part of the skull between the parietal and temporal bones.

Occlusion A closed passageway.

Occupational Therapist Medically trained person who assists in the rehabilitation process by evaluating and helping plan work, play, and self-care activities to treat the physically or emotionally ill person and to prevent or minimize disability.

Olecranon Process Large process of the ulna which projects behind the elbow joint to form the bony prominence of the elbow.

Oncologist Specialist in the treatment of cancer.

Ophthalmologist Specialist in disorders of the eye.

Optic Nerve Nerve which carries impulses for sight.

Organ A body part that has a specific function; it has specialized cells that exist only to serve its specific function and its own blood and nerve supplies.

Orthopedist Specialist in disorders of the skeleton and joints.

Os Calcis See *Calcaneus*

Oscilloscope An instrument that records electrical oscillations, or waves, on the screen of a cathode ray tube. Its medical uses include recording electrical activity in the heart, brain, and muscles.

Osteoarthritis Chronic disease involving joints, particularly weight-bearing joints, characterized by destruction of cartilage, overgrowth of bone with lipping and spur formation, and impaired function.

Osteomyelitis Inflammation of bone marrow, or of both bone and marrow.

Otolaryngologist Specialist in disorders of the ears, nose, and throat.

Otologist Specialist in disorders of the ear.

P

Paralysis Temporary or permanent loss of function, especially of voluntary movement or sensation.

Paresthesia Abnormal sensation of prickling, tingling, or numbness; heightened sensitivity.

Parietal Bones Two bones that form the top and sides of the skull.

Partial Union Condition where fragments of fractured bones do not unite properly because callus does not grow over the entire fractured area.

Patella Lens-shaped bone located in front of the knee; also called the *kneecap*.

Pathologist Specialist in the nature and causes of disease.

Pelvis Bony structure that articulates with the lower limbs and supports the spine.

Periosteum Fibrous membrane that forms the covering of bones, except at the articular ends.

Peritoneum Membrane that surrounds abdominal organs and lines the abdominal cavity.

Peritonitis Infection of the peritoneum.

Peritonitis, Aseptic Peritonitis that develops without a bacterial infection.

Peritonitis, Circumscribed Peritonitis that is confined to a small area of the peritoneum. Also called *localized peritonitis*.

Peritonitis, Diffuse Peritonitis that is spread throughout a wide area of the peritoneum. Also called *generalized peritonitis*.

Peritonitis, Primary Peritonitis that is caused by bacteria transmitted throughout the blood.

Peritonitis, Secondary Peritonitis that arises when an infection from another area spreads to the peritoneum.

Peritonitis, Traumatic Type of peritonitis that refers specifically to infection of an injury or wound.

Phalanges Toe or finger bones.

Phalanx Any one of the toe or finger bones.

Physical Therapist Medically trained person who assists in the rehabilitation process by treating injuries and diseases with physical agents such as heat, massage, and exercise.

Pia Mater The innermost layer of the meninges covering the brain and spinal cord.

Pleura Double-layered serous membrane that covers the lungs.

Pleural Space The space between inner and outer layers of the pleura.

PMF See *Progressive Massive Fibrosis*

Pneumoconiosis Fibrosis of the lungs caused by inhalation of various kinds of dusts.

Pneumothorax Presence of air in the pleural space.

Pneumothorax, Open Type of pneumothorax where the pleural space is exposed to air through an open wound in the chest wall.

Pneumothorax, Spontaneous Type of pneumothorax that is not caused by trauma; may be caused by a pulmonary disease or a rupture of some part of the respiratory system, or may simply appear in a previously healthy person.

Pneumothorax, Tension Type of pneumothorax where air is introduced into the pleural space but cannot escape; often a complication of treatment methods, such as mechanical ventilators.

Posteroanterior (P.A.) Indicates a movement or flow that occurs from back to front.

Posterior Toward the back.

Process Outgrowth of bone or tissue.

Progressive Massive Fibrosis Term used to describe the advanced stages of coal worker's pneumoconiosis.

Proximal Nearest the point of attachment to the body; opposite of *distal*.

Pubic Bone Lower, anterior part of the ilium.

Pulmonary Vein A vein that carries blood from the lungs to the left atrium of the heart.

R

Radial Nerve Nerve that originates at the brachial plexus; winds around the middle third of the humerus, and extends down into the forearm; controls sensation and movement of the entire arm.

Radiologist Specialist in interpreting x-rays and/or using x-rays to treat certain diseases.

Radiopaque Substance that will not allow the passage of radiant energy; when a radiopaque is used in an x-ray, it produces a white or light-colored area on the film.

Radius Outer bone of the forearm.

Reduction Restoration to normal position, as in a hernia or a fractured bone.

Reduction, Closed Reduction of a fractured bone by nonsurgical techniques.

Reduction, Open Reduction of a fractured bone by surgical techniques.

Regeneration Repair, regrowth, or restoration of a part.

Retina Innermost layer of the eyeball; attached to the choroid.

Retinal Detachment Complete or partial separation of the retina from the choroid.

Rib One of a series of 12 pairs of narrow, curved bones extending laterally and anteriorly from the sides of the thoracic vertebrae.

Ribs, False Three pairs of ribs that, instead of attaching to the sternum, are each attached to the rib above it.

Ribs, Floating Two lower pair of ribs that are not attached to anything anteriorally.

Ribs, True Top seven pairs of ribs that attach directly to the sternum.

Romberg's Sign Used to indicate nerve damage; positive if the patient is unable to maintain balance while standing with the feet close together and the eyes closed.

Rotation Turning on an axis.

Rupture A breaking apart, as of an organ; also called a *hernia*.

S

Sacroiliac Pertaining to the sacrum and ilium.

Sacrum Large bone that forms the back of the pelvis, located between the fifth lumbar vertebra and the coccyx.

Scapula One of two broad, flat, triangular-shaped bones that form the back of the shoulder. Also called the *shoulder blades*.

Sciatica Severe pain in the leg along the course of the sciatic nerve at the back of the thigh.

Sciatic Nerve Large nerve that runs down the back of the leg.

Sclera Outermost layer of the eyeball; also called the *white of the eye*.

Sclerosis Hardening of an organ or tissue.

Sensorineural Hearing Impairment See *Neural Hearing Impairment*

Sensory Hearing Impairment See *Neural Hearing Impairment*

Shaft See *Diaphysis*

Shock Sudden collapse of the circulatory system.

Sign Any objective evidence or manifestation of a disorder exhibited involuntarily by a patient; a predictable involuntary response to a specific stimulus.

Silicosis A pneumoconiosis resulting from long-term inhalation of free silica (quartz) dust.

Silver Fork Deformity See *Fracture, Colles*

Skull Bony frame composed of cranial bones, facial bones and teeth. Its primary function is to protect the brain.

Spasm Convulsive muscular contraction or involuntary, sudden movement.

Sphenoid Bone Large bone that extends through the skull, but is visible from both sides only as a small wedge in front of the temporal bones.

Spinal Canal Canal that contains the spinal cord. Also called *vertebral canal*.

Spinal Column See *Spine*

Spinal Cord Thin column of nerve-enriched tissue that extends from the medulla oblongata to approximately the second lumbar vertebra.

Spinal Puncture, Spinal Tap Puncture of the spinal cavity with a needle to remove fluid for diagnostic purposes, to remove fluid so that other fluids, such as radiopaque substances, may be injected, or to introduce anesthesia into the spinal canal.

Spine Protective column composed of 26 vertebrae which surrounds the spinal cord. Also called *backbone*, *spinal column*, and *vertebral column*.

Spleen Lymphatic organ located in the left side of the abdominal cavity which filters blood and produces certain types of blood cells.

Spondylolisthesis Forward displacement of one vertebra over another.

Sprain Trauma to a joint which causes pain and disability depending on the degree of injury to ligaments; in severe sprains, the ligaments are completely torn.

Spur A sharp or pointed projection; a sharp outgrowth of skin.

Sternum Narrow, flat bone in the middle, anterior portion of the thorax. Also called the *breastbone*.

Straight Leg-Raising Test Used to distinguish between sciatica and hip joint disease. While the patient is lying face up, the physician raises the patient's extended leg and, if necessary, bends the extended leg to flex the hip joint; pain while the extended leg is straight indicates sciatica; pain while the extended leg is bent indicates hip joint disease.

Strain Stretching of muscles or tendons beyond their usual limits; may be very painful at first, but does not produce lasting effects.

Stroke Abnormal interruption of blood flow to the brain caused by a hemorrhage in the brain, occlusion of an artery, or rupture of an artery. Also see *Cerebrovascular Accident*.

Subarachnoid Occurring below or under the surface of the arachnoid membrane and the pia mater.

Subdural Occurring beneath the dura mater.

Subjective Complaint A complaint that cannot be perceived or observed by another; opposite of *objective finding*.

Subluxation Partial or incomplete dislocation.

Superior Higher than; above.

Surgical Neck Constricted part of a long bone beneath the tuberosities.

Symptom A change in the body or its functions that indicates disease.

Syndrome Group of symptoms and signs that points to a particular disease or condition of the body.

T

Tachycardia Abnormally rapid heartbeat.

Talus Bone directly below the tibia which forms part of the ankle joint.

Tarsals Bones of the ankle.

Teeth, Deciduous First of two sets of teeth that erupt in a person's lifetime; usually start coming in at the age of six months and start falling out at age six. Also called *baby teeth*.

Teeth, Permanent Second of two sets of teeth that erupt in a person's lifetime; usually begin coming in at around age 6 and are completely in, except for the wisdom teeth, by around age 16.

Temporal Bones Bones located at the base of the skull and on either side of the head; terminate in the area of the temples.

Temporomandibular Joint (TMJ) Joint formed by the mandible and the temporal bone.

Temporomandibular Joint Disorders Name given to a family of disorders affecting the TMJ. Common symptoms include pain in the area of the TMJ joint, difficulty in opening the mouth, and grating or clicking sounds when opening the mouth.

Temporoparietal Area Place where the temporal and parietal bones of the skull converge above the ear.

Tendon Fibrous tissue that attaches muscle to bone.

Therapy Treatment of a disease or condition.

Thoracentesis Procedure where fluid is drained from the pleural space through a needle.

Thoracic Pertaining to the area of the thorax; also to the region of the back between the cervical and lumbar areas.

Thoracic Outlet Syndromes One of a group of disorders in which typical complaints are of pain and/or numbness in the neck, shoulders, arms and/or hands; believed to result from compressed nerve roots or blood vessels.

Thoracotomy Surgical incision into the chest wall.

Thorax Part of the body between the base of the neck and the diaphragm; also called the *chest*.

Thrombosis Formation, development, or existence of a blood clot within the vascular system.

TIA See *Transient Ischemic Attack*

Tibia Larger of the two lower leg bones; located on the inside of the leg.

Tissue Group of cells and their intercellular substance which act jointly in the performance of a particular body function.

TMJ See *Temporomandibular Joint*

Tomography Use of x-rays to capture details in a selected body structure by blurring other images or shadows that surround the part being examined.

Trachea Tube extending from the lower part of the larynx which divides to form the bronchi; also called the *windpipe*.

Traction Drawing or pulling; method used to correct bone displacement through the use of weights.

Transducer A piece of equipment designed to send and receive energy and, if necessary, convert the energy to another form to make it usable; used in ultrasound techniques.

Transient Ischemic Attack (TIA) Temporary interference with the blood supply to the brain.

Trauma Physical injury or wound caused by violence or external force.

Traumatic Caused by or related to an injury.

Tuberculosis Bacterial infection that causes inflammation of the lungs.

Tuberosity Elevated, round process of a bone.

Tumor An overgrowth of tissue.

U

Ulna Inner bone of the forearm.

Ultrasound Pertaining to sound waves of extremely high frequency, inaudible to the human ear, which have different velocities in different densities of tissue, a characteristic that permits ultrasonographic imaging.

Ultrasonography The use of ultrasound to produce images of organs or tissues.

Universal Lettering System System used to identify deciduous teeth by assignment of a specific letter to each of the 20 deciduous teeth.

Universal Numbering System System used to identify permanent teeth by assignment of a specific number to each of the 32 permanent teeth.

Urinary Bladder Hollow, muscular organ that can be stretched or inflated to hold urine.

V

Vascular Pertaining to or containing blood vessels.

Vein A blood vessel that returns deoxygenated blood to the right side of the heart.

Vena Cava One of two large veins that receives deoxygenated blood from the body and sends it to the right side of the heart. The *inferior vena cava* carries blood from the lower part of the body; the *superior vena cava* carries blood from the upper part of the body.

Ventricle Pumping portions of the left and right sides of the heart. The right ventricle pumps blood to the lungs for oxygenation, and the left ventricle pumps the oxygenated blood to the body.

Vertebra Any one of the bony segments that make up the spine.

Vertebral Canal See *Spinal Canal*

Vertebral Column See *Spine*

Vital Signs Traditional signs of life which include respiration, heartbeat, blood pressure, and body temperature.

W

Whiplash Nontechnical term used to describe a variety of injuries to the neck, most commonly a hyperextension-hyperflexion injury.

Wound A break in the continuity of the soft parts of the body as the result of traumatic injury to soft tissue.

Wound, Crushing Type of wound caused by trauma of sufficient force to smash or compress tissues, but which may not lacerate the skin.

Wound, Incised A clean, straight cut caused by a sharp-edged instrument.

Wound, Penetrating Type of puncture wound where the object breaks the skin and enters under the skin or deeper into the body.

Wound, Perforating Type of puncture wound where the object penetrates the skin or body and exits at another point.

Wound, Puncture Type of wound caused by a sharp, pointed instrument.

X

X-Ray High-energy, high-frequency radiation capable of penetrating a variety of structures and acting on photographic films and plates. Excessive exposure can damage the human body. When controlled, x-rays have both diagnostic and therapeutic uses. Also, photographic images obtained by the use of x-rays.

Z

Zygomatic Bones See *Malar Bones*

Index

Job Aids

Medical Abbreviations

Abbreviation	Meaning
b.i.d.	Twice a day
BP	Blood pressure
c̄	With
CC	Chief complaint
dos	Dosage
e.m.p.	As directed
gtt.	Drops
h.s.	At bedtime
I.M.	Intramuscular
I.V.	Intravenous
n.p.o.	Nothing By mouth
p.o.	By mouth
q.d.	Every day
qh	Every hour
q.i.d.	Four times a day
q.o.d.	Every other day
q.s.	Quantity sufficient
r	Respirations
s̄	Without
ss	Half
tab	Tablet
t.i.d.	Three times a day
v.s.	Vital signs
v.s.s.	Vital signs stable

Medical Terminology Guide

Term	Type	Meaning
A/an	Prefix	Negative condition
Aden	Root	Gland
Algesia	Root	Sensitivity to pain
Algia	Suffix	Pain
Arth/arthr	Prefix	Joint
Asthenia	Root	Weakness
Cardi/cardio	Root	Heart
Cephal	Root	Head
Chondri/chondro	Root	Cartilage
Cost	Root	Rib
Crani	Root	Skull
Derma/dermis	Root	Skin
Dynia	Suffix	Pain
Ectomy	Suffix	Surgical removal
Emia	Suffix	Presence of blood
En	Prefix	In
Encephal	Root	Brain
Epi	Prefix	On or upon
Esthesia	Root	Sensation, feeling
Gaster/gastero/gastro	Root	Stomach
Hemat/hemato	Root	Blood
Hepat/hepato	Root	Liver
Hidrosis	Root	Sweating
Hyper	Prefix	Above normal, excessive, high
Hypo	Prefix	Less than normal, below, under
Inter	Prefix	Between
Intra	Prefix	Within
Itis	Suffix	Inflammation
Myel/myelo	Root	Bone marrow
Myo	Root	Muscle
Neur/neuro	Root	Nerve
Olisthesis	Suffix	Slipping
Oma	Suffix	Tumor
Osis	Suffix	Condition or disease
Oste/osteo	Root	Bone
Ot/oto	Root	Ear
Otomy	Suffix	Surgical incision
Para	Prefix	Alongside, near

Medical Terminology Guide
(Continued)

Term	Type	Meaning
Peri	Prefix	Around
Plasty	Suffix	Form or reform
Rrhage/rrhagia	Suffix	Flow of blood
Rrhea	Suffix	Discharge of substance other than blood
Sclerosis	Root	Hardening of part of the body
Spondyl	Root	Vertebra
Sub	Prefix	Under
Supra	Prefix	Over, above
Tension	Root	Pressure
Thermia	Suffix	Heat or fever
Trophy	Suffix	Nourishment, growth, generation
Uria	Suffix	Urine

Medical Terminology Pronunciation Guide

How to Use this Guide

- All vowels and consonants in the following terms are pronounced as they are in English.

- **Primary accent marks** (') note the part of the term that receives the most vocal stress (such as *ab'ses*). Some terms also have **secondary accent marks** ("). Less stress is given to the part of the term with the secondary accent mark than the part with the primary accent (such as *ath"er-o-skle-ro'sis*).

- A **vowel followed by a consonant in the same syllable** is pronounced as a **short vowel** (such as *nom* in *anomaly* (a-nom a-le).

- A **vowel which is not followed by a consonant** is pronounced as a **long vowel** (such as *le* in *anomaly*).

- In a few terms, phonetic respelling requires that a consonant be placed after a long vowel for pronunciation purposes. For these terms, a **macron** (⁻) is placed over the vowel. An example is the phonetic spelling of *gangrene*, which is *gang grēn*.

- A vowel that stands alone is pronounced as a short vowel unless marked with a macron.

Abscess (ab'ses)
Acetabulum (as-e-tab'u-lum)
Aden (ad'en)
Adipose (ad'epos)
Algesia (al-je'ze-a)
Algia (al'je-a)
Alveolus (al-ve'ol-us)
Aneurysm (an'u-rizm)
Anomaly (a-nom'a-le)
Aorta (a-or'ta)
Aphasia (ah-fa'ze-ah)
Arachnoid (ah-rak'noid)
Asthenia (as-the'ne-a)
Atherosclerosis (ath"er-o-skle-ro'sis)
Atrophy (at'ro-fe)
Brachial (bra'ke-al)
Bronchiole (brong'ke-ol)
Bronchus (brong'kus)
Bursa (bur'sah)

Calcaneus (kal-ka'ne-us)
Capillary (kap'i-lar-e)
Cataract (kat'ah-rakt)
Catheterization (kath"e-ter-i-za'shun)
Cephal (sef'al)
Chondri (kon'dri)
Chondro (kon'dro)
Coccyx (kok'siks)
Conjunctivitis (kon-junk-te-vi'tis)
Crani (kra'ne)
Derma (derm'a)
Dermis (der'mis)
Diabetes mellitus (di-ah-be'tez mel'i-tus)
Dura mater (du'rah ma'ter)
Dynia (din'ē-a)
Ecchymosis (ek-e-mo'sis)
Ectomy (ek'to-me)

Emia (ē'me-a)
Encephal (en-sef'al)
Epiphysis (e-pif'is-is)
Esthesia (es-the'ze-a)
Foramen (fo-ra'men)
Gangrene (gang'grēn)
Glaucoma (glaw-ko'mah)
Hemat (hem'at, hēm'at)
Hemato (hem a to, hēm'a to)
Hemiplegia (hem-e-ple'je-ah)
Hepat (hep'at)
Hepato (hep'a to)
Hernia (her'ne-ah)
Hidrosis (hi-dro'sis)
Inguinal (ing'gwi-nal)
Ischemia (is-ke'me-ah)
Ischium (is'ke-um)
Keloid (ke'loyd)
Lesion (le'zhun)
Lumbar (lum'ber)

Malar (ma′lar)

Malleolus (mal-e′o-lus)

Mediastinum (me″de-as-ti′num)

Medulla oblongata (me-dul′la ob″long-ga′ta)

Meninges (me-nin′jēz)

Myel (mi′el)

Myelo (mi′el-ō)

Myo (mi′ō)

Neur (nūr)

Neuro (nu′ro)

Occipital (ok-sip′i-tal)

Olecranon (o-lek′ran-on)

Olisthesis (ō-lis″the′sis)

Oma (ōm′a)

Ophthalmologist (of-thal-mol′o-jist)

Oste (os′te)

Osteo (os′te-ō)

Otomy (ot′ō-me)

Parietal (pah-ri′e-tal)

Peritoneum (per″i-to-ne′um)

Phalanges (fa-lan′jez)

Phalanx (f āl′anks)

Pia mater (pi′ah mā′ter)

Pleural (ploo′ral)

Pneumoconiosis (nu″mo-ko″ne-o′sis)

Pneumothorax (nu-mo′tho′raks)

Retina (ret′i-nah)

Rrhage (rij)

Rrhagia (ra′je-a)

Rrhea (re′a)

Sacroiliac (sa-kro-il′e-ak)

Scapula (skap′ku-la)

Sciatica (si-at′i-ka)

Sclerosis (skle-ro′sis)

Silicosis (sil-e-ko′sis)

Sphenoid (sfe′noyd)

Spondyl (spon′dil)

Tachycardia (tak″e-kar′de-a)

Talus (ta′lus)

Temporomandibular (tem″po-ro-man-dib′u-lar)

Thoracentesis (tho″rah-sen-te′sis)

Thoracic (tho-ras′ik)

Trachea (tra′ke-ah)

Uria (u′re-a)

Vena cava (ve′na ka′va)

Zygomatic (zi″go-mat′ik)

Temporary Disability Estimate Chart

Important

The following disability estimates are based on the time it would take for an average adult to return to a full-time job that may involve some light physical activity. Individuals employed in jobs requiring heavy manual labor usually require a longer disability period.

Estimates do not include additional time that may be required for possible complications involved in the medical condition.

These estimates should be used only as guidelines, not as a set of hard-and-fast rules that apply to all individuals. Other factors, such as the individual's employment, the circumstances of his or her disability, and any ongoing medical treatment must be taken into consideration when determining the length of the disability.

Type of Fracture	Estimated Length of Temporary Disability
Ankle	3–12 weeks
Carpal Bone	1–8 weeks
Coccyx	0 days–6 weeks
Colles	1–8 weeks
Compression Fracture of the Spine	*Nonsurgical treatment:* 3 days–10 weeks *Surgical treatment:* See Physican Report
Femur	10–16 weeks
Fibula	1–8 weeks
Hip/Acetabulum	16–24 weeks
Humerus	3–8 weeks
Metacarpal	0 days–6 weeks
Metatarsal	0 days–8 weeks
Patella	2–12 weeks
Pelvis (Not Involving Acetabulum)	2–16 weeks
Phalanges (Fingers)	0 days–6 weeks
Phalanges (Toes)	0 days–4 weeks
Radius	1–8 weeks
Radius And Ulna	1–8 weeks
Ribs	0 days–6 weeks
Scapula	0 days–4 weeks
Skull (Simple)	2–8 weeks
Skull (Simple, Compound, Comminuted, or Depressed)	See Physician Report
Sternum	1–6 weeks
Tarsal (Including Calcaneus)	3–12 weeks
Tibia	2–16 weeks
Ulna	1–8 weeks
Vertebra	See Physician Report

Temporary Disability Estimate Chart
(Continued)

Type of Medical Condition	Estimated Length of Temporary Disability
Asbestosis	See Physican Report
Back Sprain/Strain	0 days–2 weeks
Burns	*1st degree, small 2nd degree:* 0 days–2 weeks *Large 2nd degree, 3rd degree:* See Physician Report
Carpal Tunnel Syndrome	*Nonsurgical treatment:* 0 days–3 weeks *Surgical treatment:* 1–6 weeks
Cataract	3 days–2 weeks
Cerebral Concussion	See Physician Report
Cerebral Hemorrhage	See Physician Report
Cerebral Vascular Accident	See Physician Report
Cervical Strain/"Whiplash"-Type Injury	0 days–2 weeks
Coal Workers Pneumoconiosis	See Physician Report
Glaucoma	*Nonsurgical treatment:* 0 days–2 weeks *Surgical treatment:* 1 day–4 weeks
Hernia, Femoral	2 days–6 weeks
Hernia, Inguinal	2 days–6 weeks
Herniated Intervertebral Disc	*Nonsurgical treatment:* 0 days–3 weeks *Surgical treatment:* 8–12 weeks
Myocardial Infarction	See Physician Report
Pneumothorax	1–6 weeks
Retinal Detachment	1–8 weeks
Silicosis	See Physician Report
Thoracic Outlet Syndromes	*Nonsurgical treatment:* 0 days–2 weeks *Surgical treatment:* See Physician Report
TMJ Disorders	Usually Not Required
Transient Ischemic Attack	Usually Not Required